The
IMAGINARY
INDIAN

Arsenal Pulp Press | Vancouver

The
IMAGINARY
INDIAN

THE IMAGE OF THE INDIAN
IN CANADIAN CULTURE

DANIEL FRANCIS

ARSENAL PULP PRESS
Suite 101, 211 East Georgia St.
Vancouver, BC
Canada V6A 1Z6
arsenalpulp.com

The publisher gratefully acknowledges the support of the Canada Council for the Arts and the British Columbia Arts Council for its publishing program, and the Government of Canada (through the Canada Book Fund) and the Government of British Columbia (through the Book Publishing Tax Credit Program) for its publishing activities.

Book design by Shyla Seller
Photograph of the author by Patrick Francis

Printed and bound in Canada

Library and Archives Canada Cataloguing in Publication:

Francis, Daniel
    The imaginary Indian : the image of the Indian in Canadian culture / Daniel Francis. — 2nd ed.

Includes bibliographical references and index.
Issued also in an electronic format.
ISBN 978-1-55152-425-2

    1. Indians of North America—Canada—Public opinion. 2. Indians in mass media. 3. Popular culture—Canada. I. Title.

E98.P99F73 2011   305.897'071

C2011-905443-4

FSC
www.fsc.org
MIX
Paper from
responsible sources
FSC® C011825

PREFACE TO THE SECOND EDITION

As the twentieth anniversary of *The Imaginary Indian*'s first publication approaches, this new edition allows me to acknowledge a debt which I did not even know was owed when the book first came out in 1992. Over the years when asked where the title came from, I answered truthfully that I did not recall. The phrase is so wonderfully concise and descriptive it is no surprise that I chose it, but who suggested it to me? I never assumed that I was the first to use it, but when the book first appeared neither was I aware of anyone else who had. (The *idea* of "The Imaginary Indian" derives from Robert Berkhofer Jr's wonderful 1978 book, *The White Man's Indian*, but Berkhofer does not use the phrase itself.) It was only after my book was published that I discovered that Marcia Crosby had written an essay titled "Construction of the Imaginary Indian," which appeared in *Vancouver Anthology: The Institutional Politics of Art*, edited by Stan Douglas and published by Talonbooks and the Or Gallery a year before my book was published and presented as a lecture a year before that (1990). Crosby, whom I have not met, is a Haida/Tsimpshian art historian. Her essay discusses the ways that Euro-Canadians consistently have appropriated Indian images to use for their own purposes. Even when the representations are positive, Crosby argues, their use reveals more about non-Aboriginals than it does about the people they are supposed to represent. "Emily Carr loved the same Indians Victorian society rejected," writes Crosby, "and whether they were embraced or rejected does not change the fact that they were Imaginary Indians." My belated discovery of Crosby's essay was embarrassing not just because I should have known about it but also because it makes my own use of the phrase appear to be an example of the appropriation which she discusses in her essay. So now I am able to plead ignorance, a slightly less serious literary crime than wilful plagiarism, and to apologize for inadvertently appropriating Ms Crosby's excellent phrase.

Another question that has arisen often over the past twenty years is why I chose to indulge in the first person narrative. Why make the book sometimes about me rather than a straightforward objective history? My intention in writing the book was to present a way of thinking about the relations between Aboriginal and non-Aboriginal people that asks non-Aboriginals like myself to re-examine their prejudices. In other words, I wanted to accomplish what every writer wants to accomplish: change the way the reader sees the world. For this reason the first-person seemed not just appropriate but necessary. I did not want to accuse readers of anything, nor to preach at them like an omniscient "Voice of God." If I hoped to engage them in an examination of their preconceptions about "Indians," it seemed like a good idea to begin with my own. As a result, I have always been a bit nonplussed when readers ask me, as they frequently do, "You've exposed all these images and stereotypes that are inaccurate. But you don't say what you think the real Indian is?" My answer never seems to satisfy but it is the only answer I have: the whole point of my book is that such a question should not be asked, at least not of me. There is no "correct" image of the Indian, or if there is I am not the person to be saying what it is. That comes from the First Nations themselves. My book presents the question; answering it is the responsibility of the reader.

The Imaginary Indian marked an important step in my evolution as a writer. While working on it I came to recognize the approach to history that would characterize most if not all of my subsequent books. I realized that I was preoccupied less with what happened in history than with what people *thought* happened (and the gap between the two is often wide). Why do we believe what we believe about the past? That became the question that I tried to answer. In the case of *The Imaginary Indian*, for example, I am examining the images and stereotypes non-Aboriginal Canadians have had about Aboriginals and wondering where they came from. In the book which followed, *National Dreams: Myth, Memory and Canadian History*, I identified some of the driving narratives of Canadian history and thought about why they had had such a strong hold on our imaginations. But even in subsequent books that were less overtly about image and stereotype, my interest tends to gravitate to the why, not the what. For example, in 2004 I published a biography about an early mayor of Vancouver, Louis D. Taylor (*L.D.: Mayor Louis Taylor and the Rise of Vancouver*). Part of what interested me about Taylor was the fact that he had disappeared so completely from the historical record. In a sense what I ended up writing was a history of a reputation. Why had Vancouverites washed their memories of their longest-serving mayor? My biography was an attempt to answer that question. It was with *The Imaginary Indian* that this tendency to investigate history as a set of unreliable narratives began. As such it has a special meaning for me and I am pleased to have a chance to present this second edition in the hope that it will find another generation of readers who share my interest in these issues.

"What was done becomes clear enough. What people thought they were doing is much less clear, but often much more important."
—J.E. Chamberlin, *The Harrowing of Eden*, 1975

"It is useless for us to become involved in a struggle to improve our image, because native people did not create these images, and they should not be concerned with trying to improve them so that whites will respect them. The society would simply create new racist images for us to work at... "
—Howard Adams, *Prison of Grass*, 1975

CONTENTS

ACKNOWLEDGMENTS

In the course of my research for this book, I acquired many debts: to archivists and librarians who gave so freely of their knowledge; to the authors of the many books I pillaged for insights and information; to family and friends who endured my harangues on the subject with tolerant patience; and to Brian Lam and his colleagues at Arsenal Pulp Press for being so supportive of the project. Special thanks are reserved for three friends: Jim Taylor, whose interest in the subject got me going in the first place; Donald B. Smith, whose knowledge of the Indian image far exceeds my own and who generously shared the contents of his voluminous files; and Stephen Osborne, editor and friend, who helped me work out my ideas in conversation, and then in prose. They get the credit for inspiring the project; I get the blame if the final result fails to live up to our shared expectations.

FOREWORD
by Randy Fred

My first contact with white kids was in grade seven, when kids from the residential school were bussed into town so we could go to a "public" school. We didn't want to be there, and it was pretty clear the white kids didn't want us to be there either. Social Studies was the worst class, because Indians were sometimes its subject. I didn't know who the Iroquois were, or who the Hurons were (no other Indians were mentioned in those classes), but I knew they were Indians, and so was I.

They were savage people, the Indians we learned about in the Social Studies class.

Residential school kids were not to associate with reserve kids—many of whom, where I lived, were my close relatives. The rule was that we couldn't go within ten feet of the chicken-wire fence separating the schoolyard from the reserve. Reserve kids, we were told again and again, were dirty and useless. This was a problem for me, because in the summer I lived on the other side of the fence: for a couple of months every year, I was a reserve kid.

I was in that school for nine years. When I got out of there it was like getting out of jail.

We saw the same movies in that school that white kids did: westerns; and, like them, we cheered on the cowboys or the cavalry. We too played Cowboys and Indians—and we all wanted to be cowboys.

I felt I had a special claim on cowboys, as I was named after Randolph Scott, one of the biggest movie cowboys.

I was twenty years old when I woke up in a hospital bed in Jasper,

Alberta, and heard a doctor say: "These Indians don't know how to take care of themselves." I had a job, I had a good wage, I had insurance. But there was nothing I could say.

At about the same time, I learned that I was slowly going blind: I had retinitis pigmentosa, as the doctors like to say. Since then my sight has been diminishing. These days I am entitled to a white cane, and when I carry it, I see how easily the white cane blinds people to my Indianness. As long as I carry the cane, I hear no slurs when I stumble; but without the cane, I hear enough that will not bear repeating. In 1976 I found myself in Stanley Park on a Sunday afternoon, down by Lumberman's Arch. There was some kind of arts and crafts show happening, and there were several booths—all run by non-Natives, to my dismay—displaying paintings of Indian-like people, all of whom had the same expression on their faces—frowning and looking very mean and stony—even though they had been painted by different artists.

Native people live within a world of imagery that isn't their own: in this book Dan Francis shows us where that world of imagery comes from, and how necessary it is that we struggle to sweep it away.

—*Randy Fred is a member of the Tseshaht First Nation and the founder of Theytus Books in Penticton. He lives in Nanaimo, BC.*

INTRODUCTION

> ... the indians are not composed of the romantic stories
> about them ...
> —John Newlove, *The Pride*

SOME YEARS AGO A FRIEND and I decided to pay a visit to Head-Smashed-In Buffalo Jump. Located where the prairie meets the foothills in southwestern Alberta, Head-Smashed-In is a high cliff over which Native people stampeded the great herds of buffalo hundreds of years ago. Archaeologists believe that people used this place as a slaughterhouse for almost 6,000 years. The United Nations has declared it a World Heritage Site, one of the most culturally significant places in the world.

We drove south from Calgary on a sunny Thanksgiving day. On our left the flat plain ran away to the horizon under a wide, blue sky; on our right the land folded into rolling hills all the way to the Rocky Mountains, faintly visible in the distance. There were few signposts along the way and we had begun to fear that we had missed the turn-off when at last we spotted the sign and left the highway on a meandering strip of asphalt heading west toward the mountains. Just about the time we once again thought we must be lost, we arrived at a gravel parking lot, seemingly in the middle of nowhere. We were there.

The site at first seemed unimpressive. The visitors' centre, actually a mini-museum, is a concrete building several stories high embedded in the face of the cliff. It appears to have been built to make as little impact on the landscape as possible. Entering at the front door, we climbed up through a series of levels and emerged at the top of the cliff, at the edge of the buffalo jump, right where the stampeding animals would have run out into empty space and begun the long, bellowing fall onto the rocks below.

The anthropologist George MacDonald has written that the three holiest places in Canada are a row of stone statues at Eskimo Point in Nunavut, Bill Reid's large cedar carving, "The Raven and the First Men," at Vancouver's Museum of Anthropology, and the abandoned Haida village of Ninstints on Anthony Island. Well, I thought, as I looked out from the clifftop across a vast sweep of undulating prairie, lightening and darkening as the billowing clouds obscured the sun and set it free again, add a fourth; if by holy you mean a place where the warm wind seems to be the earth breathing, a place where personal identity dissolves temporarily, where you can feel the connectedness of lives back through time to be a reality, and not just an opinion.

Back inside the museum, looking at the various items depicting the history of the buffalo and the people who hunted them, my attention shifted from the display cases to the people who were tending them. I became aware that the facility was staffed entirely by Indians (Peigan, as it turned out, from a nearby reserve). But I found myself thinking that they didn't look like Indians to me, the Indians I knew from my school books and from the movies, the Indians, in fact, who were depicted inside the museum displays I was looking at. That is where most of us are used to seeing Indians, from the other side of a sheet of glass. But at Head-Smashed-In, they were running the place. They stood around in jeans and dresses and plaid shirts—not feather headdresses and leather moccasins—talking and laughing. If curious visitors like myself asked them something, they answered thoroughly but not pedantically: as if this was something they knew, not something they had studied.

After a long afternoon learning about the buffalo, I left Head-Smashed-In dimly aware that I had changed my mind about something. It had been an encounter not just with an important place in the history of the continent, but also with an idea, my own idea about what an Indian was. If I thought I had known before, I didn't think I knew anymore. And perhaps that is where this book began. How had I come to believe in an Imaginary Indian?

II

In 1899, the poet Charles Mair travelled into the far Northwest as secretary to the Half-Breed Scrip Commission, appointed by the government in Ottawa to carry out negotiations related to Treaty 8 with the Native people of northern Alberta. Negotiations began on the shore of Lesser Slave Lake, before a large tent with a spacious marquee beneath which the members of the official party arranged themselves. The Native people, Beaver and Métis, sat on the ground in the sun, or stood in small knots. As the speeches droned on through the long June afternoon, Mair observed the people as they listened to what the government emissaries had to say. "Instead of paint and feathers, the scalp-lock, the breech-clout, and the buffalo robe," he later wrote:

> there presented itself a body of respectable-looking
> men, as well dressed and evidently quite as independent
> in their feelings as any like number of average pioneers
> in the East ... One was prepared, in this wild region of
> forest, to behold some savage types of men; indeed, I
> craved to renew the vanished scenes of old. But, alas!
> one beheld, instead, men with well-washed unpainted
> faces, and combed and common hair; men in suits of
> ordinary store-clothes, and some even with "boiled" if not

laundered shirts. One felt disappointed, even defrauded. It was not what was expected, what we believed we had a right to expect, after so much waggoning and tracking and drenching and river turmoil and trouble.[1]

Unlike most Canadians of his time, Charles Mair possessed extensive knowledge of the country's Native people, living as he had for so many years as a merchant trader in the future province of Saskatchewan. He knew well that the contemporary Indian no longer galloped across the plains in breechcloth and feathered headdress. However, Mair did expect to discover in the more isolated regions of the north a Native population closer to his image of the picturesque Red Man. His disappointment was profound when instead he found "a group of commonplace men smoking briar-roots."

III

Two very similar experiences, almost a century apart. Charles Mair, myself, and how many other White people, having to relearn the same lesson: Indians, as we think we know them, do not exist. In fact, there may well be no such thing as an Indian.

Indirectly, we all know this to be true; it is one of the lessons we learn as school children. When Christopher Columbus arrived in America five hundred years ago he thought he had reached the East Indies so he called the people he met Indians. But really they were Arawaks, and they had as much in common with the Iroquois of the northern woodlands as the Iroquois had in common with the Blackfoot of the western Plains or the Haida of the Pacific Coast. In other words, when Columbus arrived in America there were a large number of different and distinct indigenous cultures, but there were no Indians.

The Indian is the invention of the European.

Robert Berkhofer Jr. introduced me to this unsettling idea in his book, *The White Man's Indian*. "Since the original inhabitants of the Western Hemisphere neither called themselves by a single term nor understood themselves as a collectivity," Berkhofer began, "the idea and the image of the Indian must be a White conception. Native Americans were and are real, but the Indian was a White invention ..."[2]

The Indian began as a White man's mistake, and became a White man's fantasy. Through the prism of White hopes, fears and prejudices, indigenous Americans would be seen to have lost contact with reality and to have become "Indians"; that is, anything non-Natives wanted them to be.

IV

This book attempts to describe the image of the Indian, the Imaginary Indian, in Canada since the middle of the nineteenth century. During this time, what did Canadians think an Indian was? What did children learn about them in school? What was government policy toward them? What Indian did painters paint and writers write about? I want to make it perfectly clear that while Indians are the subject of this book, Native people are not. This is a book about the images of Native people that White Canadians manufactured, believed in, feared, despised, admired, taught their children. It is a book about White—and not Native—cultural history.

Many of the images of Indians held by Whites were derogatory, and many were not. Many contained accurate representations of Native people; many did not. The "truth" of the image is not really what concerns me. I am not setting out to expose fraudulent images by comparing them to a "real Indian." It is, after all, the argument of this book that there is no such thing as a real Indian. When non-Native accounts of Indians are at variance with the known facts I will say so, but my main intention is not to argue with the stereotypes, but to think about them. The last thing I want to do is to replace an outdated Imaginary Indian with my very own, equally misguided, version. My concern is rather to understand where the Imaginary Indian came from, how Indian imagery has affected public policy in Canada and how it has shaped, and continues to shape, the myths non-Natives tell themselves about being Canadians.

Every generation claims a clearer grasp of reality than its predecessors. Our forebears held ludicrous ideas about certain things, we say confidently, but we do not. For instance, we claim to see Indians today much more clearly for what they are. I hope that my book will undermine such confidence. Much public discourse about Native people still deals in stereotypes. Our views of what constitutes an Indian today are as much bound up with myth, prejudice, and ideology as earlier versions were. If the Indian really is imaginary, it could hardly be otherwise.

Take, for example, the controversial 1991 decision by Chief Justice Allan McEachern of the Supreme Court of British Columbia relating to the Gitksan-Wet'suwet'en land claims case. Much of what Judge McEachern wrote about Native culture in that decision could as easily have been written by another judge one hundred, two hundred, three hundred years ago. In dismissing the Natives' claim, he wrote: "The plaintiffs' ancestors had no written language, no horses or wheeled vehicles, slavery and starvation was not uncommon, wars with neighbouring peoples were common, and there is no doubt, to quote Hobbs [sic], that aboriginal life in the territory was, at best, 'nasty, brutish and short.'"[3]

It is unclear whether Judge McEachern was aware when he borrowed this well-worn phrase that Thomas Hobbes actually coined it in 1651 to describe "the savage people of America" as he believed them to be. And many Europeans agreed with him. Because Native

North Americans were so different, had so few of the "badges of civilization" as Judge McEachern calls them, it was seriously debated whether they could properly be called human beings at all. I would have thought, however, that in the 340 years separating Thomas Hobbes and Judge McEachern, our understanding of aboriginal culture might be seen to have improved. But obviously not.

Of course, non-Natives have held much more favourable opinions about Indians over the years. The Noble Savage, for instance, is a venerable image, first used by the English dramatist John Dryden in his 1670 play, *The Conquest of Granada*, to refer to the innate goodness of man in a perceived "state of nature":

> I am as free as nature first made man,
> Ere the base laws of servitude began,
> When wild in the woods the noble savage ran.

For an example closer to home, we need look no further than the aforementioned Charles Mair, who wrote in his long poem, Tecumseh:

> … There lived a soul more wild than barbarous;
> A tameless soul-the sunburnt savage free-
> Free, and untainted by the greed of gain:
> Great Nature's man content with Nature's good.

Savage, when used by Dryden and Mair, meant innocent, virtuous, and peace-loving, free of the guile and vanity that came from living in contemporary society. I don't think I have to argue the fact that many non-Natives continue to believe that Indians have an innate nobility of character which somehow derives from their long connection with the American continent and their innocence of industrial society.

Ignoble or noble? From the first encounter, Europeans viewed aboriginal Americans through a screen of their own prejudices and preconceptions. Given the wide gulf separating the cultures, Europeans have tended to imagine the Indian rather than to know Native people, thereby to project onto Native people all the fears and hopes they have for the New World. If America was a Garden of Eden, then Indians must be seen as blessed innocents. If America was an alien place, then Indians must be seen to be frightful and bloodthirsty. Europeans also projected onto Native peoples all the misgivings they had about the shortcomings of their own civilization: the Imaginary Indian became a stick with which they beat their own society. The Indian became the standard of virtue and manliness against which Europeans measured themselves, and often found themselves wanting. In other words, non-Natives in North America have long defined themselves in relation to the Other in the form of the Indian.

As time passed, colonist and Native had more to do with one another. But Euro-Canadians continued to perceive Indians in terms of their own changing values, and so the image of the Indian changed over time. Close contact revealed differences between the idealized vision of the noble savage and the reality of Native culture. As White settlement spread, conflict increased. As long as Natives remained valuable allies in the wars the colonial powers waged against each other, the image of the Indian remained reasonably positive. By the middle of the nineteenth century, however, these wars were over and whites no longer needed Native military allies. Natives had become marginal to the new issues which preoccupied Canadian colonists: how to wrest a living from the country, how to create durable political institutions, how to transform a set of isolated colonies into a unified nation.

At this point Whites set themselves the task of inventing a new identity for themselves as Canadians. The image of the Other, the Indian, was integral to this process of self-identification. The Other came to stand for everything the Euro-Canadian was not. The content of the Other is the subject of this book.

V

A word about terminology. There is much debate these days about the correct term for indigenous Americans. Some do not object to being called Indians; others do. Alternative terms include aboriginals, Natives, Amerindians, First Nations peoples, and probably others I have not heard. In this book I use the word Indian when I am referring to the image of Native people held by non-Natives, and I use the terms Natives, Native people, or aboriginals when I am referring to the actual people. What to call non-Natives is equally puzzling. White is the convenient opposite of Indian, but it has obvious limitations. So, in this age of multiculturalism, does Euro-Canadian, an awkward term anyway. I hope readers will forgive me for using all three. It is part of the legacy of the Imaginary Indian that we lack a vocabulary with which to speak about these issues clearly.

PART ONE

◇◇◇◇◇◇◇◇◇◇◇◇

Taking the Image

ONE OF THE MOST famous historical paintings ever done on a Canadian theme is *The Death of Wolfe* by Benjamin West. The huge canvas depicts the English general, James Wolfe, expiring on the Plains of Abraham outside the walls of Quebec City. In the background, his triumphant army is capturing Canada for British arms. Wolfe lies prostrate in the arms of his grieving fellow officers. A messenger brings news of the victory, and with his last breath the general gives thanks. The eye is drawn to the left foreground where an Iroquois warrior squats, his chin resting contemplatively in his hand, watching as death claims his commander. The light shimmers on the Indian's bare torso, which looks as if it might be sculpted from marble.

From its unveiling in London in the spring of 1771, *The Death of Wolfe* was a sensation. It earned for its creator an official appointment as history painter to the King, and became one of the most enduring images of the British Empire, reproduced on tea trays, wall hangings, and drinking mugs. West himself completed six versions of the painting. Today it still appears in history textbooks as an accurate representation of the past. Yet as an historical document, it is largely a work of fiction. In reality, Wolfe died apart from the field of battle and only one of the men seen in the painting was actually present. Other officers who were present at the death refused to be included in the painting because they disliked General Wolfe so much.

And the Indian? According to his biographers, Wolfe despised the Native people, all of whom fought on the side of the French, anyway. Certainly, none would have been present at his death. But that did not matter to Benjamin West. Unlike Wolfe, West admired the

This famous painting, *The Death of Wolfe*, by Benjamin West, exemplifies the Imaginary Indian. It is largely a work of fiction, not an actual recreation of the event depicted. Only one of the men attending the dying general was actually present at Wolfe's death; which took place away from the battlefield. No Indian was there; Wolfe despised them and anyway they all fought on the side of the French. But Benjamin West was an admirer of the Noble Savage and so included the contemplative Native, mourning the death of his commander. The painting enjoyed enormous popularity and has been reproduced in countless schoolbooks down through the years as an authentic view of the battlefield.

Noble Savage of the American forest. And so he included the image of a Mohawk warrior, posed as a muscular sage—a symbol of the natural virtue of the New World, a virtue for which Wolfe might be seen to have sacrificed his life.

II

When White Canadians of earlier generations asked themselves what is an Indian, how did they know what to respond? What information did they have on which to base an answer? By the end of the nineteenth century, there were about 127,000 officially-designated

Indians living in Canada. Non-Natives had little exposure to these people, most of whom lived on reserves isolated from the main centres of population. They were pretty much a forgotten people. When they gave Native people any thought at all, White Canadians believed they were quickly disappearing in the face of disease, alcohol abuse, and economic hardship.

For the vast majority of Whites, Indians existed only as images like that of the Mohawk warrior in Benjamin West's painting. These images originated with a handful of artists, writers, and photographers who made the arduous journey into "Indian Country" and returned to exhibit what they had seen there. These image-makers to a large extent created the Imaginary Indian which Whites have believed in ever since.

CHAPTER TWO

The Vanishing Canadian

As late spring of 1845 warmed into summer, a portrait paint er named Paul Kane left Toronto "with a determined spirit and a light heart" to journey into Indian country for the first time. A painter of society portraits who had studied in Rome and London, the thirty-five-year-old Kane had taken the unusual decision to dedicate his talents to making an artistic record of the Canadian Indian. Kane believed the "red man" to be disappearing: "All traces of his footsteps are fast being obliterated from his once favourite haunts, and those who would see the aborigines of the country in their original state, or seek to study their native manners and customs, must travel far through the pathless forest to find them."[1] Before the Indians vanished, Kane intended to preserve their traditional customs and appearance on canvas.

Kane's travels that summer took him by canoe to Ojibway villages and seasonal gathering places around the shores of the Great Lakes, but he was not happy with what he found. His main impression of the Ojibway was of a people debauched by their contacts with White traders and settlers. "Liquor, whenever they can obtain it, is their chief bane," he wrote, "and lays them more open to the fraudulent sickness of their despoilers."[2] His objective was to make a record of the "noble savage" in his natural setting, not to witness the unhappy effects of White encroachment. Kane hoped that farther west he would find Native inhabitants who were less tainted by contact with outsiders. Returning to Toronto, he sought support for a larger expedition from Sir George Simpson, governor of the Hudson's Bay Company. With a letter from Simpson guaranteeing free transport with the company's canoe brigades and a cordial welcome at any of its trading posts, Kane embarked for Red River and the Northwest in June, 1846.

Paul Kane was the first artist in Canada to take the Native population as his subject. "The principal object of my undertaking," he later wrote, "was to sketch pictures of the principal chiefs and their original costumes, to illustrate their manners and customs, and to represent the scenery of an almost unknown country."[3] What made him decide to paint the Indians? Not even his biographer can say for sure. "There is no clear evidence to explain Kane's almost instant conversion at this time to the cause of painting Indians," writes Russell Harper. "A cynic might suggest that he saw a good thing and anticipated fame and fortune coming to him by means of a gallery of Canadian Indians."[4] Kane himself left no explanation for embarking on his great project.

Kane had had little personal exposure to Native people when he commenced his endeavour. As a youngster in Toronto, then the town of York, he saw a few Natives about the streets. But he did not take much interest in them until he travelled to Europe to study painting. There, in London, in 1843, Kane met the American artist George Catlin, whose canvases struck him with the force of a revelation. Catlin had ventured into the trans-Mississippi West during the 1830s to record the lifestyles of the Indians. After his return, he assembled six hundred paintings, along with a large collection of ethnological material, into a mobile display which toured the United States and Europe. In 1841, he published his first book about the Indians, the two-volume *Letter and Notes on the Manners, Customs and Condition of the North American Indians.* When Kane saw what Catlin had accomplished, he determined on the spot to give up portraiture, which had so far been his artistic bread and butter, return home, and do for Canada what Catlin had done so successfully south of the border.

Kane reached Red River by canoe in the middle of June, 1846, where he witnessed a Métis buffalo hunt. "The half-breeds are a very hardy race of men, capable of enduring the greatest hardships and fatigues," he wrote, "but their Indian propensities predominate, and consequently they make poor farmers, neglecting their land for the most exciting pleasures of the chase."[5] Kane crossed Lake Winnipeg to the trading post at Norway House where he remained for a month. Then he set off up the Saskatchewan River, the historic canoe route of the fur brigades, reaching Fort Edmonton towards the end of September. Travelling as he was in the company of Hudson's Bay Company men, Kane not unnaturally formed a positive impression of the company and its trading monopoly. Allowing free traders to enter the country to compete with the HBC would be akin to signing the death warrant of the Indians, he warned. "For while it is the interest of such a body as the Hudson's Bay Company to improve the Indians and encourage them to industry, according to their own native habits in hunting and the chase ... it is as obviously the interest of small companies and private adventurers to draw as much wealth as they possibly can from the country in the shortest possible time, altho' in doing so the very source from which the wealth springs should be destroyed."[6] Kane was referring here to the debilitating effects of the liquor trade with the Natives, which he blamed on the free traders.

With winter fast approaching, Kane and his party hurried to cross the Rocky Mountains, then descended the Columbia River to Fort Vancouver where they arrived early in December. Fort Vancouver remained Kane's headquarters during his stay on the West Coast. He sketched several portraits of the local Flathead people, who were not

One of Paul Kane's dramatic Indian paintings, in the style of European romanticism, *The Man Always Rides.*

quite sure how to interpret what they saw. "My power of portraying the features of individuals was attributed entirely to supernatural agency," reported Kane, "and I found that, in looking at my pictures, they always covered their eyes with their hands and looked through their fingers; this being also the invariable custom when looking at a dead person."[7] In the spring of 1847, Kane went on a three-month sketching trip to Vancouver Island. There would not be another artist interested in recording the Native people of the Pacific Northwest until Emily Carr over fifty years later.

That summer Kane left Fort Vancouver for the East. Travelling back up the Columbia River, he made an arduous crossing of the Rockies and did not arrive at Fort Edmonton until December. He remained there for the next six months sketching on the prairie and waiting for the spring canoe brigade to depart with the season's trade of furs. Descending the Saskatchewan River, he crossed Lake Winnipeg and northern Ontario and reached Sault Ste. Marie on the first day of October. Two weeks later a steamboat carried him into Toronto harbour, home again after more than two years wandering the wild Northwest.

Kane's arrival home stirred up great interest. Within a month he mounted an exhibit much like Catlin's, including some of the five hundred sketches prepared on his travels and a selection of Indian "souvenirs." Response was enthusiastic. People flocked to the exhibit to see powerful portraits of Native hunters, scenes of the buffalo chase, and depictions of exotic pagan rituals. Critics remarked on the authenticity and exquisite detail of the work. "A striking characteristic of Mr. Kane's paintings ... is their truthfulness," reported the *British Colonist* newspaper. "Nothing has been sacrificed to effect—no exaggerated examples of costumes—no incredible distortions of features—are permitted to move our wonder, or exalt our conceptions of what is sufficiently wild and striking without improvements."[8] The Ontario public was just beginning to wake up to the existence of the far Northwest, and was already predisposed to romanticize the western Native. In Kane's paintings of picturesque Indians in elaborate costumes of feathers and buffalo hide, his audience found confirmation of a fascinating wilderness world inhabited by fiercely independent, entirely mysterious people. Everyone agreed that Kane, their own local hero, had done even better than Catlin.

Kane's ambition was to complete a series of one hundred large canvases depicting the Northwest frontier from the Great Lakes to the Pacific Coast. After closing his one-man show in Toronto, he set to work on this task. As well, he had to prepare another fourteen paintings which he had promised George Simpson. In 1850, Kane asked the House of Assembly for financial help to complete his project and the next year the provincial government agreed to buy a dozen canvases. After much prompting, these were completed in 1856 and now reside with the National Gallery in Ottawa. Meanwhile, a wealthy Toronto lawyer, George W. Allan, purchased the entire set of one hundred paintings, which were by then almost finished. Together with Kane's Indian artifacts, Allan displayed the works for many years in his home, Moss Park. After his death in 1901, the paintings were sold to Sir Edmund Osler, who in turn donated them to the Royal Ontario Museum in Toronto, where they remain.

Kane was a documentary artist, but he worked within certain conventions and manipulated his images to suit the demands of these conventions. Though he was praised for his accuracy, he often added details of setting and landscape to highlight the romantic flavour of the scenes, and he sometimes "cheated" by adding clothing and artifacts foreign to the Indians in the paintings. His most famous "forgery" is a depiction of an Assiniboine buffalo hunt which was actually modelled on an Italian engraving of two young men on horseback chasing a bull. Recently Kane has been accused of exploiting the Indians by using them as "exotic curiosities" instead of painting them realistically.[9]

But I don't think Kane can be expected to have conveyed a realistic sense of the Native cultures he visited. He was essentially a tourist among the Indians. He spoke no Native languages; he had a superficial understanding of Native customs. Despite his sympathy for what he saw to be their plight, he showed little concern for Native people after his expedition and he was surprisingly narrow-minded about many aspects of their culture. Nonetheless, the power, the beauty, and above all the uniqueness of his paintings established him as the pre-eminent artistic interpreter of the Indian for many years to come. Even today it is hard to find a history textbook that does not contain at least one of Kane's renderings of Indian life. For most of us, the Indian of nineteenth-century Canada is Paul Kane's Indian.

The Noble Savage of the Plains is depicted in this large canvas by Kane, *Big Snake, a Blackfoot Chief recounting his War Exploits.*

Like Catlin, Kane described his western adventures in a popular memoir. *Wanderings of an Artist among the Indians of North America* appeared in 1859 to laudatory reviews. A bestseller in English, it spawned French, Danish, and German editions within four years. In the preface, Kane laments the inevitable disappearance of the Indian, and though the rest of the book does not deal with this subject in any detail, most reviewers took it as their theme. "One must make haste to visit the Red Men," said a typical review. "Their tribes, not long since still masters of a whole world, are disappearing rapidly, driven back and destroyed by the inroads of the white race. Their future is inevitable ... The Indians are doomed; their fate will be that of so many primitive races now gone." [10]

In their conviction that the Native people were doomed to

disappear, Kane and his admirers were completely representative of their age. If any single belief dominated the thinking about Canadian aboriginals during the last half of the nineteenth century, it was that they would not be around to see much of the twentieth. Anyone who paid any attention at all to the question agreed that Natives were disappearing from the face of the earth, victims of disease, starvation, alcohol, and the remorseless ebb and flow of civilizations. "The Indian tribes are passing away, and what is done must be done quickly," wrote the missionary John Maclean, a noted Indian authority, in 1889. "On the western plains, native songs, wafted on the evening breezes, are the dying requiem of the departing savage."[11] Any number of other writers made the same point. Some believed that it was the Indian's traditional culture that was being eradicated by the spread of white settlement, while others believed the Indians themselves literally to be dying out. Some found the idea appalling; some found it regrettable; some found it desirable. But all were agreed that the Indian was doomed.

II

The "fact" that Indians were a vanishing breed made them especially attractive to artists. The pathos inherent in the subject appealed to White audiences. It also gave an urgency to the work. Artists like Paul Kane who chose to portray the Indian believed they were saving an entire people from extinction; not literally, of course, but in the sense that they were preserving on canvas, and later on film, a record of a dying culture before it expired forever.

This sense of urgent mission controlled the way Indians were portrayed in the work of White artists, who became amateur ethnographers seeking to record Indian life as it was lived before the arrival of White people. Artists ignored evidence of Native adaptation to White civilization and highlighted traditional lifestyles. Often the result was an idealized image of the Indian based on what the artist imagined aboriginal life to have been before contact.

Several Canadian artists tried their hand at Indian painting, but three in particular attempted, like Kane, to become the chief interpreters and preservers of Native culture. One was Frederick Arthur Verner, known especially for his paintings of buffalo. Another was Edmund Morris, a landscape painter turned Native portraitist. And the third was Emily Carr, whose brooding oil paintings of West Coast totem poles gained her sudden attention in the 1930s.

III

Born in 1836 in Halton County, Upper Canada (Ontario), Frederick Arthur Verner displayed an aptitude for drawing from an early age and was exhibiting publicly by the time he was sixteen years old.[12] He was a great admirer of Kane's work, and it must have given him a great deal of satisfaction in 1876 when a government report described him as having taken up "the mantle fallen from the shoulders of the late Paul Kane."

Unlike his mentor, however, Verner began painting Indians before he had really seen much of them. His first two Indian portraits, done in 1862, were based on photographs. Most of his research involved looking at paintings and illustrations by other artists. In 1867, he got as far as the reserve on Chemong Lake, near Peterborough, but in 1870 he exhibited a group of five oil paintings in Montreal titled "Indian landscape scenes in the far West" even though the farthest west he had travelled was the Muskoka Lakes. The tipis in his paintings were ones he had seen at a provincial exhibition in Toronto.

Verner finally went west in 1873, spending a summer in Manitoba. He witnessed the signing of Treaty 3 at Lake of the Woods that September, and the sketches he made during this brief trip supplied him with material for most of his subsequent Indian paintings. In 1875, he began the buffalo paintings for which he would become famous, although his biographer, Joan Murray, believes he probably never saw one in the wild.

Verner liked to paint scenes showing Indian figures canoeing across remote wilderness lakes or shooting down tumbling rapids. Another favourite subject was an Indian family sitting around its lodge, a model image of domesticity. His figures are seldom seen up close; rather they are figures in idyllic natural settings with no individuality. His work is beautiful but monotonous. He painted attitudes and postures, not people. In Verner's art, the Indian is merely part of the landscape. In his autobiography, A.Y. Jackson said of Verner: "Only occasionally does one feel that he painted something he had actually seen." [13]

In 1880, Verner moved to England, where he attained great success and where he remained the rest of his life. Abroad, his images of Indians and buffalo, because of their exoticism, drew even more attention than they might have at home. "His subjects are very interesting to us who live on this side of the great salt lake," wrote a British academic; "they record things which ... are doomed to pass away. The buffalo may already be classed with the Great Auk and the Dodo, and the aboriginal Red Indian, in flannel shirt and trousers, no longer reminds one of the noble savage in his war paint who stalks so majestically through the narratives of Fenimore Cooper." [14]

IV

If Frederick Verner aspired to follow in the footsteps of Paul Kane, Edmund Morris actually did so, in the sense that he made a project out of the Indians. The son of Alexander Morris, the lieutenant governor of Manitoba and the Northwest Territories who negotiated several treaties with the western tribes, Edmund was raised at Fort Garry. [15] Later the family moved back to Ontario and after studies in New York and Paris, Edmund achieved recognition in Canada prin-

Frederick Arthur Verner's vision of the Canadian Shield, *The Upper Ottawa* (1882). As in most of his paintings, the Indians are figures in the landscape.

cipally as a landscape painter. His youthful exposure to the western frontier surfaced in 1905 when he exhibited three portraits of Plains chiefs—Big Bear, Poundmaker, and Crowfoot—in Ottawa. The federal government bought the canvases and in the following year the Ontario government invited Morris to accompany a party of officials travelling through northern Ontario negotiating the James Bay Treaty (Treaty 9) with the Cree and Ojibway inhabitants. It was the treaty party's second summer in the bush and Morris went along to paint the portraits of the Native leaders who signed the treaty.

The excursion was an eye-opener for Morris, and it seems to have set him on a new artistic course. From then on, Indians provided the subject matter for most of his paintings. Early in 1907, he exhibited several of his James Bay portraits in Toronto. Impressed with his work, the Ontario government again commissioned him, this time to travel out west to paint elderly Native leaders who had been signatories to the Prairie treaties made thirty years before. Morris spent the next four summers in Alberta, Saskatchewan, and Manitoba touring the reserves, meeting the Natives and painting their portraits. In the process, he became engrossed in the history of the Plains tribes. He gathered stories and information about them from missionaries and Indian agents and from the Native elders themselves. Whenever possible, he attached detailed biographies to the portraits. As well as making paintings, he photographed many of his subjects and made an extensive collection of Native clothing and other objects.

At the end of March, 1909, Morris opened a major exhibition of his Indian paintings and artifacts in Toronto. They aroused a great deal of attention and praise. The Ontario government had decided not

Edmund Morris with Chief Nepahpenais, one of his subjects.

to commission Morris for another season and the decision earned criticism from the *Globe*. "Mr. Morris has been devoting some of the best years of his life to the painting of rapidly vanishing Indian Chiefs," the newspaper intoned, and all for a pittance. "No wonder young Canadian artists go abroad whenever they can earn passage money."[16] (Actually, Morris was independently wealthy and hardly lacked passage money to anywhere.) Meanwhile, a critic in the same paper pointed out the great service Morris was performing, recording for posterity "the sole survivors of the great race of redmen in Canada."[17] *Saturday Night* hailed the portraits as "the finest possible souvenirs of a race which will soon be no more than a tradition."[18] Critics praised the paintings for their artistic qualities, but also they approved Morris's entire Indian project. The artist was cast in the role of archaeologist, returning from his quest with evidence of cultures now defunct.

Morris himself did not necessarily agree that Indians were disappearing from the West. His concern was to preserve a record of individual Indians who were dying, the elders who had signed the treaties and lived a traditional life on the Plains before contact with White people. Time was having its way with this band of survivors, and their offspring, in the throes of adjusting to a completely different world, were losing their identities as hunters and warriors. Morris explained to Saskatchewan Premier Walter Scott "the importance of losing no time as the last of the fighting Indians will soon be gone and then it will be impossible to get true records of the old type of those who held land before the coming of the whites."[19] But Morris did not share the prevailing belief that the Indian as a separate people were vanishing.

In 1913, Morris drowned in the St. Lawrence River—whether accidently or intentionally is not certain. By the time he died he had amassed a stunning collection of Native material, much of which now resides in the Royal Ontario Museum. Unlike some of the other artists who painted the Indians, Morris seems to have had a genuine interest in his subjects as people. On a couple of occasions he gave buffalo hides to the elders and asked them to paint their own life stories on them. After his visits to the West, he kept up a correspondence with them and sent them gifts. They in turn called him Kyaiyii (Bear Robe in Blackfoot), and hoped he would take up their grievances with government officials in the East.

Morris's diaries from these western trips reveal a man who genuinely admired the traditional culture of the Plains tribes.[20] In his

Two of Edmund Morris's Indian portraits: the Assinboine chief, Opazatonka (*left*), and the Cree, Pimotat (*right*).

daily entries he neither moralized about the Indians, nor despised their customary practices as, for example, Paul Kane habitually did in his account of his expedition. But neither did Morris romanticize Native culture, or exploit it simply to make his mark as a popular artist. He was concerned primarily with recording the faces of the elders. Whatever he may have felt about the problems Natives were having in their contacts with Whites, he did not indulge in moralizing in his portraits. They are straightforward head-and-shoulder views, without the dramatic props of Kane or the picturesque settings of Verner. The faces are dignified and unsentimental and manage to convey individuality and force of character. The result is a portrait gallery of unprecedented artistic merit and historic value. "Certainly," writes the ethnographer E.S. Rogers, "they should be to all Canadians, as they were to Morris, as important as the portraits of prime ministers, lieutenant governors and generals ... "[21]

Morris was not widely valued as an artist in his own day, and was quickly forgotten after his death. "His slip from memory has been almost complete," wrote one critic in 1984.[22] Why? The rise and fall of artistic fortunes is a complicated process. There are many reasons why a painter falls into disfavour. It has been argued in Morris's case that he was old-fashioned in his obeisance to European styles, and was shunted aside by an art world looking for the "made in Canada" sensibility of the Group of Seven.[23] It might also be true that Morris's Indian portraits did not satisfy the enjoyment many Canadians got from moralizing about the Indians. Perhaps the public was disappointed in Morris for not evoking the tragic disappearance of the Indian. Morris committed the indiscretion of leaving Whites out of his Indian paintings, in the sense that he tried to paint what he saw without obvious comment. As a result, a public eager to become emotionally involved was denied the pleasure of feeling guilty about the "Vanishing Canadians." In the end they made the artist pay the price; they forgot about him.

V

At about the same time as Edmund Morris was recording the Plains Indian chiefs, Emily Carr was undertaking a similar project among the tribes on the coast of British Columbia. "I am a Canadian born and bred," she told the audience at a huge exhibit of her paintings in Vancouver in April, 1913. "I glory in our wonderful West and I hope to leave behind me some of the relics of its first primitive greatness."[24]

"These things," she continued, referring to the totem poles, house fronts, and village scenes in her paintings, "should be to we Canadians what the ancient Briton's relics are to the English. Only a few more years and they will be gone forever, into silent nothingness, and I would gather my collections together before they are forever past."[25]

As these remarks reveal, Carr initially cast herself very much in the same mould as Paul Kane; that is, a documentary artist making a visual record of a condemned people. Carr conceived her Indian project in

1907 during a summer steamer excursion to Alaska with her sister. The two women spent a week at the Native settlement of Sitka where they visited the famous Totem Walk, a collection of poles erected as a tourist attraction. While she was at Sitka, Carr met the American artist, Theodore J. Richardson, who had been painting in the village every summer for many years. She viewed his work and showed him some of the watercolours she had done of the poles. Richardson praised her abilities and Carr decided on the spot to dedicate herself to recording the heritage of British Columbia's Native peoples before it vanished.

At this time Emily Carr had been studying painting for more than a decade, in San Francisco and London, and was teaching art in Vancouver as well as pursuing her own career as a painter. Her exposure to Native people was limited to the Indians she saw around Victoria when she was growing up, and to the visit she had made in 1898 to the Native villages near Ucluelet on the west coast of Vancouver Island. Yet even as a child, she felt a strong fascination for the Indian; "often I used to wish I had been born an Indian," she later wrote. Her biographers speculate that Carr, alienated from her own family and from polite Victoria society, was attracted by the apparent freedom and unconventionality of the Indians who inhabited the fringes of her world.[26] A bit of a misanthrope, she idealized Indians as outsiders, misfits like herself.

Having resolved to paint the Indian "like a camera" for posterity, Carr set about her project with great energy. Between 1907 and 1912, interrupted by a year of study in France, she visited Native villages all along the coast, from Campbell River and Alert Bay on Vancouver Island to the Haida settlements of the Queen Charlotte Islands and the Gitksan villages in the Skeena River Valley. These were arduous expeditions, especially for a woman travelling alone. They involved long voyages by steamship and open boat, toilsome hikes with heavy packs through dense forest, overnight camping in leaky tents in iso-

House Front – Gold Harbour (1912–13), one of the paintings resulting from Emily Carr's excursions to the isolated villages of the Pacific coast.

lated villages. Through it all, her commitment to the project was total.

Carr's Indian painting came to a head in 1913 with the Vancouver exhibition. It contained almost two hundred pieces—oils, watercolours, sketches—covering fourteen years' worth of excursions. The long public lecture which she gave twice during the exhibition explained how totem poles were made and the role they played in the life of the Native people. In her talk, Carr revealed her strong affection and admiration for the Natives of the coast. Unlike Kane and the other artists who had set out to paint the Indian, Carr felt a deep personal bond with her subject. She was recording for posterity, but she was also striving for understanding.

Like many of her contemporaries, Carr interpreted contact between Native and non-Native in Christian terms. Before the White man came, she believed that the Indian lived in harmony with nature in something approaching a Garden of Eden. "In their own primitive state they were a moral people with a high ideal of right," she told her listeners. "I think they could teach us many things." When Whites arrived, they offered Indians the "apple" of a new way of life. But the apple had a worm in it. "They looked up to the whites, as a superior race whom they should try to copy. Alas, they could not discriminate between the good and bad, there was so much bad, and they copied it." [27] As a result, she believed, Indians had lost touch with their traditional culture which was speedily disappearing from the coast.

Carr's 1913 exhibition was well received, but she failed to win a hoped-for commission from the provincial government and had to return to Victoria where she assumed the life of a boarding-house keeper. Without encouragement, she could not afford to go on painting and eventually she abandoned her Indian project. Her "retirement" lasted until 1927, when a visit from Eric Brown, director of the National Gallery in Ottawa, suddenly elevated her and her Indian paintings into national prominence. Brown was looking for canvases to include in an upcoming show of West Coast Indian art at the National Museum. Stunned to discover the cache of paintings Carr had completed so many years before, he convinced her to contribute several to the exhibition. What followed—Carr's trip back east to the opening, her meeting with Lawren Harris, her discovery of the Group of Seven and their discovery of her—is one of the legends of Canadian art history.

The exhibition opened in Ottawa on December 2, 1927. A combination of Native art and modern paintings on Native themes, the show was hailed in the press as an historic occasion, the first of its kind anywhere in the world. "What a tremendous influence the vanishing civilization of the West Coast Indian is having on the minds of Canadian artists," reported the *Ottawa Citizen*. Carr received particular praise. "She is a real discovery," wrote the *Citizen* critic. Her work was "the greatest contribution of all time to historic art of the Pacific slope." [28] Early in January, the exhibition moved on to Toronto where

The Ottawa exhibition of Native art which brought Emily Carr's work to the attention of a wide audience.

the critic in the *Daily Star* described it as "a revelation" comparable to the discovery of a "Canadian tomb of Tutankaheman." The Native art and artifacts were among the country's greatest cultural treasures, he wrote, as important as the art of the Aztecs, the Mayans, or the Incans.[29] It is noteworthy that he made the comparison not to a living tradition but to other vanished Americans.

A cynic might have taken a more jaundiced view of the exhibition. After all, the art seemed to be valued chiefly as examples of a Native tradition long dead. The death of that tradition was both the theme of the work and the necessary precondition of its sudden popularity. While artists like Emily Carr lamented the fate of the Indian, their success was predicated on it. Having first of all destroyed many aspects of Native culture, White society now turned around and admired its own recreations of what it had destroyed. To the extent that they suffered any guilt over what had happened to the Native people, Whites relieved it by preserving evidence of the supposedly dying

Mrs. Douse, Chieftainess of Kitwancool (1928), one of the later paintings of Native people by Emily Carr.

culture. Whites convinced themselves that they were in this way saving the Indians. By a curious leap of logic, non-Natives became the saviours of the vanishing Indian.

Carr returned from the East with her confidence as an artist restored. She immediately resumed her painting career, and in the summer of 1928 made another excursion north to the villages of the Skeena and Nass rivers and the Queen Charlotte Islands. This trip resulted in some of her finest paintings, but it also marked an end to her Indian project. Under the encouragement of Lawren Harris, she began to feel that she had gone as far as she could as an interpreter of Native art and that it was time to concentrate on her own vision of the forest wilderness, unmediated by Native monuments.

But Carr's interest in Native people remained strong. As her health deteriorated in the late 1930s, she devoted more of her time to writing. She wrote stories about her odd assortment of pets, about her days as a landlady, about her childhood, and about her early excursions to the coastal Indian villages. A group of the latter were collected and published in 1941 as *Klee Wyck*. The book received a warm critical reception—"there is nothing to be said in dispraise of her work," commented Robertson Davies—and the next year it won a Governor General's Award for non-fiction.

Carr's style in *Klee Wyck* is unique and charming, at its best when she describes her deep affection for the coastal forest, "the twisted trees and high tossed driftwood."[30] With few exceptions, though, her Indians lack individual character. They are noble figures, living in tune with forest and sea. But they are exotics—servants, street pedlars, subsistence fishermen who speak broken English—living outside White society and apparently having no place in it. Carr is never patronizing. She herself was alienated from mainstream Canadian society and her stories romanticize the poverty and dignity of the social outcast. She describes the harsh reality of life for the contemporary Native, but she is no social worker. Her stories ask the reader to admire the character of the Indian, just as her painting asks the viewer to admire the spirituality and art. Nowhere does she ask her audience to confront social reality. As a result, although she had great personal sympathy for the Indian, she nevertheless belongs to the tradition of artists who took for granted that Indians were vanishing and sought to preserve an idealized image of them, and not the reality of Native people.

VI

The Vanishing Indian was by no means an exclusively Canadian concept. South of the border, Americans also considered Native people an endangered species. James Fenimore Cooper's "last Mohican" was for many a symbol of all Indians. Prior to World War I, the Vanishing American achieved cult status. In 1911, in California, a lone Native appeared out of the wilderness near Oroville, the last member of his tribe known to exist. Ishi, the so-called last of the Yaki, was more or less adopted by a museum at the University of California where the anthropologist Alfred Kroeber worked with him to reconstruct the culture of his people. Like Cooper's fictional Indian, Ishi became a public symbol of "the last Indian." His death in 1916 represented for many Americans the demise of an entire race.

Another highly-publicized attempt to preserve a record of the Vanishing American was launched in 1908 by Rodman Wanamaker, the wealthy son of a Philadelphia dry goods merchant. Believing that Indians were disappearing, Wanamaker financed three film expeditions into the western states. The first resulted in a film version of the Hiawatha story using Native actors. The second expedition, in 1909, invited members of the western tribes to attend a council where their stories were transcribed and their photographs taken. The result was an illustrated book, *The Vanishing Race*, written by Wanamaker's associate, Joseph Dixon. By the time of the third expedition, in 1913, the Wanamaker project had abandoned any pretense of science in favour of showmanship on a grand scale. Called the "Expedition of Citizenship to the North American Indian," this travelling caravan visited dozens of reservations to ask Natives, with much fanfare, to sign a declaration of allegiance to America and to listen to a recorded message from President Woodrow Wilson. Wanamaker's expeditions, which produced 11,000 photographs and fifty miles of movie film, represent the most ambitious private attempt to preserve a record of the "Vanishing American."[31]

One person who was not amused by Wanamaker's showmanship was the Seattle photographer, Edward S. Curtis. About 1900, Curtis had set out to accomplish in photographs what George Catlin and

Paul Kane had attempted to do in paint—to capture the image of the Indian before it disappeared without a trace. Visiting Native tribes from Alaska to the American Southwest, Curtis attempted to make a complete record of Indian life. He published his photographs in a monumental series of twenty books, *The North American Indian*, published between 1907 and 1930. The series included a total of 1,500 prints. Each volume also came with a corresponding portfolio of copperplate photogravures, 722 in all. The cost of an entire set was anywhere from $3,000 to $4,500.

The very first photograph in the set was titled "The Vanishing Race." It depicted a group of Navajo on horseback disappearing into a desert haze. Curtis explained that he meant the photograph to show "that the Indians as a race, already shorn of their tribal strength and stripped of their primitive dress, are passing into the darkness of an unknown future."[32] This image attained huge popularity in its own right, so Curtis understandably was put out when the Wanamaker-Dixon project published its book of the same name, filled with illustrations reminiscent of his own photographic style. Curtis accused his rivals of plagiarism, but he needn't have worried. Their efforts were quickly forgotten, while his own work includes some of the most powerful and popular images of Indians ever produced. (*The Vanishing American* continued to echo down through the years. In 1925, the western novelist Zane Grey borrowed the phrase for the title of one of his novels, which in turn inspired a silent film of the same name.)

Curtis's project consumed thirty years of his life and all of his resources. The financier J.P. Morgan was a major backer, but even so Curtis was constantly on the verge of bankruptcy, seeking ways to finance the next volume. He lectured tirelessly on Indian subjects and exhibited collections of his photographs. Many of his pictures were reproduced for sale as fine-art prints and postcards. He collected prominent patrons to tout his work, including President Theo-

Edward Curtis taking one of his carefully-staged photographs.

dore Roosevelt who, despite being an out-and-out racist—"The most vicious cowboy has more moral principle than the average Indian," he once said—loudly praised the photographs. In 1911, Curtis even mounted an elaborate touring musical entertainment to raise money. Called alternatively "The Curtis Indian Picture Opera" or "The Curtis Picture Musicale," the show featured Curtis's standard lecture on the "Vanishing American" illustrated with hand-tinted lantern slides, moving pictures, and a twenty-two-piece orchestra playing an original score based on "Indian" music. Apparently Curtis overreached himself with this extravaganza and had to close partway through the initial tour.[33]

It was partly to raise money for *The North American Indian* that Curtis produced his pioneering documentary motion picture, *In the Land of the Head-Hunters.* This film, which was shown publicly only twice and then disappeared, was a lurid tale of love and warfare among the Kwakiutl of northern Vancouver Island. Head-hunting was not an important part of the film, nor was it a significant part of Kwakiutl culture. The title was chosen for its appeal to the film-going public, as were many of the events in the movie, including a vision quest, a whale hunt, a romantic love affair, an evil sorcerer, and an elaborate battle scene. A copy of the film has been restored and provides a remarkable record of Kwakiutl ceremonialism.[34]

If the camera never lies, neither does it tell the whole truth. Critics praised the authenticity of Curtis's photographs. People admired the way they showed Indians "as they really were." But in fact, the photographs were carefully posed renderings designed to convey a particular view of the Indian. Curtis equipped his subjects with props—wigs, for example, and items of clothing—and doctored the photographs to eliminate evidence of White culture. He was trying to present Indians as they existed before the White Man came; or, more accurately, as he thought they existed before the White Man came. Like most non-Natives of his day, Curtis believed in a timeless Indian past where nothing much really changed. His photographs were tiny time machines intended to take the viewer back before history began into a romantic world of a technologically primitive people. Any evidence of contact with White culture contaminated this image and Curtis worked to eliminate it. Native people as they actually lived did not interest him because in his eyes they were no longer Indians. Only in his photographs might one find the real Indian, which is to say, the Imaginary Indian.

When Curtis finally completed his Indian project in 1930 he was depressed and almost penniless, his marriage and his health broken. By the time he died in 1952, his work had fallen into neglect and he was largely forgotten. But then in the 1970s came the great revival. The civil rights movement, the environmental movement, the anti-materialism of the counterculture, all combined to bring Indians back into fashion. A kind of "neo-noble-savagism" was all the rage and Curtis provided the movement with some of its most striking icons. *The North American Indian* became "the most profound document of pure Indian culture ever made" as the introduction to a new book of his photographs put it.[35] His Indian images papered the walls of university dorms, head-shops, galleries, and cafes. Young people in particular were seduced by the nostalgic images of a spiritual people, innocent of polluting machinery, existing in what appeared to be a pristine state of nature. It is an irony of Curtis's career that when he took them he intended his photographs to be appreciated by the rich and the powerful, but twenty years after his death they found a much wider audience as symbols of rebellion and anti-consumerism.

VII

Douglas Sladen was a British tourist who crossed Canada by rail in 1894. In his memoir of the trip, *On the Cars and Off*, Sladen remarked on the sudden democratization of photography. Quite clearly, Edward Curtis wasn't the only one photographing the Indian. Everyone on the train seemed to be busy with a camera. "Whenever you stop at a station," he wrote, "all the steps getting down are packed with people taking pot shots with Kodaks. American children learn kodaking before they learn to behave themselves ... Crossing the prairie, every operator imagines he is going to kodak an Indian; but the wily Indian sits in the shade, where instantaneous photography availeth not, and, if he observes himself being 'time exposed,' covers himself with a blanket."[36]

This reluctance of Native people to be photographed recalls Paul Kane's description of his Native subjects covering their faces when they looked at their portraits. It has been said that aboriginal people unfamiliar with the technology of the camera believe the photographer to be capturing their souls in his little box. And in a manner of speaking, they are right. "To photograph is to appropriate the thing photographed," writes Susan Sontag. "It means putting oneself into a certain relation to the world that feels like knowledge—and, therefore, like power."[37]

When they drew the Indians or took their photographs, artists like Kane, Curtis, and the rest were taking possession of the Indian image. It was now theirs to manipulate and display in any way they wanted. The image-makers returned from Indian Country with their images and displayed them as actual representations of the way Indians really were. Fanciful as they were in so many respects, these images nevertheless became the Indian for most non-Native Canadians who knew no other.

CHAPTER THREE
Writing Off the Indian

P AUL KANE AND HIS FELLOW artists were not the only people at work on the Indian image in the latter half of the nineteenth century. They were accompanied into Indian Country by a veritable stampede of travellers, surveyors, sportsmen, and missionaries, from Europe as well as Eastern Canada, attracted by the opportunity to see the wild "redskin" in his natural setting before he passed away into history. They came with sketchbook open and pen at the ready, poised to record every impression. Many described their adventures in articles and books which were devoured by audiences back home curious about what the Indian was "really like."

Travellers whose imaginations had been nurtured on the paintings of Catlin and Kane and the novels of Fenimore Cooper held high expectations of the Red Man. Actual Native people could not hope to measure up to the standards set by art. As a result, visitors often felt betrayed in their efforts to find a real Indian: "I was disappointed in these Indians," wrote the Earl of Southesk about his encounter with a band of Saulteaux at Pembina in 1859. "They too much resembled commonplace Europeans." Southesk was a wealthy nobleman travelling in western Canada partly for his health and partly because he had nothing better to do. At Fort Garry, he met a party of Cree and dismissed them as "an ugly, hard-featured set ... dirty, gypsylike people, neither handsome, interesting, nor picturesque." Noticing a young Native boy shooting toy arrows at his father's horse, Southesk remarked: "From his very childhood the Indian learns inhumanity to animals"—this from a man who was himself an avid trophy hunter. Southesk further informed his readers that the older generation of Indians was beyond redemption. "All with whom I have conversed agree in thinking that little or nothing can be done to improve the adults of the Cree, Ojibway, Assiniboine or Blackfoot tribes, and believe that the only hope lies in teaching and influencing the young, before evil and reckless habits become a part of their nature." [1]

Southesk was the first of a long line of writers who milked the confrontation between Indian and industrialism for all its symbolic possibilities. At Fort Garry on the banks of the Red River he witnessed the arrival from St. Paul of the *Anson Northup*, the first steamboat in the Northwest. "Crowds of Indians stood silently on the shore, watching the arrival of this strange, portentous object," he reported. "Little thought they how ominous a sight it was for them, fraught with presages of ruin for all their wandering race!" [2] In this oft-repeated image, contempt for Native culture gives way to pity and even sometimes regret. Viscount Milton and W.B. Cheadle, two transcontinental travellers, observed a "Red Indian" at a railway station in the United States in 1862:

> He wore leather shirt, leggings and mocassins, a blanket thrown over his shoulders, and his bold-featured handsome face was adorned with paint. He was leaning against a tree, smoking his pipe with great dignity, not deigning to move or betray the slightest interest as the train went past him. We could not help reflecting—as, perhaps, he was doing—with something of sadness upon the changes which had taken place since his ancestors were lords of the soil.... And we could well imagine the disgust of these sons of silence and stealth at the noisy trains which rush through the forests, and the steamers

Travellers loved to take the railway west where they could see the noble Red Man in his natural setting before he disappeared forever.

which dart along lakes and rivers, once the favourite haunt of game, now driven far away. How bitterly in their hearts they must curse that steady, unfaltering, inevitable advance of the great army of whites, recruited from every corner of the earth, spreading over the land like locusts ...[3]

Seldom has the clash of cultures been described so poignantly. The noble Indian, the forest philosopher, stands by stoically while the forces of civilization invade and disrupt his land and foreshadow his ultimate destruction. But as Milton and Cheadle continued their expedition across the Canadian Plains, their sentimental regret at the corruption of the wilderness was soon forgotten. They became instead excited boosters of the very process they seemed to condemn. Come to Canada, they encouraged their fellow Britons: "This glorious country, capable of sustaining an enormous population, lies ut-

terly useless, except for the support of a few Indians, and the enrich-
ment of the shareholders of the Last Great Monopoly [the Hudson's
Bay Company]."[4] However much they regretted the extermination
of an entire people, Milton and Cheadle believed in the inevitability
of progress. They were convinced that their own civilization must
prevail, that the Red Man could not adapt to the new world taking
shape around him.

Another representative of western civilization, William Francis
Butler, visited the Northwest in 1870. Butler, too, emphasized the
emptiness of what he memorably termed "The Great Lone Land."
"There is no other portion of the globe in which travel is possible
where loneliness can be said to live so thoroughly," he wrote. Butler was sent west by the government to assess the effects of a recent smallpox epidemic. He returned with harrowing tales about the
fate of the Native people at the hands of predatory white traders and
hunters who were beginning to enter their land. "It is the same story
from the Atlantic to the Pacific. First the white man was the welcome
guest, the honoured visitor; then the greedy hunter, the death-deal-
ing vendor of fire-water and poison; then the settler and extermina-
tor—everywhere it has been the same story."[5]

To Butler, the western Indian represented natural man, proud,
independent, virtuous—and doomed. "The most curious anomaly
among the race of man, the red man of America, is passing away
beneath our eyes into the infinite solitude. The possession of the
same noble qualities which we affect to reverence among our nations
makes us kill him ... If he would be our slave he might live, but as
he won't be that, won't toil and delve and hew for us, and will per-
sist in hunting, fishing, and roaming over the beautiful prairie land
which the Great Spirit gave him; in a word, since he will be free—
we kill him." Butler described the fearful impact of smallpox on the
people of the Plains who had no immunity to it. At Fort Pitt on the

North Saskatchewan River, dozens of Cree had died outside the post, their corpses devoured by wolves. The Natives believed they could rid themselves of the disease by transferring it back to the Whites and they crowded around the stockade, touching their pustules to the walls and spitting on the door handles.[6]

For Butler, the demise of the Indian was not the byproduct of the impersonal forces of progress. In his best-selling account of his expedition, *The Great Lone Land*, he blamed the White whiskey peddlers, buffalo-robe traders, and wolfers, most of them American, who were spreading disease and mayhem among the Plains tribes. "It is a useless struggle, that which these Indians wage against their latest and most deadly enemy" he wrote, "but nevertheless it is one in which the sympathy of any brave heart must lie on the side of the savage."[7]

George Grant agreed. Grant, a Presbyterian minister from Nova Scotia, travelled across the Northwest in 1872 as secretary to Sandford Fleming's transcontinental railway survey. On his return, he wrote a best-selling account of the expedition, *Ocean to Ocean*, in which he enthused about the prospects for western settlement. Like Butler, he believed that the future did not include the Indian. "Poor creatures! Not much use have they ever made of the land; but yet, in admitting the settler, they sign their own death warrants." Grant, however, wrote to reassure prospective immigrants, not to make them feel guilty. He reported that the Indian was docile and harmless, posing no threat to the peaceful settlement of the land by outsiders. "Poor whites, were they about in equal numbers, would give ten times as much trouble as the poor Indians." Grant's view of the Indian was brisk and sensible. He did not spend a lot of time lamenting what could not be helped. He saw the Indian as a problem to be solved. "It may be said that, do what we like, the Indians as a race must eventually die out. It is not unlikely." However, Reverend Grant had faith in the power of Christian education to transform and preserve the Indian: "as the Indian has no chance of existence except by conforming to civilized ways, the sooner that the Government or the Christian people awake to the necessity of establishing schools among every tribe the better. Little can be done with the old, and it may be two, three or more generations before the old habits of a people are changed; but, by always taking hold of the young, the work can be done."[8]

II

The job of christianizing the Natives fell to the missionaries. During the last half of the nineteenth century, a flood of churchmen washed over the Northwest. Anglicans, Methodists, and Catholic Oblates engaged in a fierce struggle with Indian "superstition," and each other, to bring the word of God to the aboriginals. Many of the missionaries wrote books and articles and gave lectures about their frontier adventures. Churned out by the religious presses, these books were devoured by the Eastern-Canadian faithful. At the same time as they romanticized the missionary effort on a distant frontier among a heathen people, these writers helped to create the Imaginary Indian in the public mind.

The three most influential missionary image-makers were John Maclean, John McDougall, and Egerton Ryerson Young.[9] All three were Methodists who spent time living with Native tribes west of Ontario. Maclean, a native of Scotland, worked among the Blood Indians at Fort Macleod during the 1880s. He had a Ph.D. in history and along with his missionary activities he wrote books and articles and published a short-lived newspaper. Two of his books, *The Indians of Canada* (1889) and *Canadian Savage Folk* (1896), were considered standard authorities on their subject. Young's sojourn among the Indians was briefest of the three. He arrived at Norway House in northern Manitoba in 1868, remained eight years, then spent most of the rest of his life writing and lecturing about his experiences. He published eleven books, including memoirs and stories for boys, and toured the United States and Britain giving public lectures about Indians. At the turn of the century Young was considered one of the most successful writers in Canada. John McDougall was a different case altogether. He devoted his entire life to his Indian work, seldom leaving his Alberta mission. He helped prepare the Plains Natives for the arrival of the North-West Mounted Police in 1874, sat in on the signing of Treaty 7 three years later, and rode with the mounted troops during the Northwest Rebellion. His most influential books were a series of five volumes of memoirs about his life on the Plains, published between 1895 and 1911. A sixth volume appeared after his death.

It is misleading to generalize about the missionary writers. Each had his own point of view. McDougall genuinely admired many aspects of Plains culture. He grew up in the backwoods of Ontario and was much more at home in a log cabin or a Native tipi than a Toronto drawing room. In his books he did not bother to disguise his contempt for effete Easterners who could not endure long days in the saddle and long nights huddled around a campfire. His Christianity was decidedly muscular and he disdained what he called "spurious civilization": "too much coddling, too much comfort, too much false sympathy, and the result a misconception of life and its responsibility and the further result is moral and physical degeneracy. No wonder the Lord has every little while to bring trouble upon a nation or people."[10] Many of the qualities he missed in his own society McDougall recognized in the Plains people. He found them intelligent, brave, eloquent in their speech, handsome to look at, honourable, proud and dignified, unspoiled by an over-reliance on creature comforts.

John Maclean likewise praised the Indian character in his books. He pleaded for sympathetic understanding. "Underlying the blanket of the red man beats a noble heart, that shows true affection

This photograph of a Plains chief and his industrial-school-educated children was used by missionaries to show White audiences that the Indians were becoming "civilized."

for his own kin, can be moved deeply by a brave action, and is true to the principles of honor, justice and truth." According to Maclean, Indians were going through a transition stage "between losing faith in their native religion and accepting Christianity and civilization."[11] In the process, many were suffering. But in the long run, he believed, the Indians who accepted the new way of life would be better for it.

Unlike his colleagues, Egerton Ryerson Young found little to commend Native culture. In his lectures he dwelled on the evil effects of polygamy, the brutalization of women, unrestrained drunkenness and gambling. He admired Indians chiefly for their picturesque qualities. He liked to tell an anecdote about going fishing one day with a friend, a doctor, who was deeply impressed with the beauty of the lake country around Norway House. "'Wait a moment, doctor,' I said. 'I can add to the wild beauty of the place something that will please your artistic eye.'" Young had two Natives paddle out to a nearby island where he asked them to strike poses on the rocks, their fishing lines in the water, while Young and his friend admired them. "I confess I was entranced by the loveliness of the sight," he wrote.[12] For Young, Indians were figures in a landscape, placed there by an all-knowing God to enhance the romanticism of the scenery.

Despite their differences, the missionaries agreed on one thing— they were agents of a superior civilization, and in order to survive contact with it the Indians were going to have to give up their pagan superstitions and embrace the White Way. "As we rode these many miles," wrote John McDougall, "we saw in prophetic vision the settling up of this wonderful country—schoolhouse and church, village and homestead, presently the iron horse, and then the mine and factory ... As sure as God had made such a world, so we felt certain it would be peopled."[13] The White Way was superior because it challenged and conquered nature. As described by the missionaries, Natives were slaves to their environment, roaming aimlessly across the Plains in pursuit of game, worshipping gods which inhabited the wind and the trees. Because they did nothing with the resources of the land—built no cities, tilled no fields, dug no mines—Indians deserved to be superceded by a civilization that recognized the potential for material progress.

Missionaries offered the Indians salvation. They dismissed Native religious beliefs as pagan superstition, describing the shamans as clever charlatans who terrorized the people through a mixture of primitive psychology, folk medicine, and magic tricks. But salvation was cultural as well as religious. Personal appearance, family relations, table manners—the smallest details of daily life had to be transformed if the Indian was going to take his place in the new society.

Even those missionaries who were sympathetic to Native culture preached that the only way for Indians to survive contact with White society was by acculturation. In order to save themselves as individuals, they must give up everything that defined them as a people. This was the choice offered by the missionaries. Even John McDougall, who abhorred eastern urban lifestyles in so many ways, believed with a messianic fervor that it was his task to prepare the Indians for the inevitable. "We were 'path-finders' for multitudes to follow; we were foundation builders of empire; we were forerunners of a Christian civilization." [14]

Their White audiences listened raptly as the missionaries assured them that the Indian was hungry for the new religion and way of life. "An almost universal desire to accept the white man's way had taken possession of these Indians," claimed E.R. Young. [15] With the slightest encouragement, he said, the Indian leaped at the chance to convert not just to Christianity but to the sedentary, agricultural lifestyle being offered them. Missionaries encouraged no second thoughts, no guilty consciences, among their supporters. The Indian was being given an opportunity to join a superior civilization. Those who did not take it were doomed to ultimate extinction by their own inexplicable attachment to an inferior, obsolete way of life.

III

The early image-makers all agreed that Indians were disappearing. This "fact" was why it was so important to capture a record of their culture before it died away. This fate was what made Indians so interesting to the public at large.

The imminent disappearance of the Indian was an article of faith among Canadians until well into the twentieth century. For years people could point to the census to prove their case. The "Vanishing Canadian" was rooted in demographic reality. The population of Native people, afflicted with disease, alcohol abuse, and social dislocation, fell in the post-Confederation period, from roughly 108,500 in 1881 to 103,750 in 1915, at the same time as the non-Native population was booming. By itself, the influenza epidemic which followed World War I claimed 3,700 Native lives. Tuberculosis, the "white death," was especially virulent.

This precipitous decline was reversed, however, in the years following the war when the aboriginal population actually began to increase. The 1921 census counted 110,814 registered Indians; ten years later, the number had climbed to 122,911. By the 1950s, the Native population was growing at an annual rate of four percent, faster than the general population. This trend was due chiefly to the control of epidemic diseases like tuberculosis among the Native population, and it has continued to the present. Yet for many years, census figures had little impact on the stereotype of the Vanishing Canadian. "Authorities" continued to predict that all Indians, or at least an identifiable Indian culture, would soon disappear.

The humourist Stephen Leacock was typical. Acknowledged to be the funniest man in the Dominion, Leacock was also a respected economist, a professor of political economy at McGill University. In the first years of World War I, he contributed two volumes to the prestigious *Chronicles of Canada*, a thirty-two-volume history of Canada. The series was edited by Hugh Langton, librarian at the University of Toronto, and George M. Wrong, head of the university's history department. In other words, it was the work of some of the country's leading intellectuals. In a volume titled *The Dawn of Canadian History*, Leacock gave his view of Native culture.

According to Leacock, Canadian history began with the arrival of Europeans. Before that time the continent was inhabited by a few Indians mired in a state of primitive barbarism. "The continent was, in truth, one vast silence, broken only by the roar of the waterfall or the cry of the beasts and birds of the forest."[16] Like most of his contemporaries, Leacock ranked civilizations on an ascending scale, with modern industrial society at the top. He believed that North American Indians at contact did not even make it onto the bottom of the scale. They had none of the attributes which characterized civilized people: they did not live in permanent houses in permanent settlements; they knew nothing of metal or the wheel; they could not write; most of them did not practise any form of agriculture; they did not recognize the Christian God. Leacock graded some tribes superior to others to the degree that they lived in houses and engaged in agriculture. He admitted, for instance, that the Iroquois had some virtues. But the hunter-gatherer societies of the northern woodlands earned his complete scorn.

Leacock did not lament the passing of the Indian for one moment. In his opinion they represented an early stage in the evolution of civilization in North America, one best forgotten. Nor did he change his mind with time. In 1941 he wrote another history of Canada, a lavishly illustrated book sponsored by The House of Seagram. It took as its theme "the struggle of civilization against savagery" and confirmed Leacock's dismissive, even vicious, attitude toward Native people. "We think of prehistoric North America as inhabited by the Indians, and have based on this a sort of recognition of ownership on their part," he wrote. "But this attitude is hardly warranted. The Indians were too few to count. Their use of the resources of the continent was scarcely more than that by crows and wolves, their development of it nothing." [17]

If Stephen Leacock occupied one end of the spectrum of White opinion, Marius Barbeau occupied the other. Barbeau was an ethnologist with the Museum of Man in Ottawa. He devoted much of his long career to collecting stories and artifacts among the Northwest Coast Indians. Considered an authority on the totem pole, he published a two-volume study of the poles, as well as a popular 1928 novel, *The Downfall of Temlaham*, based on Native legend. Despite his great respect for aboriginal culture, which clashed so markedly with Stephen Leacock's racist views, Barbeau agreed with Leacock that Indians were doomed. In a 1931 article in *Queen's Quarterly*, "Our Indians—Their Disappearance," he summarized his view of their plight.

"The popular notion about the vanished American races is not very far wrong," Barbeau argued: disease and mistreatment had reduced the Natives to a shadow of their former selves, and miscegenation had so altered their physical characteristics that an Indian didn't even look like an Indian anymore. On the Plains, the Indians "are known mostly for their casual appearance in stampedes and parades for the benefit of western fairs. Their war paint and regalia belongs to the circus. Those responsible for their survival, and perhaps improvement, are the railways and the tourists." The buffalo, the salmon, and all the other wild game on which the people depended for their survival had been depleted by the casual sportsman, he said, and the disheartened, impoverished Natives were confined to reserves where they spent their time pining over past glories. "At present," concluded Barbeau, "the indications point convincingly to the extinction of the race."[18]

In 1932, a colleague of Barbeau's at the National Museum, the anthropologist Diamond Jenness, lent his authority to the prevailing image of the Indian. Jenness did field work among several Native tribes during the 1920s, and in 1932 summed up his findings for the popular audience in *The Indians of Canada*, which is still in print. For Jenness, the contact experience was totally negative for almost all native groups in Canada. He listed the forces which had battered the Indian: disease, alcohol, increased warfare, depletion of game resources, alien religious beliefs. The situation was different for each tribe, he wrote, but he was pessimistic about the future which awaited most of them. He presented a portrait of a completely demoralized people who felt, as he wrote about the Pacific Coast tribes, "that their race is run and calmly, rather mournfully, await the end." His final conclusion: "Doubtless all the tribes will disappear."[19]

Jenness, Barbeau and every other White writer on the subject emphasized the negative results of the contact between industrial civilization and Native Americans, and from that extrapolated their conclusions: the Indian was ravaged by disease and neglect; his traditional culture was destroyed and he could not adapt to the new White way— so he faltered, and died. Contact was a curse, a sentence of death.

IV

If Indians were truly vanishing, they seemed to be taking a long time doing so. From Paul Kane in the 1850s, to the scientific authorities of the 1930s, the prediction was repeated. Yet there were still Native people around, and by the 1920s anyone who cared to look could see that they were in fact growing in numbers. But the image of the Vanishing Indian was perhaps just too convenient to give up—appealing as it did so strongly to sentimentalists who wanted to indulge a guilty conscience while feeling there was nothing they could do about it. It appealed as well to social critics eager to berate governments for their shameful policies of neglect. It appealed to expansionists because it disposed of a major obstacle to the extension of White civilization across the continent. And, of course, the image appealed to racists who found in it a welcome reassurance that their own way of life was superior. For everyone, the most important thing to know about Indians in the century before World War II was that they were disappearing. When Canadians said "Indian," they meant doomed.

Eventually, the image of the Vanishing Indian did begin to die out. As a literal fact, it could no longer be substantiated. Canadians had to find another way of thinking about their future. Not only were their numbers increasing, but Native people were asserting themselves more and more strongly. In the post-World War I period Natives joined together into political organizations to lobby the government for improved education, secure hunting and fishing rights, an end to land surrenders, and many other issues which affected their political rights and economic security. In B.C. in 1916, the Allied Tribes of British Columbia campaigned for recognition of aboriginal land title. Two years later the League of Indians of Canada began on the Six Nations reserve in Ontario, then spread across the country. The League petered out, but for a while it was influential enough that the Indian Department used the RCMP to try to discredit its founder, F.O. Loft. Far from being a vanishing people, Native Canadians seemed to be increasingly alive and kicking, determined to speak for themselves, and to be heard. It was hard to characterize them as passive, doomed people when they were in the headlines and in the courts. Despite a century of being told about their own disappearance, Indians were here to stay.

In another sense, though, the Vanishing Indian still persists: the stereotype did not disappear so much as change content. Evidently,

Native people have survived, but the essential core of the Indian way of life is now considered to be at risk. Since the 1960s, we have been inundated with books and films celebrating the spiritual side of Indian life, the wisdom of the elders, the secret practices of sorcerers and shamans. Feeling an absence of the sacred in modern life, many non-Natives look to Indian culture for values they find lacking in their own. The environmental movement has given a boost to this new image by adopting the Indian as symbolic of a culture which lives in harmony with the natural world. This is the new Vanishing Indian, the Indian as spiritual and environmental guru, threatened by the forces of consumer culture.

The belief in the inevitable disappearance of the Indian was genuinely held by many Canadians. It was a piece of conventional wisdom that was never questioned. It is interesting, however, that almost no one ever suggested doing anything about it. Aside from assimilating the Indians for their own good, there were no plans presented for halting their seemingly inexorable plunge toward extinction. In part, this was because such plans were unthinkable. Canadians believed firmly in progress, and progress demanded that the inferior civilization of the Indian had to give way to superior, White civilization. Progress had its price, and the Indian was expected to pay it. In part also, the Vanishing Indian was a very expedient notion. It was reinforced by the perception that Indians seemed to serve no useful purpose in the modern world. They occupied land of value to farmers. In the minds of many Whites they presented a threat to the peaceful expansion of settlement. In the more populated Eastern provinces they were an intractable social problem. It was convenient that they should simply disappear. Encouraged by their image-makers to believe that this was the direction in which events were unfolding naturally, Whites had little reason to question the process.

Canadians did not expect Indians to adapt to the modern world.

Their only hope was to assimilate, to become White, to cease to be Indians. In this view, a modern Indian is a contradiction in terms: Whites could not imagine such a thing. Any Indian was by definition a traditional Indian, a relic of the past. The only image of the Indian presented to non-Natives was therefore an historical one. The image could not be modernized. Indians were defined in relation to the past and in contradistinction to White society. To the degree that they changed, they were perceived to become less Indian. Remember Edward Curtis retouching his photographs to remove all evidence of modern life. White society was allowed to change, to evolve, without losing its defining cultural, ethnic, and racial characteristics, but Indian society was not. Indians were considered strangers to progress. They were fixed in a traditional mode and could not change without becoming something else, something not Indian. The Imaginary Indian, therefore, could never become modern.

Canadians prided themselves on the fact that they, unlike their American neighbours, did not believe that "the only good Indian was a dead Indian." But in practice this is exactly what they did believe. True enough, Canadians did not engage in the outright extermination of their Native population. However, they wholeheartedly endorsed the assimilation of the Indian, which in the long run meant the same thing, an end to an identifiable Indian people. In this view of the world, the only good Indians were traditional Indians, who existed only in the past, and assimilated Indians, who were not Indians at all. Any other Indian had vanished.

CHAPTER FOUR

Red Coats and Redskins

THE STORY OF THE North-West Mounted Police is one of the great romances of Canadian history. Few events have evoked as much admiration as the Great March of 1874, when the scarlet-clad Mounties, farmboys from eastern Canada, left civilization behind them and trekked off into the western wilderness. For many Canadians, the Mounties came to stand for the very essence of our national character—a healthy respect for just authority. "In large measure, world opinion took for granted that lawlessness must accompany pioneer conditions," wrote R.G. MacBeth in his history of the police in 1931. "Canada's Mounted Police Force was the challenge to that idea."[1]

MacBeth's history was just one of several that took their inspiration from the memoirs and memories of men who had served with the Mounted Police during the first decades of its existence.[2] Authors of popular fiction also recognized a good story when they heard one, and, with their help, the saga of the NWMP "winning an empire for civilization" soon became as important to the myth of Canadian nationhood as the Battle of the Plains of Abraham.

It was the fate of the Indian to play the role of villain in this western romance. In the classic American western story, the cowboy hero has a faithful Indian companion. The Lone Ranger has Tonto; Red Ryder has Little Beaver. But north of the border the Mountie's sidekick is a "half-breed." Jerry Potts, the mixed-blood scout who led the Mounties in search of whiskey pedlars, provides the archetype of this faithful retainer, transformed in fiction into Blue Pete, the mixed-blood hero of the many pulp novels of William Lacey Amy. The Indians, on the other hand, are a breed apart in the Mountie legend. Wild and unruly, they supposedly prompted the creation of the Mounted Police in the first place (without disorder, there would be no need to impose order). As a result, in the vast literature of the Mountie produced between 1885 and World War II, the Indian is the "bad guy," savage and ungovernable, a symbol of the dark forces of anarchy which had to be subdued before civilization could flourish in the West.

II

The romance of the Mounted Police really begins in pre-history, before the police came. "Many persons of high attainments ... are under the erroneous impression that there never has been in Canada, as in the United States, what is commonly called 'The Wild and Woolly West,'" wrote the legendary Mountie Sam Steele in his 1915 memoirs. But this was not the case, said Steele; the Canadian West used to be every bit as wild as the American frontier: before the coming of law and order, murder and mayhem ruled the plains. War between Indian tribes raged ceaselessly: "Only the traveller who courted death went west of where Regina now prospers, in the midst of smiling farms, without an escort." Steele described how unprincipled whiskey traders stirred up the Indians to unimaginable horrors—"orgies, brutalities and crimes beyond description." "Murder was common and the perpetrators stalked abroad in open day without the slightest fear of arrest." [3] Steele's West was a region where civilized people dare not set foot.

Every other chronicler of the Mounted Police agreed with Steele. "The steed of the far West was riderless, the reins had been thrown away and the country was running wild," wrote Rev. MacBeth.[4] "Violence was in the saddle over Canada's West," cried Cecil Denny, another historian riding the same equestrian metaphor, "—battle, murder, and sudden death, a composite of evils which, from the Red River to the Rocky Mountains, year by year, exacted a grisly toll. Red man warred upon red man, tribe upon tribe, and the white man warred and preyed upon them all."[5] Whiskey traders, usually Americans, preyed on the Indians, who were powerless in the grip of their unquenchable thirst. "Crazed by the poisonous stuff, they virtually threw away their robes," explained Denny, a former member of the force; "quarrels and fighting inevitably broke out, and terror and devastation ran through the camps."[6] To make matters worse, the great herds of buffalo were fast disappearing from the plains and the Indians were starving and afflicted with epidemic diseases.

Into this hellish scene, the reality of which is highly debatable, galloped the Riders of the Plains, celebrated in a popular poem by one of the young constables:

> Our mission is to raise the Flag
> Of Britain's Empire here,
> Restrain the lawless savage,
> And protect the Pioneer;
> And 'tis a proud and daring trust,
> To hold these vast Domains,
> With but three hundred Mounted Men,
> The Riders of the Plains.[7]

And with the raising of the flag, the dark ages ended and history began. Quite literally, the chroniclers of the Mounted Police claimed that the West, and its Native inhabitants, had no past. They agreed with William Butler who compared the West to an empty ocean, existing out of time. "This ocean has no past," Butler wrote in 1872,

"time has been naught to it; and men have come and gone, leaving behind them no track, no vestige, of their presence ... One saw here the
world as it had taken shape and form from the hands of the Creator."[8]
There was no denying that events had taken place here. But these
were to be seen as the chaotic happenings of uncivilized people. History began with civilization, and civilization could only begin with
order. The romance of the Mounted Police knew little and cared less
about the Indians. The people who created it were not anthropolo-
gists; they were imperialists, and nationalists.

According to historians of the early days, the arrival of the Mounted Police completely, and almost instantly, transformed life in western
Canada. Whiskey traders went out of business. Indian tribes stopped
fighting each other. Justice prevailed for White man and Red. "In
the space of a few years," boasted A.L. Haydon in his 1912 history
of the police, "the north-west had witnessed a revolution take place
within its borders, a bloodless revolution of a most remarkable kind.
Over thirty thousand Indians, at war with one another and hostile to
the white invasion, had been transformed into a peaceful community
showing every disposition to remain contented and law-abiding."[9]
The frontier was ready for the next stage in its development, the arrival of thousands of industrious farmers. It was nothing short of a
miracle.

The Indians who emerge from this history of peaceful conquest
share many of the characteristics of children. "Children of the plains,"
Rev. MacBeth called them.[10] Like children, they cannot control their
own behaviour. Their main pleasures in life seem to be drinking and
fighting, and both activities are engaged in with little regard for personal safety. Every history describes how Indians besieged the traders'
shacks looking for whiskey. So great was their thirst that when the
doors were locked against them, they reportedly climbed onto the
sod roofs and slid down the chimneys. "They had been a free and

happy race, knowing no law or restraint but their own will or the tribal rule," lamented Cecil Denny, "and were now like people suddenly shut off from light, having blindly to grope their way towards a new and unknown condition of which they had no conception." [11] It was the job of the police to take their hands and guide them gently toward the light.

In these stories, Indians are characterized as harbouring ancient bloodlusts, latent but threatening to burst forth at any time. It was widely believed by White historians that in 1885, during the rebellion led by Louis Riel, the West had come perilously close to a general Indian uprising. "The hereditary instincts of the savage had been aroused," wrote A.L. Haydon. "There had been war—red war, with its opportunities for fighting, for revenge, and for the many other outlets of energy so dear to the primitive mind. These instincts are hard to eradicate." [12] Unlike Whites, who apparently only waged war for sensible reasons, Indians were seen to engage in war as a kind of vicious sport to satisfy an instinctual love of violence. This double standard was seldom questioned by White writers. Modern historians give the Indians credit for having their own political agenda during the troubled season of 1884-85. They believe that leading chiefs were attempting to unite their followers to force better treatment from the government in Ottawa. According to this interpretation, there was no threat of a general Indian rising. [13] Earlier historians, however, did not admit that Indians had policies. Like children, Indians had appetites, and they followed them. Most Canadians were convinced that only the presence of the Mounted Police kept Indian ferocity in check in 1885.

Like children, too, Indians were portrayed by White writers as superstitious and credulous. Those who came under the influence of a Christian missionary were, of course, much improved. But many were untouched by Christianity and continued to practise rituals which deeply offended White observers. Historians picked on the Sun Dance ceremony in particular. Banned by the federal government in 1885, the Sun Dance was an important summer ceremonial for the Plains Indians. Whites, on the other hand, were horrified at the self-mutilation involved, which did not stop them from describing in great detail the tearing flesh, the spine-tingling shrieks of the women, and the eerie chanting and drumming of the onlookers. Readers were meant to experience a real thrill of horror before they were asked to condemn the practice as "debasing and cruel," "revolting," and "barbarous." No White writer attempted to put the ceremony into the context of Indian religious beliefs.

Like young children, Indians in Mountie literature are readily cowed by a display of authority. Easily the most common scene in the romance of the Mounted Police is the confrontation between an unarmed officer and a gang of angry Indian braves. Looking for a lawbreaker, the policeman coolly dismounts from his horse. Appearing to take no notice of the rifle barrels aimed at his heart, he marches up to the leading Indian and demands that the fugitive give himself up at once. Completely disarmed by this mixture of reckless courage and self-confidence, the Indians meekly do as they are told.

The confrontation scene appears in many versions of the Mountie story, but the most common rendering features the Cree Chief Piapot, who, with hundreds of his followers spoiling for a fight, has pitched camp across the CPR tracks in an attempt to obtain food. When a train arrives, the chief refuses to move and the police are called. Two young officers ride up. "Two men entrusted with the task of bringing a camp of several hundred savages to reason!" gasped Ernest Chambers in his account. "It appeared like tempting Providence—the very height of rashness."[14] When Piapot refuses to move, Corporal William Brock Wilde pulls out his watch and tells the Indians they have fifteen minutes to clear out. As the minutes slowly pass,

Indian braves try to intimidate the Mounties by bumping their horses and firing guns into the air. Finally, when the time is up, Wilde calmly gets down from his horse, walks over to Piapot's tent and kicks down the lodge pole, collapsing the tent in a heap. He proceeds to knock over another tipi, and then another, until Piapot gets the message and shamefacedly orders his braves away.

Despite its symbolic importance, this incident seems never to have taken place. It was first described by William A. Fraser, a journalist and novelist, in an article he wrote for *McClure's Magazine* in 1899. The article, which reappeared in *Canadian Magazine* the next year, gives no source for the story and a search of the records has turned up no earlier, first-hand account. Nonetheless, Fraser's tall tale was repeated by most writers celebrating the history of the Mounted Police.[15]

Another famous, but real, incident, this one involving a Cree named Almighty Voice, reveals what is implicit in these confrontations: White writers believed that Indians had a code of ethics inferior to that of the Mounted Police and White civilization, but nevertheless were easily to be cowed by it. Jailed for cattle killing, Almighty Voice broke out of prison in 1895. Sergeant Colebrooke of the Mounted picked up the trail and ran the fugitive to the ground. Instead of giving himself up, however, Almighty Voice pointed his rifle at the Mountie and warned him to stay back. Colebrooke did not draw his gun, apparently convinced that it was his duty to take the escapee alive. As Chambers explained in his account of the confrontation, "a man does not serve long enough in the Mounted Police to win the three-barred chevron without acquiring a sense of duty fairly idolatrous in its intensity." Apparently Almighty Voice was not as impressed as Chambers by Colebrooke's display of resolution (or maybe he hadn't read any Mountie stories). In any event, he shot Colebrooke dead on the spot. The police had until now been protected as if by "miraculous intervention" in their confrontations with the

Indians, Chambers told his readers, but this day God must have been looking the other way. Almighty Voice made his escape, only to die later in a shoot-out with his pursuers, while Colebrooke's valour (or foolishness) won him a special place in the romance of the Mounted Police. "The death of Colebrooke," wrote Ernest Chambers, "was as clearly a case of self-sacrifice on the alter of stern, manly duty as any recorded in the pages of history."[16]

Integral to the Mountie myth was the notion that the police were protecting the Indians from the depredations of unscrupulous Whites. "The first business our Mounted Police did was to stand between the Indians and the vile creatures who would give them drink and rob them of all they possessed," explained Rev. MacBeth. As a result, again like children, "the Indians recognized the police as their friends and not as their enemies."[17] This belief, that they were acting in the best interests of the Indians, was an article of faith with the police, and with their chroniclers, and served to explain why such a small body of officers, vastly outnumbered by aboriginal inhabitants, was able to pacify a territory as large as some European countries. The police were not invaders; "… the Indians welcomed our residence among them, and looked upon us as their friends and deliverers from the many evils they had suffered at the hands of unprincipled white men."[18]

What looked like friendship and protection to White observers may well have seemed to be something else to the Native people. From their point of view, the Mounted Police were agents of a foreign government. The Red Coats arrived on the Plains without warning and began enforcing alien laws and stamping out long-held cultural practices. It is hard to imagine what Natives must have thought when customs which had served them well for generations suddenly landed them behind iron bars. As government policy became increasingly repressive following the 1885 rising, Natives were not even allowed to leave their reserves without permission. Police became more coercive in their application of draconian laws, which soon came to form, according to historian John Jennings, a system of apartheid.[19]

According to the legend, however, Mounties were completely impartial in their administration of justice. They brought to the West that most precious of gifts, British law, and applied it to all residents irrespective of social class or skin colour. It was taken for granted that the law itself was fair. White writers marvelled at the impartiality with which the police were seen to apply it. The Indians, they report, marvelled as well, and were completely won over. "It was a subject of comment among the redmen," as Ernest Chambers, who characteristically quotes no Native informants, put it, "that however other white men might lie to them and cheat them, those wearing the red coat could be trusted with implicit confidence."[20] Or, as Rev. MacBeth described it, the police "stood for the square deal."[21] This image of the grateful Indian was an essential ingredient in the myth of national identity which was taking shape in Canada around the turn of the century. The image allowed Canadians to nurture a sense of themselves as a just people, unlike the Americans south of the border who were waging a war of extermination against their Indian population. Canadians believed that they treated their Natives justly. They negotiated treaties before they occupied the land. They fed the Indians when they were starving and shared with them the great principles of British justice. The story of the Mounted Police had a powerful influence on the way Canadians felt themselves to be distinct from, and morally superior to, the United States. Crucial to this process was the story of Sitting Bull, the Sioux war chief who is almost as important a figure in Canadian history as he is in American.[22]

Sitting Bull crossed the border into Canada at the end of May, 1877, eleven months after his victory over General George Custer at Little Big Horn, Montana. He had been preceded by several bands of Sioux and his arrival increased the number of American Natives in Canadian territory to more than 5,000. The story of the initial meeting between Sitting Bull and police major James Walsh conforms to the familiar confrontation stereotype. In this version, Walsh rides unannounced into the Sioux camp, astonishing the Indian leader with his apparent lack of fear. Offering his hand in friendship, Walsh welcomes Sitting Bull onto British territory and tells him he can stay as long as he doesn't conduct raids across the border and as long as he obeys the law of the land. Sitting Bull, so the story goes, is nonplussed by the courage of the policeman, and agrees to live at peace while in Canada.

The Cypress Hills in southern Saskatchewan had become the grand rendezvous for the Plains tribes—both Canadian and American—who were drawn there by the last remaining buffalo herds and other game animals. The resulting congregation was a powder keg in the eyes of Canadian authorities. Canadian Natives resented the new arrivals from south of the border, worrying that there was not enough food to go around. American Natives seethed with anger at the treatment they had suffered at the hands of American authorities and sought to forge an alliance with Canadian tribes to drive the White man from the plains. The Sioux in particular had a reputation for violence. Canadians held their breath while they waited to see if a full-scale Indian war would break out in the West.

Under intense pressure from American, and some Canadian, officials to return to the United States, Sitting Bull preferred to remain where he was. He wanted to be recognized as a Canadian subject, but the government of John A. Macdonald refused. It did not want to take responsibility for several thousand more Natives. At the same time, it could not try to expel them for fear of precipitating a war. Events were at an impasse. But as the buffalo continued to disappear, the situation of the refugee Sioux deteriorated, and finally they began drifting back across the border to settle on the reservations set aside for them in North Dakota. Sitting Bull did not try to stop them, and in July, 1881, convinced that there was no alternative, he led the last of his followers out of Canada.

In the Canadian version of these events, a holocaust had been averted: despite an overwhelming advantage in numbers, the Indians had declined to take to the warpath. But they received none of the credit for choosing the path of peace: that was reserved for the Mounted Police. While the success of Canada's expansion into the West hung in the balance, "to the utter amazement of Eastern Canadians" wrote Rev. MacBeth, "and to the more profound surprise of the Americans, our handful of Mounted Police, with masterly diplomacy, endless patience and steady, cool courage were able to handle the whole situation and solve it without the loss of a single life on either side. There are few such chapters anywhere in the records of history."[23]

What makes the episode particularly significant is that it has given Canadians an opportunity to feel superior to the Americans ever since. Had he been given a choice, Sitting Bull would have chosen to remain in Canada—Canadians were convinced of it. According to the legend, after years of harassment at the hands of American soldiers and settlers, the Sioux received fair treatment from Major Walsh and the Mounties—and what was seen to be true for Sitting Bull was held to be equally true for all of the western Indians. For most Canadians, the American attitude was summed up in General Philip Sheridan's famous remark: "The only good Indians I ever saw were dead." Canadians believed that their way was quite different. As Rev. MacBeth put it, "It is inevitable in the progress of human history that higher civilizations should supersede the lower"—but within the context of British justice, this process would take place without injustice or hardship.[24]

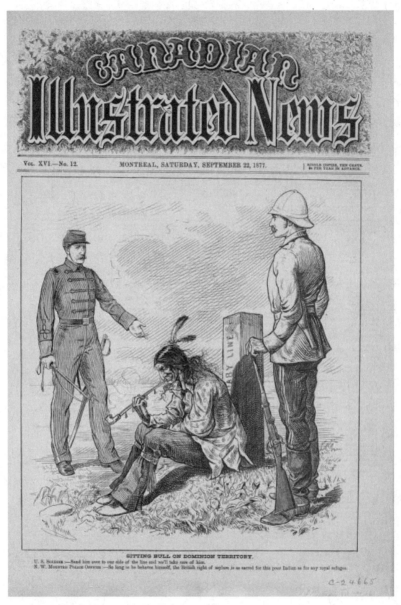

This cartoon appeared in the *Canadian Illustrated News* during Sitting Bull's sojourn in Canada. It reflects the view of the Mounted Police as the protectors of the Indian. The NWMP officer on the right is telling his American counterpart: "So long as he behaves himself, the British right of asylum is as sacred for this poor Indian as for any royal refugee."

Following the 1885 Northwest Rebellion, a band of disaffected Cree fled to the United States. American authorities wanted the two hundred Natives back in Canada and a large force of cavalry was dispatched to escort them to the border where the Mounted Police would take over. Arriving at the rendezvous, the American commander was astonished to find just four Mounties. "Where's your regiment?" he asked. We're all here, explained one of the young officers; "you see, we wear the Queen's scarlet." And of course, the story goes, the four horsemen were sufficient to lead the Cree well away from the border.[25] Writer after writer offered this incident as proof positive that the Canadian approach to the Indian "problem" was superior to the American. Otherwise, how could such a small number of Mounties have kept the peace on a distant frontier seething with discontent with so little recourse to force?

III

The history of the North-West Mounted Police was too good a story to leave to the historians. As early as 1885, writers of popular fiction seized on the straight-backed, clear-eyed, scarlet-jacketed members of the force as ideal subjects. Until the 1940s, when the rage for Mountie fiction died down, hundreds of stories and novels mixed fact and fiction in a heady brew of high adventure on the Canadian frontier. Indeed, one critic has called Mountie fiction "the nearest approach we have to a popular art form of the Canadian West analogous to the American Western."[26]

There was an international market for these Canadian adventure yarns. The British loved to read about life in their far-flung colonies, especially when it was spiced with exotic scenery and violent action. Authors of stories for boys particularly appreciated the colonial West; magazines like *The Boy's Own Paper* and *Chums* invariably included a story with Canadian content, and the exciting adventures of the Mounties were tailor-made for young readers. "The scarlet tunic! What a story!" enthused one of these authors in a 1908 issue of *Chums*.[27]

Americans had been hungry for stories about their own West since James Fenimore Cooper began publishing his *Leatherstocking Tales* in 1823. Cooper spawned a host of less-skilled imitators in the US, and also in Europe where "the cult of the western" swept countries such as Germany, France, Poland, and Norway.[28] Balduin Mollhausen, a German writer, produced 150 pot-boilers about the West; during the 1860s and 1870s he was the best-read writer in his native country. In France, Gustave Aimard published a book a month to satisfy a huge appetite for "westerns." But no one could rival the popularity of Karl May. A native of Germany, May never even visited the American West, but this didn't stop him from setting dozens of his novels there, featuring Indians that read Longfellow and spoke German. Ridiculous as they may seem in retrospect, May's books were translated into twenty languages and were read by an estimated 300 million people. Both Adolph Hitler and Albert Einstein said he was their favourite writer.

In the 1870s, the dime novel phenomenon swept the United States. Written by prolific hacks for a mass audience, these cheap, lurid, "penny dreadfuls" featured Indians, pioneers, detectives, scouts, and cowboys. Not surprisingly, writers looking for new material discovered in the Canadian Mounted Police a convenient novelty for their readers. It was an easy matter to shift the action north of the border and to make the protagonist one of the "Scarlet Jackets" making the frontier safe for civilization.

Like the early histories of the force, Mountie fiction depends on an image of the Indian. The whole point of these adventure stories, with their glamorous heroes, sinister villains, and lots of blood-curdling action, is to chronicle the triumph of White civilization over the wilderness. And with few exceptions, Indians are identified with the wilderness: portrayed without subtlety as savage, blood-thirsty, superstitious enemies of White society. Not surprisingly, fictional Mounties are derived from the same impartial arbiters of justice familiar from the history books (the only source of material available to most of these fictioneers). And the Indians are seen as the same child-like denizens of the plains and forest. In fact, the line between history and fiction becomes very blurred. Many of the tall tales, legends, and myths recorded as fact in the histories of the Mounted Police reappear in the pages of Mountie fiction.

The apotheosis of the Imaginary Indian in fiction of this type occurs in the work of the hugely popular novelist, Ralph Connor. Connor was the pen name of the Reverend Charles Gordon, a prominent Presbyterian clergyman and social reformer. His career as a fiction writer began in 1896, when he wrote a story for a church paper describing some of his experiences as a missionary in Western Canada. "My sole purpose was to awaken my church in Eastern Canada to the splendor of the mighty religious adventure being attempted by the missionary pioneers in the Canada beyond the Great Lakes," he explained in his memoirs.[29] The initial story became the basis for his first novel, *Black Rock* (1898), which launched one of the most successful writing careers in Canadian history. Connor began to produce a book a year, rousing stories of big-hearted, two-fisted muscular Christians busting heads for God. In the United States, where Ralph Connor became a household name, sales of his morality tales ran into the millions. His books were tremendously influential in shaping an image of the Canadian West, and, necessarily, the image of the Indian.

Connor wrote two novels featuring the Mounted Police. In the first, *Corporal Cameron of the North West Mounted Police*, published in 1912, he introduces Allan Cameron, a young Scotsman who emigrates to Canada in the early 1880s when his chances for advancement at home seem blocked. Cameron goes west with a survey crew and meets his first Mountie in a gambling joint frequented by "bad men from across the line." One of the ruffians is waving his gun around when "a tall slim youngster in the red jacket and pill-box cap of that world-famous body of military guardians of law and order, the North West Mounted Police" enters. "Put the gun down," orders the young Mountie, without drawing his own. Realizing that he has met his match, the bad guy drops his firearm onto a table, then slinks from the room. "Irresistible authority seemed to go with the word that sent him forth, and rightly so," writes Connor, "for behind that word lay the full weight of Great Britain's mighty empire! It was Cameron's first experience of the North West Mounted Police, that famous corps of frontier riders who for more than a quarter of a century have ridden the marches of Great Britain's territories in the far northwest land, keeping intact the Pax Britannica amid the wild turmoil of pioneer days."[30]

Connor treats his readers to a brief (and by now standard) history of the Mounted Police bringing peace and order to the wild frontier, while protecting and befriending the Indians. The Indians are presented as wild, savage people, gullible and inept in their relations with White traders and pathetically addicted to alcohol. Cameron is impressed at how the police impose order on "thousands of savage Indians, utterly strange to any rule or law except that of their own sweet will."[31] "This police business is a big affair," he says to the NWMP commissioner. "You practically run the country." "We see that every man gets a fair show," the commissioner modestly answers.[32]

Later, some incredulous Americans wonder how so few Mounties are able to "keep the Indians down." Connor's attitude to the Indians is summed up in the commissioner's response: "We don't keep them down," he says. "We try to take care of them."[33]

Allan Cameron joins the Mounted Police, and in his next novel,

The Patrol of the Sun Dance Trail, Connor places his hero in the middle of events leading up to the rebellion of 1885. The story focusses on Indian involvement in the rising, and the possibility of a full-scale Indian war, a possibility "so serious, so terrible, that the oldest officer of the force spoke of it with face growing grave and with lowered voice."[34] According to Connor, the Métis have just claims against the government, even if their leader, Louis Riel, is a crazed megalomaniac. The Indians in the novel, on the other hand, appear to have no cause for complaint. Connor pays no attention to Native concerns about land, or the government's failure to live up to the commitments it made in the treaties signed a decade earlier. As far as Connor is concerned, the Indians are simply bored and spoiling for a fight. "The fiery spirit of the red man, long subdued by those powers that represented the civilization of the white man, was burning fiercely within them. The insatiable lust for glory formerly won in war or in the chase, but now no longer possible to them, burned in their hearts like a consuming fire."[35]

Indians in the novel are hardly human. Connor depicts them at satanic campfire meetings, their savage, painted faces lit hideously by the flames, engaged in some strange religious ritual or mesmerized by the rhetoric of a demagogic leader. When they speak, the Indians use a form of mangled English that makes them sound brain-dead. Usually all they say is "Huh," apparently an all-purpose expletive. On one occasion, Cameron is hiding in the bushes watching one of the campfire meetings and thinking to himself that "the situation held possibilities of horror unspeakable in the revival of that ancient savage spirit which had been so very materially softened and tamed by years of kindly, patient and firm control on the part of those who represented among them British law and civilization."[36]

In the end, it is only "a feeling that they have been justly treated, fairly and justly dealt with by the Government, and a wholesome respect for Her Majesty's North West Mounted Police" that averts a tragedy too horrible to contemplate.[37]

In his day Connor was a respected social reformer, a moderator of the Presbyterian Church. His views were not those of a gutter racist, though at times they read like it. He spoke for many of the most thoughtful Canadians of his generation. Of course, he was oblivious to his distortion of Native aspirations. In his memoirs, he ingenuously claims that his novels were so popular because they "gave an authentic picture of life in the great and wonderful new country in Western Canada ..." "The pictures were from personal experience," he assured his fans. "I knew the country. I had ridden the ranges. I had pushed through the mountain passes. I had swum my bronco across its rivers."[38] As was so often the case, Native people had most to fear from writers who claimed to know them best.

IV

During the 1920s, Canada's fledgling motion picture industry tried to capitalize on Ralph Connor's celebrity by turning some of his novels into movies. The country's leading film entrepreneur at the time was Ernest Shipman, a theatrical promoter and publicist turned filmmaker. In 1919, Shipman and his wife Nell made a hit film version of James Curwood's novel, *Back to God's Country*. He followed up this success with four movies based on Connor's books, including *Cameron of the Royal Mounted*. But the profits from these movies were unspectacular and Shipman moved on to other film ventures.[39]

If Canadians failed to have much success with the Mountie movie, the genre proved to be a durable staple for Hollywood's film industry. Pierre Berton calculates that almost half the movies that Hollywood made about Canada featured the Mounted Police. "The movie industry's unrequited love affair with the force has been passionate and long-standing," writes Berton.[40] The first Mountie movie appeared in

A Hollywood Mountie braves a bar-room full of desperadoes to apprehend a suspect in this scene from *God's Country and the Law* (1921).

1909, and by 1922 Hollywood was churning them out at a rate of two per month. Mountie movies featured some of Hollywood's brightest stars, including Tyrone Power, Gary Cooper, Shirley Temple, Randolph Scott and, of course, Nelson Eddy and Jeanette MacDonald in the 1936 classic, *Rose Marie*. The critics grew bored, but filmgoers could not seem to get enough of the red-coated boy scouts from the north.

As with popular fiction, the Americans simply produced westerns with Mounties in the saddle instead of cowboys. Though the image of the force was usually positive, filmmakers were less than scrupulous when it came to accuracy. Canadian history was rewritten to satisfy the demands of Hollywood. In the 1926 feature, *The Flaming Forest*, viewers learn that the NWMP was formed to put down the first Métis rebellion (which actually took place five years before the force appeared in the West).[41] Three films dealt with Sitting Bull's sojourn in Canada—*Fort Vengeance*, *Saskatchewan*, and *The Canadians*. In each, the Sioux are depicted as continuing their warlike ways north of the border, looting, burning, and massacring innocent white settlers in attacks that never actually took place.

In 1940, Cecil B. DeMille made a feature about the second Riel rebellion, *North West Mounted Police*, starring Gary Cooper. DeMille prided himself on his historical authenticity, though he shot the film in a Hollywood back lot and got almost everything about the rebellion wrong. He misrepresented the Métis scandalously, and portrayed the police in their familiar fictional role as the saviours of the Canadian West. The picture, said the *Motion Picture Herald*, dramatized the rebellion, which "was put down by fifty North West Mounted Police in a manner celebrated by Canadians in song and story."[42] So much for General Frederick Middleton's five thousand militiamen. So much also for Louis Riel, who was portrayed as a weak-willed figurehead, controlled by sinister "halfbreeds" who wanted a free hand to sell whiskey to the Indians.

The Hollywood image of Native people has been well documented by Berton and others. Certainly the Mountie movie was no exception. There was no attempt made to portray aboriginal cultures accurately. In *Rose Marie*, a film set in northern Quebec, an Indian festival features huge West Coast totem poles and Natives wearing Plains Indian feather headdresses, a style of headgear unknown to the eastern woodlands outside the movies. Indians in these movies were wholly imaginary; that is, they were based on images inherited from popular art, fiction and history, images which themselves were the product of White imaginings about Indians.

In the style of the shoot-'em-up western, Indians in the Mountie movies attacked wagon trains, burned settlers' cabins, and roasted captives at the stake, all things which never took place in the Canadian

West. The Canadian frontier had its problems: the illicit trade in alcohol, the disappearance of the buffalo, the spread of disease. But these were not the problems moviegoers saw. Rather the Mountie movie provided another opportunity for the Hollywood dream machine to act out its melodramatic fantasies about the American Wild West. And these fantasies involved an image of the Indian which was patronizing and degrading.

V

Books and movies about the Mounties began to go out of fashion in the 1940s. A world at war had need of other, more up-to-date, role models. But the romance of the Mounted Police by that time had served Canadians well. It had given them a way to interpret their history, and to take pride in the apparently peaceful, lawful way their West was settled. The romance validated the dispossession of the western Natives by turning events into an allegory, describing the extension of civilization into the wilderness. In the beginning, there was only a savage landscape. Then the police came and made the world safe and familiar so that the railway could be built and settlers might feel at home. "There is absolutely no doubt that the tide of humanity flowed freely into the vast new frontier land by reason of the fact that the scarlet-coated riders had made the wilderness a safe abode and a place of opportunity for the law-abiding and the industrious."[43]

The glorious story of the Mounted Police required Indians who were marginal, their history to be not so much ignored as completely denied. Indians belonged to the wilderness—wild, savage, brutal, unpredictable, ahistorical—and, like other impediments to progress, they had to be cleared away like so many trees, or broken like the hard prairie sod. Writers of history and fiction alike were more or less optimistic about the Indians' willingness and ability to give up their old patterns of living; all agreed that they would have to. There was no room on the settlement frontier for wandering hunters. The Indians would have to settle down on their reserves and learn to till the soil. All of this was a necessary part of the romance of the Mounted Police. Indians were being offered progress, the gift of civilization. They should be thankful, not resistant.

The romance of the Mountie comes dressed as an adventure story, an adventure in nation-building, but it is far more than that. Like all treasured national stories, myths if you prefer, it validates and affirms important cultural values; in this case, the primacy of law and the subservience of the individual to social order. These Euro-Canadian cultural values are necessarily not shared by the Indians, who nevertheless play many roles in the romance: they obstruct the spread of civilization; they provide a reason to feel superior to the Americans; they provide an excuse to feel good about British justice. But they never play themselves. They have no reality. They are imaginary.

The Mounted Police are held in history and in fiction to have pacified the western Indians at little expense and with almost no bloodshed, and Euro-Canadian society has been showing its gratitude to the force ever since. It has also been living ever since with the image of the Indian as an impediment to national progress and civilized values. Such is the legacy of the romance of the Mounted Police.

PART TWO

◇◇◇◇◇◇◇◇◇◇◇◇◇◇

Presenting the Image

NOT LONG AGO, one of my relatives, our family's unofficial historian, told me that she suspected another of our relations, long dead, of being at least part-Indian. Surprised, I asked why. She gave several reasons, but one of the most compelling clues was that she remembered our relative as being particularly dour and humourless. "As everyone knows," she said, "Indians have no sense of humour."

My relative is a good-hearted person who did not mean her comment to be taken as a slur. She was merely stating what she took to be a fact: Indians have no sense of humour.

I used to know this "fact" myself. One of the earliest cartoons I can remember depicts the Lone Ranger and Tonto surrounded by hostile Indians. The Lone Ranger turns to his faithful companion and says something like, "It looks like we're done for, Tonto." To which Tonto responds, "What do you mean *we*, White Man?"

That cartoon was a shock to me, which is presumably why I recall it all these years later. First of all it was a shock because I had always assumed that Tonto was one of Us. Now I had to recognize the obvious, that in fact he was one of Them. The world was a less comfortable place than I had imagined.

But just as importantly, the cartoon is shocking because in it Tonto cracks a joke. It violates one of the most common stereotypes non-Natives have about Indians. They are considered stern, emotionless, stoical. We believe that they don't have a sense of humour.

The cigar store wooden Indian is the prototype for this image. It has been around for hundreds of years, and refers to the association between Native North Americans and tobacco, a product which originated in the New World. But long since, the wooden Indian has come to represent certain 'truths' about Indians. On the negative side, the wooden-Indian stereotype suggests a lack of emotional range, a failure of feeling. Indians are made of wood, this stereotype tells us; they do not experience emotions with the same sensitivity that a non-Native person does. On the positive side, this stereotype says that Indians do not wear their hearts on their sleeves; they do not reveal their emotions capriciously. They suffer injustice with a stoic resignation. They say little, but feel deeply. On the surface we might think they appear apathetic, even dull-witted, but inside we are convinced that they contain all the world's wisdom. Once again the Imaginary Indian is almost anything Whites want it to be.

The wooden Indian is an artifact of the image-makers. Once the artists and writers who had been to Indian Country reported back with news of what they had seen, others began shaping and reshaping the images, presenting them to the public as authentic representations of what the Indian was really like. This is how non-Native Canadians came to know the Indian: in books, in public performance, at country fairs, in museums and schoolrooms, at summer camp and in the movies. There were very few places, in fact, that Canadians did not encounter someone who was ready to tell them exactly what an Indian was.

CHAPTER FIVE

Performing Indians

IN THE SUMMER OF 1885, Sitting Bull, the great Sioux chief, returned to Canada. It was his second visit. The first had lasted four
years. At that time he and his followers, fresh from victory at Little Big Horn, hoped to find a permanent refuge in the territory of the
"Great Mother," Queen Victoria. Ultimately that hope was dashed.
Under pressure from both the American and Canadian governments,
the Sioux returned to the United States, surrendered their guns, and
went to live on the lands set aside for them in North Dakota.

It did not take long for the entertainment industry to capitalize
on Sitting Bull's great celebrity, and in 1885 he was visiting Canada
not as a hunted refugee but as a headliner in one of the greatest show
business productions of all time, Buffalo Bill's Wild West Show.

It took eighteen train cars to haul Buffalo Bill Cody, his entou-
rage of 150 "cowboys, Mexicans and Indians" and assorted animals
to Toronto. According to advertisements, the show was "the Greatest Novelty of the Century." Along with Sitting Bull and his "staff
of fifty-two braves," it featured sharpshooter Annie Oakley, "the
phenomenal Boy Shot, Johnny Baker," the "novel equestrianism" of
Buck Taylor (King of the Cowboys), music by the Cowboy Band, and
"the largest herd of buffalo ever exhibited." [1]

The show kicked off with a long procession through the streets
of the city to Woodbine Park. Buffalo Bill himself drew the most attention. "His fine appearance on horseback and handsome features

were admired by the vast crowds who lined the streets to witness this interesting parade," gushed a reporter for the *Globe*.[2] Once the show got underway, a sold-out audience applauded a varied display of trick shooting, horse racing, bronco riding, buffalo hunting and Indian dancing. "To call Buffalo Bill's exhibition a show is scarcely affording a just idea of it," wrote the *Globe* reporter. "The people employed are not actors trained for the work, but for the most part men who have spent their lives in just such scenes as they are called upon to represent before the audience."[3]

Of all the acts, the most thrilling were the set battles between Buffalo Bill's cowboys and Sitting Bull's Indians. The first of these was a replication of an incident from Cody's own life. Once, when he was scouting for the cavalry, he shot and killed a Cheyenne chief named Yellow Hair, then scalped the corpse. For the purposes of the Wild West Show, this encounter became a hand-to-hand fight to the death between Cody, armed with a knife, and an actor-Indian armed with a spear. After Cody killed his opponent, he brandished the dead warrior's war bonnet, shouting "The first scalp for Custer!" (He dropped this act from the show after a couple of seasons when he realized it wasn't doing his reputation any good.)[4]

The next highlight was an attack on the Deadwood Coach—advertised as an actual stagecoach once used in the Black Hills of Dakota—by a band of whooping Indians who are eventually chased away by mounted cowboys. The show ended with a similar act, "a wonderfully life-like representation of an Indian attack on a settler's cabin, and a brilliant rescue affected by Buffalo Bill and his cowboys."[5]

After the show, the *Globe* reporter paid a visit behind the scenes to the Indians' tents where he described Natives smoking their pipes and performing a curing ceremony for one of their sick comrades. "The Indians have been so isolated from the outside world," he explained, "that they are to-day precisely the same in manner, dress, habits and ways of thinking as they were when first taken from their reserves."[6] At the Wild West Show, in other words, one saw real Indians, real life.

II

The Buffalo Bill Show which entertained Canadian audiences in 1885 was only in its third season. It was still seeking the format which would turn it from a modest western variety show into an amusement extravaganza, wildly popular on two continents.[7] Its founder, William F. (Buffalo Bill) Cody, was a famous frontiersman. Born in Iowa in 1846, Cody had a personal history that itself reads like a fantasy of the Wild West: he rode for the Pony Express, served in the Civil War, hunted buffalo for railway construction crews, fought hand to hand with the Indians as a cavalry scout. Dime novelist Ned Buntline used these exploits as material for a series of adventure stories which transformed Buffalo Bill into a household name. After retiring from the frontier, Cody used his celebrity to launch a career on the stage, performing dramas also based loosely on incidents from his life. It is interesting that such an important creator of the Imaginary Indian should be in many ways an imaginary character himself.

In the summer of 1882, while visiting his home in North Platte, Nebraska, Cody was surprised to learn that the town had no plans for a Fourth of July celebration. To mark the holiday, he organized an "Old Glory Blow Out," featuring demonstrations of buffalo hunting and conventional cowboy events such as pony races, roping, and displays of marksmanship. This is apparently when Cody got the idea to mount a touring Wild West Show, mixing elements of the rodeo and the circus. That winter he and a partner, the sharpshooter "Doc" Carver, put a show together. Titled "The Wild West, Hon. W.F. Cody and Dr. W.F. Carver's Rocky Mountain and Prairie Exhibition," it featured the marksman and inventor of the clay pigeon, Captain Adam Bogardus; Major Frank North and his band of Pawnee Scouts;

Buck Taylor, "King of the Cowboys"; and a finale called "A Grand Hunt on the Plains" using herds of wild animals. After opening in Omaha in May, the show travelled to Illinois, Boston, and Coney Island, earning enough gate receipts to cover expenses and to convince Cody that he was on to something.

The visit to Canada in 1885 was a trial run for greater things to come. The following year the show settled into New York's Madison Square Garden for an extended winter stay. Called "The Pageant of Civilization," this multi-act production featured huge painted scenic backdrops, hundreds of performers, a small railway, and special effects that included a prairie fire and a cyclone. The show began with an Indian war and ended with an enactment of Custer's Last Stand, Buffalo Bill himself playing the role of General Custer. Then, in the spring of 1887, Cody loaded his all-star cast, 200 animals and ninety-seven Indians onto a boat and sailed to England for his first European tour. In London, Queen Victoria attended two command performances, and the show played to more than 30,000 patrons a day. It was the closest most Britons would come to the Wild West, and the only time they would ever get a chance to see an actual Indian.

Buffalo Bill's Wild West spawned many emulators, from small exhibitions performing at county fairs to touring companies which entertained the crowned heads of Europe. There seemed to be an insatiable appetite for cowboys and Indians in the cities of North America and Europe at the end of the century. Adam Forepaugh's Wild West Combination, Pawnee Bill's Historical Wild West Exhibition and Indian Encampment, the 101 Ranch Wild West Show—these were just a few of Cody's competitors. Every show had its featured cowboys and cowgirls—Annie Oakley, Buckskin Joe, Round-up Bob, Oklahoma Al, Deadshot Dick, Carazo the Female Crack Shot of the World. As they grew, they added more exotic acts. Pawnee Bill began presenting curiosities from the Far East, and Buffalo Bill introduced his famous Congress of Rough Riders of the World, including gauchos from Argentina and Cossacks from the Russian steppes.

But the real stars of the show were the Indians. On the American and Canadian Plains, authorities were still pacifying the Native population. Newspapers were full of stories about Indian wars. Dime novels were purveying a romantic version of events in the West to a mass audience. There was an intense interest in the Indians which the Wild West phenomenon exploited. The show purported to be much more than simple entertainment. Along with the rope tricks and the sharpshooting, Cody and his imitators claimed to be presenting actual events, as fresh as yesterday's headlines. Not only that, they were using actual characters, notorious for the part they played in the events they portrayed. Sitting Bull was only one example. Another was the Sioux holy man, Black Elk, who as a youth went to Europe with Buffalo Bill in 1886-1887. Gabriel Dumont, the Métis military leader during the 1885 rising, also joined the Buffalo Bill show. After the disturbances at Wounded Knee in 1890, the government forced thirty Native malcontents to go on tour in lieu of jail. And there were many others. These defeated Native leaders gave an air of historical authenticity to the proceedings. Patrons who had never been any closer to an Indian than the pages of a dime novel now had the thrill of watching Indians who had once terrorized an entire nation and brought the US army to its knees. Bill Cody's genius was that he managed to convince his audiences that he was giving them a first-hand look at what an Indian was really like. "No description can convey an adequate idea of the striking realism of this show as a picture of Western frontier life ... There is no pasteboard, no tinsel, no gaslights, no shifting of scenes, nothing to mar the realism of the scenes enacted."[8]

Natives performed as bareback riders, marksmen, and dancers, but most importantly they participated in the historic set-pieces which were the hallmark of Buffalo Bill's Wild West. These were wild and wooly enactments of events, real and imagined, featuring large numbers of actors mounted on horses performing in realistic settings that evoked the western frontier.

One of these was the famous Battle of Little Big Horn. A troop of Indians entered the arena, pitched their camp, and performed a war dance. When the cavalry burst onto the scene, an armed skirmish followed, after which the Indians exited, leaving dead cavalrymen and their horses heaped on the ground. A solitary Cody then arrived centre stage to mourn the dead while a voice intoned, "Too late!"

Cody arrived a little sooner in another set-piece, the Battle of Summit Springs, again based on an actual encounter, this time between soldiers and Cheyenne in 1869. The Wild West version showed the Indians torturing two White women captives when the cavalry appeared. During the battle, which the cavalry won, Cody rescued one of the maidens. (It is true that in 1869, the Cheyenne had a couple of women prisoners, and that one of them survived the actual battle, but it is doubtful that the Cheyenne tortured them. The Natives apparently took hostages because American soldiers earlier had taken away some Cheyenne women.)

Other acts included the "Attack on the Deadwood Stage," in which members of the audience rode in a stagecoach. Passengers usually included whatever celebrities were attending the show that day. "The mounted Indians swarmed around on both sides of the coach," described the Toronto reporter, "swerving around on their horses' necks to avoid the shots from the occupants of the coach and discharging their rifles in the most unheard of positions. It looked very much as if the coach and its occupants must fall into the hands of the redskins when suddenly Buffalo Bill and a band of cowboys came up and in an incredibly short space of time the redskins were put to flight."[9] A variation was the "Attack on the Wagon Train," in which

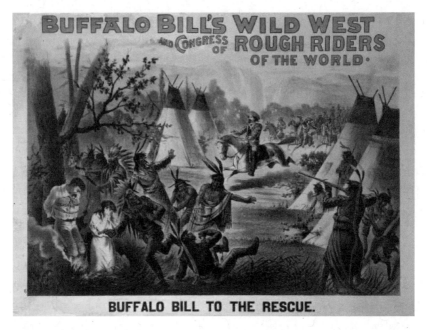

The posters for the Wild West Show contributed to the stereotype of the Indian as a bloodthirsty savage.

captives were forced to run the gauntlet and were tied to stakes while the Indians did a terrifying scalp dance. Again, the cowboys arrived in the nick of time.

Prior to the Hollywood movie, no other entertainment medium was as popular a purveyor of the Indian image as the Wild West Show. The impact of the show on the creation of the Imaginary Indian was twofold. First of all, as American historian John Ewers has pointed out, Bill Cody and his imitators fixed the Plains Indian firmly in the public's mind as typical of all Indians.[10] Audiences saw only representatives of the Plains tribes, with their horses and skin tipis and feather headdresses. This process was already underway, thanks to the efforts of the dime novelists with their lurid tales of Indian fighting on the Plains, and Western painters such as George Catlin and Paul Kane. Along with these other influences, the Wild West Show reduced the complexity of Native cultures in North America to a single image in the popular mind, the mounted, war-bonneted Plains chieftain. In the winter of 1886, a party of nine Kwakiutl from Bella Coola on the coast of British Columbia toured Germany exhibiting their traditional costumes and ceremonies. The German public was convinced that these people were Chinese or Japanese, not Indians, and accused tour organizers of a swindle. Where were the tomahawks and headdresses, the skin tipis, the aquiline features of the noble savage? Where was Buffalo Bill's Imaginary Indian?[11]

Secondly, the Wild West Show presented an Indian who was aggressive and blood-thirsty, an attacker of wagon trains, a torturer of innocent captives. Curiously, Cody himself, despite a lifetime spent fighting the Indians, was sympathetic to their plight and his show conveyed a respect for their traditional skills with horse and rifle. Certainly, it appealed to a nostalgia for the supposed "good old days" in the American West before the arrival of civilization. But the show was primarily an allegory depicting the ultimate triumph of civilized values over the anarchy of the wilderness. The Indian wars, the attacks on stagecoaches and settlers' cabins, the torture scenes, all ended with the cowboys putting the Indians to rout. The Wild West Show was not a platform for Native grievances; nor was it a travelling museum of aboriginal culture. It was dramatic entertainment, offering non-Native urban audiences a chance to see their fantasies about the American West brought to life. "Some of what they saw was authentic," writes one Wild West historian, "but audiences were not encouraged to see Indians as a people with an advanced civilization or as a group deserving treatment that was any different from what they were receiving."[12]

Native people participated in the shows for a variety of reasons. They were proud of their traditions and happy to get a chance to ride and shoot again, if only for a couple of hours a day in a crowded arena using blanks. Some were coerced by government officials who wanted to rid the reserves of "troublemakers," however temporarily. The money attracted others. Sitting Bull, for example, received $50 a week from Cody, plus a $125 signing bonus, not a huge sum, but a lot when compared to the limited opportunities on the reserves. Natives who were not well-known received far less. Black Elk joined the tour out of desperation. As he said in his memoirs, "I thought I ought to go, because I might learn some secret of the Wasichu [Whites] that would help my people somehow ... I know now that this was foolish, but I was young and in despair."[13] Not many of the Natives stayed with the tour for very long. They missed their families and their familiar country. Sitting Bull lasted just one summer season. Black Elk got lost in Europe and remained there for three years, where he was miserable most of the time.

The Wild West Show enjoyed its greatest popularity during the decades preceding World War I. Cody's show eventually merged with Pawnee Bill's Wild West, then went bankrupt in 1913, more a victim of Buffalo Bill's bad investments than a lack of public interest. Other shows survived the war period, but certainly popular interest in the Wild West Show was abating. Partly this was because the movie western was emerging as the dominant popular art form to express the myth of the Wild West. As well, the Wild West Show had its greatest popularity in a period when most eastern Canadians, and Americans, shared an anxiety about the Native people of the West. Plains Natives had not yet been pacified. In the summer of 1885, when Sitting Bull came to Toronto with the Buffalo Bill show, the Northwest Rebellion was barely over. Louis Riel was still alive, waiting in his prison cell in Regina to hang for his part in the affair. Canadians believed that a full-scale Indian war had been narrowly averted, and was still a distinct possibility. They were very nervous about events in the West and must have been reassured to visit Buffalo Bill's show and watch the forces of law and order subdue the Indians. The Wild West phenomenon reflected a cultural anxiety about the Indians in much the same way that the proliferation of television police shows reflects a modern anxiety about urban crime. As the threat of Native violence decreased toward the end of the century, so did the interest in the Wild West Show. A certain residue of nostalgia for the vanishing frontier remained, strong enough to sustain the shows into the 1930s. But after the turn of the century they no longer seemed to reflect history in the making, which was the source of their strongest fascination for audiences.

III

During the first week of July, 1908, the city of Calgary was proud to host the biggest agricultural fair ever seen in Alberta. The Dominion Exhibition kicked off on July first with a huge parade through the streets of the city. Native tribes from all over the province accepted the invitation to take part. Dressed in feathers and buckskin, they were, according to the *Calgary Herald,* "the great feature of the parade."[14] Natives camped at the exhibition grounds and people could visit their lodges and watch their demonstrations of traditional singing and dancing. As part of the fair, the Miller Brothers 101 Ranch Wild West Show arrived in town for a one-night stand.

Agricultural exhibitions were a common feature of the Prairie West early in the twentieth century. They were staged to display and promote economic development in the region. They were also a celebration of the progress which had taken place in the West since the arrival of the White man. Native participants played an exemplary role. Encouraged to appear in warpaint and buckskin and to perform the customs of their forefathers, Natives appeared as Indians representing a primitive past against which the progress of White settlers could be measured. "In their glorious blaze of color, their traditional war paint, their gorgeous feathers and their many blankets," reported the *Herald*, "the Indians brought back vividly the long and romantic history of Canada's great western land, the struggle of barbarism with civilization, the eternal contest between what has been and what is to come."[15]

Native involvement at Calgary in 1908 was not unusual. Natives regularly participated in local fairs and exhibitions.[16] But there was growing opposition on the part of officials within the federal Indian Department who believed that participation in the fairs encouraged Natives to retain their traditional culture instead of assimilating into the Canadian mainstream. The federal government wanted to wean Native people away from "the old ways" and gradually introduce a settled, agricultural lifestyle. Officials frowned on anything that served to revive or celebrate traditional practices. They did not want to convey an image of Canada as a place where wild Indians with painted faces still roamed the Plains.[17] Much more to the government's liking was the exhibit organized by Indian Department officials at the Chicago World's Fair in 1893. This included young Natives from Western Canada performing "civilized" trades and household chores against a backdrop of artifacts from the "warpath" days, including some dried scalps. The exhibit was meant to illustrate how far Indians had progressed under government tutelage.[18]

Back in Canada, officials attempted to convince organizers that Natives should not attend country fairs. If they must, why not dressed in modern clothing and exhibiting agricultural products like everyone else? But Indians were a popular part of the fairs and the government had little success. In 1914, the senior official in the Indian Department, Duncan Campbell Scott, drew up a regulation forbidding the performance of what he called "senseless drumming and dancing" outside reserves in the western provinces, as well as the wearing of "aboriginal costume" in exhibitions and fairs. The penalty was a $25 fine or a month in jail.[19] But for the most part Natives and fair organizers ignored the restrictions with impunity.

Government attempts to eradicate displays of traditional Native culture were part of a larger policy aimed at stamping out all practices which the Indian department believed stood in the way of the assimilation of Native people. Chief among these were the potlatch on the West Coast, and the sun dance among Plains Natives.

The government of Sir John A. Macdonald (who called the potlatch "a debauchery of the worst kind") banned the potlatch in 1884—on the grounds that it and similar ceremonies encouraged barbarity, idleness, and waste, interfered with more productive activities, and generally discouraged acculturation. For a variety of reasons the law was not enforced with much consistency until Scott became deputy superintendent of Indian Affairs in 1913. Scott believed that "the potlatches are attended by prolonged idleness and waste of time, by ill-advised and wanton giving away of property and by immorality."[20] He encouraged agents in the field to be more aggressive about suppressing the potlatch, with the result that several Natives were arrested.

On the Prairies the government took similar steps to outlaw traditional Native dancing, especially the Blackfoot sun dance and the Cree thirst dance. Initially, missionaries and government officials feared the potential these ceremonies had for inciting warriors to acts of violence. In the excitement of the moment, it was argued, young men might decide to return to the warlike days of old (as described in dime novels and Mountie histories). As the threat of violence faded, the dances, which sometimes featured self-mutilation, came to be seen as relics of barbarism, impediments to the assimilation of the Natives.[21] Dancing was supposed to promote indolence and immorality and was considered antithetical to the sedentary, agricultural life which the government was encouraging Natives to adopt.

Government attempts to stop the dances were no more successful

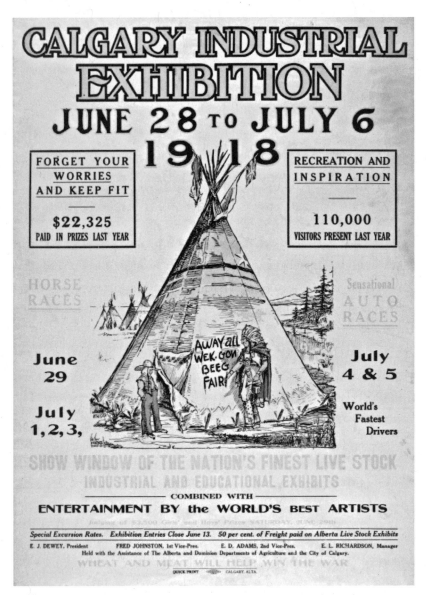

This poster for the Calgary Exhibition in 1918 highlighted the participation of Native people. The writing on the tipi, of course, reinforced the image of the Indian as unsophisticated and not very bright.

than attempts to end the potlatch. Natives modified some of their practices and abandoned others, but they usually managed to come to some *modus vivendi* with the Mounted Police and government agents who allowed dancing to continue.[22] One of the chief antagonists of the government in this regard was the Methodist missionary John McDougall. McDougall had established a mission to the Stoney Indians at Morley, Alberta, in 1873, and his influence among the Alberta Natives was strong. Unlike most other missionaries, he saw nothing wrong with Native involvement in exhibitions, nor in Native dancing. He recruited most of the Natives who attended the Calgary exhibition in 1908, and two years later he staged a five-act play at the Exhibition involving 2,000 Indians commemorating the signing of Treaty 7. Indian Affairs officials and even his own church criticized him, but McDougall continued to argue that Natives "have as much right to join in the sun dance or the thirst dance as a Methodist has to join in a camp meeting."[23]

The government assault on Native ceremonies and public performances peaked in the 1920s when William M. Graham became the senior Indian Department official on the Prairies. Graham was determined to stamp out dancing and enlisted the RCMP's help in combatting this "vice." Dances were broken up and several Indians jailed. But once again, enforcement was uneven and the Natives found ways around the regulations.

Meanwhile, Commissioner Graham also objected to the continued involvement of Natives in fairs and exhibitions like the one at Calgary. In his opinion Native participation in these events contradicted the government's policy of assimilation by reaffirming the value of Native culture. Plus, he argued, the tribespeople who took part lost precious time that they should be devoting to their crops. They should be staying at home and concentrating on learning to be good farmers. If they came to the exhibitions, it should be to display livestock and produce from their farms, like everyone else.

In 1925, Graham decided to ban Indians from the Calgary Stampede. The Stampede had evolved from the annual summer exhibition and local Natives played a prominent role. They marched in full regalia in the opening-day parade, then camped at the stampede grounds in their own village of tipis where visitors could pose for photographs with an authentic Indian chief. There were pony races, handicraft displays, and exhibitions of traditional dancing. Graham and more senior officials consistently denied Stampede organizers permission to include Indians in the festivities. And organizers just as consistently ignored the ban and invited the Indians. Graham wanted to adopt more heavy-handed measures to confine Indians to their reserves during the Stampede period, but his superior, Duncan Scott, counselled the need for patient persuasion. The 1925 ban particularly upset Stampede organizers. The theme of the exhibition that year was the fiftieth anniversary of the arrival of the North-West Mounted Police in the West. A grand historical pageant was planned. It was unthinkable to do it without aboriginal participants. Under pressure, Commissioner Graham agreed to allow elderly Natives to attend the fair, but he insisted that able-bodied young men had to remain working on the reserves.[24]

Government attempts to coerce the Indians into abandoning their traditional practices failed. Native people continued to celebrate the potlatch and their ceremonial dances, and they continued to take part in the annual Calgary Stampede festivities. Their determined resistance frustrated the government's attempts to carry out its program for assimilation. Making it even more difficult was the opposition of White officials and missionaries who believed that Native ceremonies were harmless and represented an authentic reminder of frontier days in the Canadian West.

Rev. John McDougall *(right)* parading through Calgary with Indian participants at the 1912 Stampede. McDougall was a thorn in the side of government officials who believed that the Stampede, and other exhibitions like it, perpetuated an outdated image of the Indian.

Evidently when Indians came out in public, whether in the wild west show or the country fair, they exposed divergent views about their role in contemporary Canadian society. Much as the government did not like it, many Whites preferred their Indians in feathers and warpaint. The Performing Indian was a tame Indian, one who had lost the power to frighten anyone. Fairs and exhibitions represented a manipulation of nostalgia. They allowed non-Natives to admire aspects of aboriginal culture, safely located in the past, without confronting the problems of contemporary Native people. Frozen as they were in an historical stereotype, Performing Indians invoked a bygone era. By implication, they celebrated the triumph of White civilization. They were a comfort to many people who worried that

Indian violence might still be a threat, particularly in the West. No wonder fair organizers resisted attempts to delete such a soothing reminder of White superiority from their programs.

On the other hand, Indian Department officials tried to impose a different version of the Imaginary Indian. Officials thought that the stereotype promoted by the Performing Indian excluded Native people from modern life. They preferred to emphasize the transition many Native people were making to a settled, agricultural lifestyle. They wanted Indians in public to be dressed in suits and dresses, not buckskin and feathers. Their objective was assimilation of the Native people into mainstream Canadian society. Support for traditional Native ways only made that objective more difficult to achieve. Government officials were promoting their own allegory of progress, just as much as impresarios like Buffalo Bill and the businessmen who sponsored the Calgary Stampede promoted their allegories. Government officials wanted Indians to become a part of the modern world by giving up whatever it was that made them Indians, while the others preferred Indians to affirm progress by remaining a picturesque example of what it was not. Either way, the Performing Indian was playing the role of extra in somebody else's story.

IV

At the same time as the government was trying to stamp out vestiges of traditional aboriginal culture in everyday life, it was creating a new institution devoted to the preservation of that culture. The ethnological museum filled with Indian relics is a fairly recent phenomenon. It developed from the "cabinets of curiosities" gathered by people like George Catlin, Paul Kane, and early explorers and traders. In the mid-nineteenth century, a museum mania seemed gradually to take hold of the western world. Ethnological museums opened their doors in several major cities in Europe and North America, including the

Smithsonian Institution in Washington, the American Museum of Natural History in New York, and Chicago's Field Museum.

These museums dispatched collectors to the distant regions of the world, including Canada, to buy, barter and in some cases steal artifacts from the Native people. This so-called "museum scramble" was a competition between different institutions to have the largest, best collections. In British Columbia, coastal villages were pillaged of material until by World War I there was almost nothing left: the material culture of the Northwest Coast people had been transported to museums in Chicago, New York, and Berlin.[25]

Canada was not immune to museum mania. Concerned that they were losing their heritage to foreign institutions, Canadians created their own museums in an attempt to keep some of the artifacts at home. In 1910, the federal government created a Division of Anthropology within the Geological Survey and expanded its small Geological Survey museum into the Victoria Memorial Museum, a handsome castle on the outskirts of Ottawa, the forerunner of the modern Museum of Civilization. Provincial governments in Nova Scotia, Ontario, and British Columbia earlier established their own local museums. All these museums were created in a climate of urgency. Not only were foreigners looting the country of its finest artifacts, but it was firmly believed that the Indian people themselves were vanishing and would soon be gone. The museum was created as an institution to preserve their remains so that future generations would be able to see what had once existed.

An ethnological museum and a Wild West Show are obviously quite different things. The Wild West Show was unashamedly low brow: pure show business exploiting Indian culture for the sake of entertainment. The museum, on the other hand, collected and displayed specimens of aboriginal culture in a formal, educational setting, without the three-ring-circus atmosphere of the Wild West, and could claim to be dedicated to the study and the understanding of Indian culture. But the two settings are not that disparate: both assumed that Indians were disappearing and both treated them as historical artifacts. As far as the audience was concerned, the Wild West Show was a living history museum, every bit as authentic as the beads and basketwork occupying display cases in the museum. Each presented an Imaginary Indian, one in the name of science, the other in the name of entertainment.

V

Audiences which had been exposed to the Imaginary Indian through the Wild West Show and the dime novel found their familiar stereotypes confirmed when movies made their appearance early in the twentieth century. Movies immediately seized on the Indian as an ideal subject and every year dozens of Indian pictures, usually Westerns, lit up the silver screen in theatres across the US and Canada. Movies required plenty of dramatic action in exotic locations, and Indians provided both. The Indian frontier became the setting for a continuous stream of movies which impressed the Imaginary Indian onto the popular culture of North America.

Movies aimed to amuse, not to edify: they used Indians for their entertainment value, chiefly as villains. Hollywood Indians attacked wagon trains, scalped soldiers, slaughtered settlers, and generally created mayhem wherever needed by a script. Little thought was given to historical or cultural accuracy. Indian roles invariably went to White actors. It was assumed audiences wanted "stars," not unknown Native performers. So viewers got to see Sal Mineo and Ricardo Montalban and Anthony Quinn, in bathing trunks and braids, pretending to be Indian warriors, or Loretta Young and Dolores Del Rio dressed up as Indian princesses. When Native actors did get roles, they had to conform to the stereotype of the Hollywood Indian as much as their

A West Coast totem pole is transported to Quebec for this scene from the 1936 version of *Rose Marie*. The beaded headband worn by the women was another invention of Hollywood. The actors needed something to keep their braids in place.

White colleagues. In *Geronimo* (1939), for example, a Cherokee actor named Chief Thunder Cloud played the leading role, but he had to be heavily made up because in the judgement of the director he didn't look enough like an Indian.

Costumes were seldom authentic and the movie Indians usually spoke a form of drunken English consisting mainly of "How" and "Ugh." Occasionally they spoke an actual Native language, or something that sounded like one. In one case a director simply ran the English sound track backwards to get authentic-sounding Indian "gibberish." Movies also played fast and loose with historical fact, seldom giving any realistic sense of why Native groups behaved as they did.

Following in the footsteps of the Wild West Show, Hollywood's careless treatment of the Indian reduced the complexity of Native cultures to a few familiar stereotypes. North Americans were force-fed images of painted, tomahawk-wielding warriors in feather head-dresses mounted on horseback. They could be forgiven for not know-ing that more Native Americans were farmers than buffalo hunters and knew nothing of cavalry posts and wagon trains. Yet it was the image of the Plains chieftain that made its way onto the US "Indian head" nickel and the original television test pattern.

The stereotypes were not all negative. Much has been made of the way the movies portrayed Native people as incorrigible savages, and many did. But there have always been movies which presented a more sympathetic view. The Wise Elder, for example, has been a durable stereotype. Whether it was Dan George playing Old Lodge Skins in *Little Big Man* (1971) or the Sioux shaman in *Thunderheart* (1992), the Wise Elder embodies the natural wisdom and rooted presence that non-Natives have always believed Indians to possess. From *The Van-ishing Indian* (1925) through *Broken Arrow* (1950) to *Dances with Wolves* (1990), the movies romanticize Indians when they are not demon-izing them.

Movies invariably situate Indians in the past, usually on the west-ern frontier. The result is that Indians in the movies seem marginal to modern life. Sympathetic regret or retrospective outrage are the feel-ings these movies seem most likely to evoke. In a sense, Indian mov-ies have never really been about Indians at all. They have been about White concerns: White guilt, White fear, White insecurity. The per-sistent popularity of Performing Indians—whether in the Wild West Show or in the movies—suggests that these forms of entertainment respond to a deep anxiety that non-Natives have about our place in North America, and a deep need to legitimate our presence here. Some movies have dealt with this anxiety by dehumanizing Indians, turning them into savage monsters, or drunken buffoons, who have

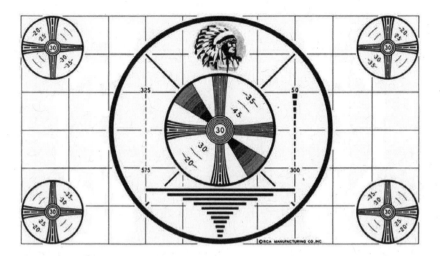

The Indian Head Test Pattern was a black and white television test pattern broadcast when there was no regular programming on air. It was introduced in 1939 by RCA and used by the CBC.

to be eradicated before civilization can take root. Other movies have romanticized Indians for their wisdom and natural virtue. Either way, the movies project onto Indian characters the uncertainty non-Natives feel about the justice of our history and our right to occupy the land.

CHAPTER SIX

Celebrity Indians and Plastic Shamans

ON-NATIVE CANADIANS HAVE always formed their impressions of the Indian without much reference to actual Native people, and especially without hearing what Native people might have to say about their own situation. There have been exceptions, however. Every once in a while a Native voice emerges from the background—or, as it were, the margins—and gains a wide audience among non-Natives, who then project onto it the voice of the "typical Indian" in the non-Native imagination.

These voices are often inauthentic. Whites have never been very good at distinguishing "real" Indians from non-Natives who appropriate an Indian persona and claim to have special insight into the Indian way of life. These "plastic shamans" speak with great authority and achieve wide recognition. They are accepted so easily because they conform to the image of the Indian held by the White world. They are the Indian that Whites wish the Indian to be: the Imaginary Indian come to life.

A particularly bizarre example of the "plastic shaman" phenomenon occurred as recently as 1991, much to the embarrassment of *The New York Times*, which for several weeks listed at the top of its nonfiction bestseller list a book called *The Education of Little Tree*. Supposedly the autobiography of a young Indian orphan named Little Tree, who had been raised by his Cherokee grandparents during the 1930s in the hills of Tennessee, the book sold more than a half million copies.

Little Tree enjoyed great success among environmentalists and New Age mystics who appreciated its message of respect for the natural world and contempt for the acquisitive values of modern society.

But it soon turned out that Forrest Carter, author of *Little Tree* (along with several western novels, including one that became the movie *The Outlaw Josey Wales*), was not an Indian at all: the autobiography was fiction. And there was more: Forrest Carter, who died in 1979, had in real life been a man named Asa Earl Carter, a Ku Klux Klan thug and virulent racist, author not only of western novels but also of anti-Semitic pamphlets and some of former Alabama governor George Wallace's strongest anti-Black speeches. When this information became public, the publisher (The University of New Mexico Press) removed the phrase "True Story" from the book's cover, and *The New York Times* quickly slid the title across the page to its list of fiction bestsellers.[1]

This kind of thing happens with surprising regularity. Don Juan, the Yaqui wise man in the set of books by Carlos Castaneda which became classics of the 1960s counter-culture, turned out to be a figment of the author's imagination. Self-proclaimed Indians with names like "Chief Piercing Eyes" and "Beautiful Painted Arrow" routinely pass themselves off as experts in Native spiritual traditions. In 1981, Jamake Highwater, claiming to be of mixed Cherokee-Blackfoot ancestry, wrote a very popular book about Native spirituality called *The Primal Mind*. So many questions were raised about the facts of his background that he agreed to stop calling himself an Indian. Apparently the public hungers for aboriginal wisdom and is none too discriminating about where it finds it.

The search for representative voices which seem to speak for the Indian goes back a long way in Canada, too. Certainly, not all "celebrity Indians" have been fakes. In the early years of the twentieth century, the most famous Indian in Canada was Pauline Johnson, whose father was a chief of the Grand River Mohawk. Two other celebrity Indians, Grey Owl and Chief Buffalo Child Long Lance, turned out not to be who they said they were. But whether or not their messages were authentically "Indian," their audiences thought they were and therefore the careers of these three writer-performers are small case studies in the presentation of the Imaginary Indian.

II

On a January evening in 1892, the overflowing crowd in the Gallery of Art at Toronto's Academy of Music was growing restive. Things had begun promisingly enough, with the poems of Agnes Machar and Wilfred Campbell. But then William Lighthall had droned on for far too long with his humourless reflections on nation-building. High-minded views on the future of Canada were expected at an event sponsored by the Young Men's Liberal Club, but this was supposed to be a literary get-together. Organizer Frank Yeigh had promised some of the leading writers of the day, but next on the program was a little known poetess from Brantford. It looked like it was going to be a long evening.[2]

Gathering her courage, Pauline Johnson emerged nervously from the wings and took her place on the platform. She was thirty years old, the daughter of a Mohawk chief, an uncelebrated writer of stories and poems who lived quietly with her mother in a provincial backwater. She knew Frank Yeigh as a classmate from school. He had seen a couple of her canoeing poems, and on the strength of them had asked her to appear at the Toronto recital. Neither of them realized that they were about to launch one of the most successful careers in Canadian entertainment history.

Above the rustling of the crowd and the murmur of whispered conversations, Pauline Johnson began to recite.

My forest brave, my Red-skin love, farewell;
We may not meet to-morrow; who can tell
What mighty ills befall our little band,
Or what you'll suffer from the white man's hand?

The poem was "A Cry from an Indian Wife," the lament of a Native woman whose husband is going off to fight alongside the Métis in the 1885 Northwest Rebellion.

They but forget we Indians owned the land
From ocean to ocean; that they stand
Upon a soil that centuries agone
Was our sole kingdom and our right alone.

Here was something different; the rebellion from the Native point of view, told dramatically, without apology, by a "daughter of the forest" herself. The audience was rivetted by the wild pathos of her words and when she finished it broke into enthusiastic applause, bringing her back for an encore.

Johnson chose another Indian poem, "As Red Men Die," a lurid story about a Mohawk captive who chooses death by hideous torture over life as a slave.

Up the long trail of fire he boasting goes,
Dancing a war dance to defy his foes.
His flesh is scorched, his muscles burn and shrink,
But still he dances to death's awful brink.
Then loyal to his race,
He bends to death—but *never* to disgrace.

Once again her audience responded with a long ovation. She had clearly taken literary Toronto by storm. "It was like the voice of the nations who once possessed this country, who have wasted away be-fore our civilisation," wrote the *Globe* reviewer, "speaking through this cultured, gifted, soft-voiced descendant."[3]

Frank Yeigh was elated. An enterprising promoter who knew when he was on to a good thing, he convinced Johnson that together they must take advantage of her sudden popularity. Hiring Toronto's Association Hall, he advertised an evening recital by "the Indian po-etess." Once again the sold-out audience, and the critics, loved her. "Another triumph," enthused the *Globe*.[4]

Johnson was an instant celebrity. She embarked on a hectic, fifty-stop tour of Ontario, giving 125 recitals in just eight months. That autumn she teamed up with a British vaudeville performer, Owen Smiley, and following the Ontario tour they took their show to the Maritimes and into the northeastern United States. Boston, New York, Toronto, Halifax, Ottawa—everywhere the critics raved. "She is perhaps the most unique figure in the literary world on this con-tinent," claimed the *New York Sun*.[5] *Canadian Magazine* called her "the most popular figure in Canadian literature."[6] To the poet, Charles G.D. Roberts, she was "the aboriginal voice of Canada." Critic Hec-tor Charlesworth went so far as to call her "the greatest living poetess."

Her fame accompanied her to England in the spring of 1894 where she performed at house parties and found a publisher for a slim vol-ume of her verse. Next year The Bodley Head released her first book, *The White Wampum*.

Johnson returned to Canada and resumed her whirlwind touring schedule, this time whistle-stopping all the way to the Pacific Coast aboard the Canadian Pacific Railway. For the next fifteen years, she was on the road almost constantly, enduring long, tiresome trips by rail, steamboat, stagecoach, and wagon. Living out of a suitcase in hotels, rooming houses, and police outposts, she performed wherever there was a hall to hold an audience, from the gas-lit theatres of To-

The two sides of Pauline Johnson—the White Man's Indian wearing an English dinner gown (*left*), and the Princess dressed for performance in her Indian costume (*right*).

ronto to the out-ports of Newfoundland to the backwoods camps of British Columbia. "There is hardly a town or settlement in Canada that we did not visit several times during those years," recalled her longtime partner, Walter McRaye.[7] Once she even mounted a billiard table to recite to a roomful of miners, changing costume behind a Hudson's Bay blanket strung on a line. The discomfort of this routine was increased by recurring bouts of ill health which Johnson suffered all her life. Despite her hectic schedule, she was unable to save much money, and spent whatever spare time she had writing adventure stories for boys' magazines and melodramatic tales for the women's market. This was the pattern of her professional life until she retired from the stage and settled in Vancouver in 1909.

From her first public performance, the critics identified Johnson as "the voice of the Indian," a label on which she quickly capitalized. Yeigh began billing her as "the Mohawk Princess," and in November 1892 she donned the Indian dress that became a hallmark of her performances. Her costume consisted of a buckskin dress, fringed at the hem to reveal a lining of red wool and decorated at the neck with silver brooches, buckskin leggings, and moccasins. Later she added a necklace of ermine tails. At her waist she carried a hunting knife and an authentic Huron scalp inherited from her great-grandfather. A red wool cloak hung from one shoulder. One sleeve was a long piece of fringed buckskin, attached at the shoulder and the wrist; the other was a drape of rabbit pelts. Johnson seems to have come up with this polyglot costume herself. She wore it during the half of her program devoted to Indian poems. For her non-Indian material, she wore a simple dinner gown.

In 1886, Johnson took the name Tekahionwake, which apparently meant Double Wampum. The naturalist, Ernest Thompson Seton, recalled that she complained to him once, "Oh, why have your people forced on me the name of Pauline Johnson? Was not my Indian name good enough?"[8] Actually, if anyone "forced" her name on her, it was Pauline's father, a chief at the Brantford reserve. He was a fervent admirer of Napoleon, and named his daughter after the French emperor's sister. (He nicknamed his eldest son "Boney" and his second son "Kleber" after one of Napoleon's generals.) Technically, the name Tekahionwake did not belong to Pauline. It was her great-grandfather's name; she adopted it as a gesture of identification with her Native background.

Johnson's White audiences loved these "authentic" Indian props. They thrilled at the war whoops, the dangling scalp, the name they could not pronounce, the poems of torture and war. She enjoyed immense popularity. Campers recited her poems by memory around their fires at night. "The Song My Paddle Sings" became an anthem for outdoors enthusiasts and a fixture in schoolbooks. It is possible that more Canadian children have memorized it than any other piece of verse. Her first biographer, Mrs. Garland Foster, claimed that a copy of her first book of poems was found in the packsack of a gold-seeker trekking into the Klondike over the Chilkoot Pass.[9]

The poet herself was ambivalent about her Indian "image." She recognized that her act depended on its exoticism. The public paid to see a Mohawk princess as much as a talented writer and recitalist. And she welcomed the opportunity to carry her message to a large audience. However, she did wonder from time to time if pandering to public taste was not stifling her growth as an artist. Writing to a friend, she confided that "the public will not listen to lyrics, will not appreciate real poetry, will in fact not have me as an entertainer if I give them nothing but rhythm, cadence, beauty, thought." Plaintively, she continued, "I could do so much better if they would only let me."[10]

Johnson could not abandon her Indian themes for fear of losing her audience. Nor did she want to. The purpose of her career, after all, was to proclaim the nobler aspects of Canada's Native people. "My aim, my joy, my pride is to sing the glories of my own people," she told Seton.[11] But in order to fulfill this purpose, Johnson had to make compromises with the expectations of her White public.

Johnson was a "White Man's Indian" in the sense that she had the polished manners of a well-bred, middle-class Victorian gentlewoman. "There are those who think they pay me a compliment—saying that I am just like a white woman," she once complained.[12] She had no desire to be considered anything but Native, but there is no question that Johnson was admired by so many Whites because she made it easy for them. Everyone she met remarked on her manners, her charm, her good looks. "She is tall and slender and dark, with grey eyes, beautifully clean cut features, black hair, a very sweet smile, and a clear, musical pleasant voice," Sara Jeanette Duncan informed her readers in the *Globe* in 1886. "I have always thought her beautiful and many agree with me. She has certainly that highest attribute of beauty, the rare, fine gift of expression. She is charmingly bright in conversation, and has a vivacity of tone and gesture that is almost French."[13]

Born to a Mohawk father and a white mother, Johnson grew up at their home, Chiefswood, a gracious colonial mansion set apart from the rest of the Six Nations Reserve on the Grand River at Brantford. Perched on a bluff overlooking the river, the house was surrounded with spacious, landscaped grounds. French windows opened onto the lawn where visitors played croquet. Each room had a fireplace, and there was a rosewood piano in the parlour. The family had three servants. Her father was the chief, but young Pauline had few friends from the reserve. She was encouraged to believe in the family's social superiority and because of her father's position she had many opportunities to mix with the White dignitaries who visited the reserve. Such an upbringing equipped Johnson with the refined sophistication that impressed so many of her White admirers and helped win acceptance for her Indian performances.

At the same time, Johnson was raised to be proud of her Native heritage. From her father she learned the great events of Mohawk history and heard the names of Brant and Pontiac and Tecumseh. From her grandfather, John Smoke Johnson, a veteran of the War of 1812 and a gifted orator, she learned the legends and stories of her people. It was his father's name she took as her own. No matter how far the music hall was from the longhouse, Johnson believed she was fulfilling an inheritance both racial and familial when she mounted the platform each night.

Critics and public alike admired in Johnson many traits which they believed to be distinctively Indian. Her stage presence and rhetorical skills were thought to derive from Native traditions of oratory. The image of Indian leaders giving eloquent speeches around the council fires was deeply ingrained in the White imagination. Likewise her simplicity was described as typically Indian, reflecting the innocence of a people uncorrupted by modern civilization. And the quiet dignity of her bearing betrayed the proud stoicism for which her race was famous.

To White critics, her poems and stories showed their Indian origins, not just in content but also in style. "Her singing sense she did not get from her white blood," remarked Mrs. Foster. "It is too evidently the product of the swinging paddle, the choral dance of the redman."[14] Most Whites thought that Indians were closer to nature than other people. Critics saw this reflected in the rhythms of Johnson's work, along with the intense passion which supposedly characterized all Indians, whether a passionate love of nature or a passionate sense of injustice. "Intense feeling distinguishes her Indian poems from all others," wrote Charles Mair; "they flow from her very veins, and are stamped with the seal of heredity ... Begot of her knowledge of the long-suffering of her race, of iniquities in the past and present, they poured red-hot from her inmost heart."[15]

What gave Johnson's work an added poignancy was the belief shared by most members of her audience that they were listening to the voice of a disappearing people. "The race that is gone speaks with touching pathos through Miss Johnson," was how the *Toronto Globe* put it.[16] In her stage performances, she personified the Vanishing Race and people strained to hear the final whispered message before it faded away completely.

Johnson, of course, was not the "voice" of the Indian. There were many Indians, many voices. She herself knew that. "The term 'Indian,'" she once wrote, "signifies about as much as the term 'European,' but I cannot recall ever having read a story where the heroine was described as 'a European.'"[17] Johnson, however, happened to possess the only voice that White society *could* hear. Other Native poets and orators did not speak English, did not have the appropriate manners for genteel socializing, did not aspire to a career on the concert stage. Natives were politically quiescent at the turn of the century. Pushed to the margins of public life, they could not get their concerns on the national agenda. Johnson, on the other hand, succeeded in capturing White attention, and while she had it, attempted to plead the cause of the Native.

Johnson did not always sustain the angry sense of injustice present in some of her most popular poems. Occasionally she allowed herself to become as patronizing towards her own people as any White writer. In 1906 she paid a second visit to England, where the editor of the *London Daily Express* asked her to contribute some articles, one of which was called "A Pagan in St. Paul's." Recollecting a visit to St. Paul's Cathedral, Johnson defends the dignity of Native religious practices and beliefs, but instead of doing so from the perspective of a sophisticated woman with some experience of the world, she adopts the persona of a naive "Redskin" who seems never to have ventured beyond the edges of the northern forest. "So this is the place where dwells the Great White Father, ruler of many lands, lodges, and tribes," her narrator marvels. "I, one of his loyal allies, have come to see his camp, known to the white man as London, his council which the whites call his Parliament, where his sachems and chiefs make the laws of his tribes, and to see his wigwam, known to the palefaces as Buckingham Palace, but to the red man as the 'Teepee of the Great White Father.'"[18] Whatever the worth of her argument about Native religion, Johnson was clearly pandering to a stereotypical notion of the Indian as an artless, childlike innocent.

This need to satisfy the demands of a White audience stultified Pauline Johnson's development as a writer and limited her effectiveness as a spokesperson for Native people. Many of her stories appeared in *Mother's Magazine*, a popular women's magazine based in

Sheet music for one of the songs in a popular musical, *A Madcap Princess*. A transplanted Plains Indian serves as a symbol of Ontario.

Illinois. "We want to picture only the best and highest," the editor told Johnson, "but we do want the good attractively presented." Johnson's stories conform to the melodramatic literary conventions of the period, but with a difference. Her brave heroines have to overcome not only social and sexual obstacles to win the man of their dreams, but racial obstacles as well. She often portrayed the traumatic effects of contact between Native and European in terms of a tragic love affair between a Native woman and a White man. One of her most famous stories was "A Red Girl's Reasoning," which she turned into a play-let for use in her performances. It is the tale of a marriage between a White man and a mixed-blood woman. The woman shocks polite society by divulging that her parents were wed according to Indian custom without the blessing of a priest. Their marriage is every bit as legitimate as any White marriage, she argues, but her friends are scandalized, her husband furious at her for being so candid. Her love for him dies and she leaves him. Realizing his hypocrisy, he tracks her down, but she is adamant, and does not return to him.

Pauline Johnson represented a shining example of Indian woman-hood for her non-Native audiences, who saw in her the personification of Pocahontas, the Indian princess. According to legend, Pocahontas saved the life of Captain John Smith, a leader of the Virginia colony, when he was threatened by her people, the Powhatan. A paragon of virtue, Pocahontas later converted to Christianity. Her marriage to John Rolfe, a White settler, helped to forge an alliance between the Powhatan and the colonists. The romantic story of Pocahontas in-spired countless works of art, both low and high, idealizing the image of the Indian woman. She was painted often in European dress, much as Pauline Johnson appeared on stage wearing a formal gown: the Indian turned gentlewoman. The original Miss America, Pocahontas came to represent the beautiful, exotic New World itself. Her story provided a model for the ideal merger of Native and newcomer.[19]

Of course, not all the stereotypes of Indian women were this positive. Opposed to the princess there was the *squaw*, a derogato-ry epithet widely applied to Native women by non-Natives. In all ways the squaw was the opposite of the princess, an anti-Pocahontas.

Where the princess was beautiful, the squaw was ugly, even deformed. Where the princess was virtuous, the squaw was debased, immoral, a sexual convenience. Where the princess was proud, the squaw lived a squalid life of servile toil, mistreated by her men. Non-Native writers described Indian women hanging around the margins of White settlement, drinking and prostituting themselves. This stereotype of the Indian woman as a low, sexual commodity—a "bit of brown" as the fur trade governor George Simpson put it—became increasingly common as Native people were pushed to the fringes of White settlement, neglected and powerless. Its tragic consequences were revealed in the case of Helen Betty Osborne, a young Native woman whose brutal murder by a gang of young Whites in The Pas, Manitoba, in 1971 was hushed up by the community for years.

In her own life, Pauline Johnson conformed to the princess stereotype. She gave great dignity to the Native characters in her poems and stories. They appear as honourable, proud people with strong family ties and long traditions. This was a rarity at the time. "Half of our authors who write up Indian stuff have never been on an Indian reserve," she complained in the *Toronto Sunday Globe*, "have never met a 'real live Redman,' have never ever read Parkman, Schoolcraft or Catlin; what wonder that their conception of a people they are ignorant of, save by hearsay, is dwarfed, erroneous and delusive." [20]

But Johnson herself only went so far. She presented the plight of the Red Man, but she demanded little from her White audience beyond sentimental regret, which was easy enough to give. The land may once have belonged to her people, but she was not asking for it back. Indeed, she was a fervent Canadian patriot who liked to mix her Indian material with odes to the National Policy, made-in-Canada manufacturing, and the North-West Mounted Police. "White race and Red are one if they are but Canadian Born," she wrote in *Canadian Born*, her second book of verse, published in 1902. These nationalist poems were among her most popular performance pieces. What could be more comforting for an Anglo-Saxon audience than to hear a Native woman singing the praises of Canada and the British-Canadian way of life?

Pauline Johnson wrote and performed at a time when the dominant image of the Indian in White culture was changing. No longer was the Indian the primitive savage. By 1900, most of Canada's Natives were pacified and living on reserves. The western frontier was closing. A wave of immigrant settlers was washing over the prairies, transforming grassland into farmland. Civilization had conquered the West and it was no longer necessary to mobilize public opinion against the frontier's original inhabitants. Having successfully subdued the Indians, Whites now could afford to get sentimental about them.

At the same time, many Canadians were beginning to have second thoughts about the industrial revolution which was transforming the country. Cities, they felt, were becoming polluted, crime-ridden, and overcrowded. Jobs were becoming tedious and enslaving. There was a growing feeling that Indian character and culture had something positive to teach Euro-Canadians. Even as they reviled the Indian as brutal and ungovernable, many Whites had admired the nobility and independence reflected in the image of the "Redman." Indians were identified with the freedom, healthfulness, and simplicity of the natural world. In the early decades of the twentieth century, Canadians who were unhappy with trends in their own society discovered in the Indian what they thought was an alternative lifestyle founded on an alternative set of values. Celebrity Indians like Pauline Johnson seemed to give voice to these alternatives and enjoyed enormous public appeal.

III

On August 24, 1928, a remarkable book appeared in New York. It was entitled *Long Lance* and purported to be the autobiography of a Blackfoot Indian chief named Buffalo Child Long Lance. The book began with the author recalling his earliest memory, a skirmish between his people and their Crow Indian enemies when he was just fourteen months old. Then Long Lance launched into a detailed reminiscence about growing up on the Plains at the end of the nineteenth century, just as the buffalo were disappearing and the first White settlers were arriving. He described how Blackfoot boys were prepared for their lives as hunters and warriors. "To toughen our bodies, our fathers used to whip the boy members of each family as we arose in the morning. After they had whipped us they would hand us the fir branches and tell us to go to the river and bathe in cold water. If it was winter they would make us go out and take a snow bath."[21] According to Long Lance, the boys thrived on this regime of beatings and cold showers, reminiscent of a British public school, and compared their welts with pride. The book was full of ethnographic detail and stories about famous Native leaders, all the time following the fortunes of a particular band of wandering Blackfoot as it moved across the Plains and into the Rockies in search of game animals.

Long Lance is not a conventional autobiography; indeed, it is hardly autobiography at all. The author pays little attention to the development of his own personality, the traditional preoccupation of autobiographers. Instead he offers an account of the transformation of Native culture. He begins with a sympathetic description of the independent life of the Blackfoot on the Plains, and laments that it is doomed by its encounter with the settlement frontier. By the end of the book, the buffalo are gone and the people are adjusting to life as farmers on the reserves. The author regrets the passing of the old days, much as he regrets the passing of his childhood. His book is a look back at Eden. "But the new day is here: it is here to stay. And now we must leave it to our old people to sit stolidly and dream of the glories of our past. Our job is to try to fit ourselves into the new scheme of life which the Great Spirit has decreed for North America. And we will do that, keeping always before us the old Blackfoot proverb: Mokokit-ki-ackamimat—Be wise and persevere" [22]

Long Lance was a huge success. Originally conceived as a book for youngsters, it achieved wide popularity among all ages. Readers believed they were getting a unique glimpse into the life of pre-contact Native people, told by an author who was raised in a Plains tipi, then crossed the cultural boundary into the White Man's world where he became an accomplished writer. Critics loved it, agreeing with Ernest Thompson Seton that it provided "one of the best pictures ever offered of the old-time Indian at his best." The book spoke to the disillusionment so many people felt with modern civilization. The first printing quickly sold out, a British edition appeared, and the following year *Long Lance* appeared in German and Dutch.

Although his autobiography contained no details of his adult life, the world already knew of Chief Buffalo Child Long Lance. War hero, journalist, socialite, sportsman, Long Lance was a self-declared Cherokee from North Carolina who had landed up in Canada after World War I.[23] As a reporter for the *Calgary Herald* and later as a freelancer, he wrote articles about different Native groups and the difficulties they were having adjusting to the White world. Educated and sophisticated, he was accepted readily as a spokesperson for the Red Indian. In 1922, the Blood people near Cardston adopted him and gave him the name Buffalo Child. Shortly afterward he began promoting himself as a Blackfoot chief.

Soon Buffalo Child Long Lance was touring the continent, lecturing about the fate of the Indian and preparing articles for such popular magazines as *Cosmopolitan*, *Good Housekeeping*, and *Maclean's*. Handsome, debonair, and charming, he was taken up and feted by high society in New York. A Noble Savage in white tie and tails, he was welcome at house parties on Long Island and cocktail parties on Park Avenue, entertaining his fellow guests with stories about life among the Plains tribes and displays of Indian sign language. He was even elected a member of New York's prestigious, and exclusive, Explorers Club, where he stayed when he was in the city.

In his lectures and articles, Long Lance's message was a simple one. He sounded a lot like an aboriginal Horatio Alger. "I have reached no dizzy heights of material success," he wrote in a long piece published in *Cosmopolitan* and *Maclean's* in 1926, "but I have succeeded in pulling myself up by my boot straps from a primitive and backward life into this great new world of white civilization. Anyone with determination and will can do as much." [24] Long Lance might have added that a flair for the dramatic never hurt. In July, 1927, for example, he published an article in *Cosmopolitan* which claimed to completely rewrite the story of the Battle of the Little Big Horn, the most famous incident in the history of the American West. There had been no "last stand," he claimed: General George Custer committed suicide when he saw his cause was lost. By libelling an American hero, Long Lance assured himself of instant notoriety.

In 1929, less than a year after the publication of his autobiography, Long Lance added actor to his list of achievements. Douglas Burden, an American explorer-filmmaker, taken by the author's portrait in the frontispiece of *Long Lance*, asked him to take a leading role in his upcoming film, *The Silent Enemy*. Made in northern Quebec and Ontario, the picture was a dramatic documentary about the Ojibway people of the northern woodlands. As part of his attempt to make the film completely authentic, Burden hired Native people to play themselves, an innovative idea at the time. The film tells the story of a love affair and a rivalry between a great hunter and an Ojibway shaman, set against a terrible famine, "the silent enemy" of the title. Long Lance played Baluk, the hunter who after much suffering saves his people by finding the caribou.

The film opened in New York in May, 1930. Though it never caught on with a wide public, the critics acclaimed it as an instant classic, remarking particularly on the strong performance of Long Lance. "Chief Long Lance is an ideal picture Indian," wrote the correspondent for *Variety*, "because he is a full-blooded one…"

But even as *The Silent Enemy* prepared to open to lavish praise, friends and acquaintances of Long Lance were beginning to discover that he was a better actor than any of them had suspected. Rumours about his origins had surfaced in the past, but Long Lance had always been able to quiet them. Then, during the filming of the movie, his co-star, the Sioux chief Chauncey Yellow Robe, a descendant of Sitting Bull, began to suspect that Long Lance was not the full-blooded Blackfoot he claimed to be. Yellow Robe made some inquiries which led him to the Bureau of Indian Affairs in Washington. Officials at the Bureau had carried out their own investigation of Long Lance two years earlier when his autobiography came out. They shared their findings with Yellow Robe, who in turn went to see Will Chanler, co-producer of *The Silent Enemy*. Chanler himself continued the investigation, and what he learned was not the life story Long Lance had presented in his book and shared with his friends.

It turned out that the best-selling autobiography was a fabrication. Long Lance had borrowed most of the stories from a Blood friend. He had not even been alive when many of the events in the book took place. For years he had been concocting stories about his life, like a fugitive on the run from himself. He was no Blackfoot from the northern plains. He was Sylvester Long, from Winston-Salem, North Carolina, born in 1890 to parents of mixed Indian, White, and probably Black ancestry. Whatever their actual background, the

Long Lance dressed as a Blackfoot chief, 1923.

Longs were known locally as "colored." Young Sylvester was required to attend a school for Blacks and made to suffer all the vicious in-dignities of racial segregation. His father was a school janitor. His mother was a midwife. His brothers remained in Winston-Salem all their lives. One ran a smoke shop, then managed the coloured section of a movie theatre; the other became a private detective. Both lived as members of the Black community.

Sylvester, on the other hand, chose to escape the oppression of the South by creating a new identity for himself. At age thirteen he left home to join a Wild West Show. This is where his Indian masquerade began. Because of his appearance, he was taken for an Indian and soon began to think of himself as one. When he returned home after five years on the road, he applied to the Carlisle Indian School in Pennsylvania as a Cherokee and was accepted. Other Cherokee at the school recognized the fraud, but Sylvester excelled in his studies and at sports and he graduated in 1912 at the head of his class. After military college, he won one of six presidential appointments to write the entrance examination to attend the West Point Military Academy, a remarkable achievement for an "Indian," and ironically, an opportunity which would have been denied him as a Black man. However, World War I was underway and Long Lance, as he was now known, wanted to join the fight. The United States was not yet at war so he came to Canada, enlisted, and fought on the front lines until he was wounded in the legs and invalided to England.

During the 1920s, through his many articles and lectures, Long Lance established himself as a public authority on the Indian. Like Pauline Johnson, he achieved the role of an "exceptional Indian," exceptional not just because he seemed to represent the best of his race, but mainly because he was so far ahead of other Natives in adapting to White culture. The "exceptional Indian" played, and plays, a dual role. He or she is an interpreter and defender of Native culture. At the same time, by succeeding so well as a White Man's Indian, the "exceptional Indian" implicitly confirms the superiority of White society.

Long Lance played his dual role tirelessly. He presented a sympathetic account of Native culture as it had existed for generations before the arrival of the White Man. His descriptions of exotic customs, of buffalo hunts and battles and the satisfactions of a simple life lived close to nature, enthralled his White audience. He described the devastating impact contact had had on "his people" and pleaded for understanding. "Struck as by a thunderbolt with an entirely new set of ideals and living conditions in the heyday of their supremacy as rulers of the western plains," he wrote in *Maclean's* in 1923, "the Indians of Saskatchewan and the neighbouring territory have within less than a generation evolved from roving bands of semi-barbarians to settled communities of self-respecting, industrious Canadian subjects. The impact of this sudden change has left its mark upon the health and native moral fibre of the race ..." Long Lance blamed the decline of the Indian on the disease, liquor, and immorality "thrust upon him by the lower elements of the incoming race." But time was proving that the Indian could adapt, he wrote. "The North American Indian has been described as the finest raw material civilization ever had presented to it for working into a better product. His native qualities earned for him in the old days the appellation noble. What will his acquired abilities earn for him? With better education, better medical attention and with more contact with the better elements of the white race, I would say, a substantial place in Canada's man and womanhood." [25]

Long Lance did not dispute the superiority of the White way, which perhaps accounts for his popularity. In another article in *Maclean's*, entitled "I Wanted to Live Like the White Man," he explains how as a young performer with the Wild West Show he was taken along to visit the home of a "wealthy and cultured" White family. "This was the first time I had ever met people of real culture and seen how they lived in their homes—and I liked them," he wrote. "These people so impressed me with their bearing and their environment that I decided on the spot, 'I am going to be like that!'" According to

Long Lance, this encounter set him on the path to self-improvement, by which he means assimilation. He describes himself as he came out of the army as "an Indian trying to fight his way from college into civilization." And he concludes with an expression of the duality which characterizes the exceptional Indian: "I'm proud to be as much like a white man as I am—but I'm proud, too, of every drop of Indian blood that runs through my veins. I'm proud of my Indian heritage—and I'm proud, too, of the land and people of my adoption." [26]

For Long Lance, there was no shame in being Indian. But neither was there any future in it. He told his audiences that within 150 years the "full-blooded Indian" would be gone, a victim of assimilation and miscegenation. As they became better educated, he believed, Indians would naturally gravitate towards White society. Generation after generation would intermarry until "Indian blood" became too thin to distinguish any longer. [27]

For Long Lance personally, the price of living as an Imaginary Indian was eventually too high. As the web of deceit he had wound around himself began to unravel, he became more and more unstable, drinking heavily and suffering through bouts of deep depression. In the spring of 1931, he went to California where he took the job of secretary and bodyguard to a wealthy divorcee and philanthropist, Anita Baldwin. It was in the library of Baldwin's opulent mansion in the early morning hours of March 20, 1932, that Sylvester Long, alias Buffalo Child Long Lance, shot himself fatally through the head.

IV

At about the same time that Buffalo Child Long Lance took his own life, another spokesperson for the Indian emerged from the Canadian backwoods. His name was Grey Owl and he claimed to be an adopted Ojibway trapper from northern Ontario who had given up trapping under the influence of his Iroquois wife to become a fervent conservationist.[28] In 1931, Grey Owl published his first book, *Men of the Last Frontier*, a tribute to the life of the "wilderness man" and at the same time a warning that our wild spaces were fast disappearing before the juggernaut of industrial civilization. The book struck a responsive chord with the public on both sides of the Atlantic and Grey Owl became a popular speaker on the lecture circuit. Dressed in a buckskin jacket and moccasins, his black hair hanging in two long braids, he appeared to his audiences to be the personification of the North American Indian. "Grey Owl is no stuffed Indian," declared *The New York Times*. "He is real and honest."[29] Lloyd Roberts, son of Sir Charles G.D. Roberts, called him "the first Indian that really looked like an Indian—an Indian from those thrilling Wild West days of covered wagons, buffalos and Sitting Bulls."[30] Grey Owl's British publisher, Lovat Dickson, described the effect that Grey Owl had on his depression-era listeners:

> This voice from the forests momentarily released us from some spell. In contrast with Hitler's screaming, ranting voice, and the remorseless clang of modern technology, Grey Owl's words evoked an unforgettable charm, lighting in our minds the vision of a cool, quiet place, where men and animals lived in love and trust together.[31]

Grey Owl followed up his initial literary success with his autobiography, *Pilgrims of the Wild*, which described his personal transformation from trapper to naturalist. *Pilgrims* appeared in 1934 and was an instant bestseller. The public gobbled it up at a rate of five thousand copies a month; it had to be reprinted eight times in the next year. Grey Owl capitalized on this success with a lecture tour of the United Kingdom where he spoke to nearly a quarter of a million people at more than 200 meetings. "We were nearly swamped in the flood of public enthusiasm that acclaimed him," wrote Dickson.[32]

Grey Owl in 1936 with two of his prominent admirers, Sir William Mulock (*left*), chief justice of Ontario, and Sir Charles G.D. Roberts.

Meanwhile, the Canadian government decided to take advantage of Grey Owl's sudden fame. The Parks Branch made a series of films showing him at work with his tame beavers. The films enjoyed enormous popularity with schools, clubs, and organizations across the country, and Grey Owl incorporated them into his lecture format. In 1931, the Parks Branch hired him to be "caretaker of park animals" at Riding Mountain National Park in Manitoba. The move was more or less a publicity stunt: Grey Owl's presence was expected to attract visitors to the park while at the same time publicize the government's own interest in animal conservation. After six months, he moved to Prince Albert National Park in Saskatchewan, where he made his home at Beaver Lodge on the shores of Lake Ajawaan. There he continued his work with wildlife, wrote his books, and welcomed a steady stream of visitors attracted by his fame. During the 1930s, Lake Aja-

Archie Belaney as a young boy in Hastings, England, long before he became Grey Owl.

waan was one of the most well-known spots in Canada.

By this time, the details of Grey Owl's autobiography were public knowledge. He was, he said, part Apache, born in Mexico to a Jacarilla woman. His father was George MacNeil, a Scot and a former Indian scout in the American southwest. His parents went to Britain as members of Buffalo Bill's Wild West Show, then returned to the United States. The family moved gradually north and Grey Owl grew up as an Apache on the Plains. When he was not yet a teenager he briefly joined the Wild West Show himself as a knife-thrower, then struck out for the silver mines of northern Ontario. There he remained, living as a trapper and guide, until, encouraged by his Iroquois wife, Anahareo, he adopted a conservationist ethic and devoted himself to preserving the wilderness.

From his base at Lake Ajawaan, Grey Owl kept up an exhausting schedule of writing, touring, and lecturing. In the fall of 1937 he began a gruelling speaking tour of Britain. In four months he made 138 speeches, including a command performance for the British Royal Family at Buckingham Palace. He was accompanied by his new White wife, Yvonne Perrier (by this time he and Anahareo had separated), whom he introduced as Silver Moon, an Indian like himself. The tour, which at times seemed more like a triumphal procession, ended with three more months of appearances in the United States and Canada.

From Quebec City to Regina, from New York to Milwaukee, Grey Owl spread his message of concern for the wilderness. And everywhere he went he was acclaimed as the finest Indian of them all.

But the tour took its toll. Always a heavy drinker, Grey Owl stopped eating properly and grew exhausted from the hectic pace. "A month more of this will kill me," he told a reporter. At the end of March, 1938, he finally returned to his home on Lake Ajawaan. After three days he had to be hospitalized in Prince Albert for a combination of fatigue and pneumonia. On April 13, he died at age forty-nine.

No sooner had Grey Owl's many fans and supporters around the world absorbed the news of his sudden death than they were stunned by an even bigger surprise. The man who had impressed audiences as the very epitome of an Indian, the man who said "I feel as an Indian, think as an Indian, all my ways are Indian, my heart is Indian"—this man turned out not to be an Indian at all.[33]

Within a week of his death, the newspapers had the whole story. The half-Apache Grey Owl was in reality Archie Belaney, an Englishman born and raised. His father, George Belaney, was a drunken wastrel who was such an embarrassment to his family that his mother finally paid him an annuity to keep him out of England. Archie was raised by his grandmother and two aunts in the town of Hastings. A solitary boy, he played for long hours in the woods by himself and kept wild animals as pets. He was extremely interested in North American Indians, and read as much as he could find about them. In 1906, at the age of seventeen, he left England with the stated intention of going to Canada to live the life of a "wilderness man."

Belaney headed for northern Ontario, where he apprenticed himself to a local guide and trapper and to the Ojibway of Bear Island in Lake Temagami. An avid learner, the young Englishman soon became an accomplished woodsman. He grew his hair long, wore moccasins and leather clothing, married an Ojibway woman, and in general "went native." But he was still Archie Belaney. When the war broke out he joined the Canadian Army and went to France where he fought in the trenches. Wounded in the foot, he returned to northern Ontario with a limp and a dark, moody side to his character. Quarrelsome and violent when drunk, he routinely got into scraps in the small mining and logging settlements.

In the mid-1920s, Belaney married Gertrude Bernard, the Iroquois woman better known to his readers as Anahareo. It was she who influenced him to give up beaver trapping and to dedicate himself to conservation instead. Belaney recorded the events leading up to this decision in *Pilgrims of the Wild*. In the spring of 1928, he was, he said, engaged in his usual beaver hunt when he came upon a pair of orphaned kits. Anahareo begged him to keep them as pets rather than killing them, and he agreed. "I was getting sick of the constant butchery," he wrote. As he got used to having the little animals around, Belaney underwent a dramatic change of heart. "To kill such creatures seemed monstrous. I would do no more of it. Instead of persecuting them further I would study them, see just what there really was to them. I perhaps could start a colony of my own; these animals could not be permitted to pass completely from the face of this wilderness." [34]

Belaney turned to writing as a way of making a living and as a way of getting his message out to a wide public. He realized that his descriptions of life in the backwoods would be taken more seriously if they seemed to be written from a Native perspective. In November, 1930, he used the name Grey Owl for the first time, and the following year began claiming for himself an Indian identity. [35] The masquerade had begun.

Grey Owl's most recent biographer, Donald Smith, has pointed out that aboriginal people who met him knew that Grey Owl was not a Native. His eyes were too blue, his skin too pale, and his attempts

To most Canadians, Grey Owl looked more Indian than an Indian. In this 1937 photograph, he seems to be striking a cigar-store pose.

at drumming and dancing too comical. But they didn't care. He was strongly sympathetic to their cultures and to their political struggle and they needed all the allies they could find, especially high-profile ones who had the ear of important government officials.

But Whites, almost without exception, believed in Grey Owl's Indian identity. Why shouldn't they? First of all, he said he was an Indian. Many would not think to contradict him. More importantly, he looked so much like what Whites thought an Indian should look like. With his long braids (which he died to keep black), dark skin (which he coloured with henna), and glowering stare (which he practised in front of a mirror), he seemed to have stepped right out of the pages of Fenimore Cooper. Even his drinking was seen as confirmation of his Native identity. "I am sorry to hear that Grey Owl has been indulging too freely in liquor," wrote a senior official in the Parks Branch on one occasion. "As a matter of fact, with so much Indian blood in his veins I suppose it is inevitable that from time to time he will break out in this connection."[36] There is something wonderfully ironic about the stereotype of the drunken Indian being used to explain away the conduct of an English gentleman.

After Grey Owl's death, and the revelation of his true identity, it soon became clear that no one much cared. The general opinion seemed to be that what he stood for was more important than who he was—and this being the case, so what if he wasn't really an Indian? What mattered was his work as a writer and as a tireless promoter of wilderness preservation. As for the rest, it seemed a harmless enough hoax. The superintendent of Prince Albert Park, Major J. A. Wood, wrote: "I care not whether he was an Englishman, Irishman, Scotsman or Negro. He was a great man with a great mind, and with great objectives which he ever kept before him."[37]

But while he lived, being Indian was crucially important to the success of Grey Owl's self-appointed mission. In his books and lectures, Grey Owl preached a message that sounds very familiar to modern ears. Man is not above nature, he said. Man belongs to nature. "That he should take his share of the gifts she has so bountifully provided for her children, is only right and proper ..."[38] But too often, heedless of the future, man is greedy and takes more than he needs. The results are everywhere to be seen—forests laid waste by logging, ground torn up for mines, lakes and rivers choked with filth, animals slaughtered to the edge of extinction. We have lost our reverence for the natural world, Grey Owl warned, and as a result we have lost touch with our essential selves. "The Wilderness should now no longer be considered as a playground for vandals," he wrote:

> or a rich treasure trove to be ruthlessly exploited for the

personal gain of the few—to be grabbed off by whoever happens to get there first. Man should enter the woods, not with any conquistador obsession or mighty hunter complex, neither in a spirit of braggadocio, but rather with the awe, and not a little of the veneration, of one who steps within the portals of some vast and ancient edifice of wondrous architecture.[39]

But the key to Grey Owl's popularity was that he kept such high-minded philosophizing to a minimum. For the most part, he told stories: about the animals which came and went around his forest cabin; about canoe trips across glassy northern lakes; about Indians and rivermen and wolves and caribou; about a rugged, idyllic, uncomplicated country beyond the reach of civilization. "I could think of no writer in Canada who had caught so truly the essential boom-note of this huge, rocky, monolithic land," wrote Lovat Dickson. "He made pure Canada, the Canada outside the concrete urban enclosures, come alive." [40]

And the thing that made these stories so authentic was the fact that Grey Owl, so far as anyone knew, was an Indian. His writings and his talks were not to be taken as the sentimental maunderings of some weekend canoeist. Grey Owl spoke with the accumulated wisdom of the people who had inhabited the eastern woodlands for thousands of years. Canadians considered Indians to be creatures of the wilderness who possessed innate knowledge of wild ways. If Grey Owl was one of them, his words demanded special attention.

Grey Owl was very calculating about exactly what image of himself he wanted to present to the public. "I do not want to go down as a soft-hearted missionary type, or animal evangelist," he wrote to his publishers, "but a man of action, having a story to tell ..." He urged them in their publicity to emphasize his activities as a woodsman, and to play down the saint in buckskin angle. Read Longfellow's poem, "Hiawatha," he urged, and use it in the publicity. "I think the truest definition of my status ... is that of a modern Hiawatha."[41]

Grey Owl proposed a special role for the Indian; his own position as an animal caretaker with the Parks Branch was the prototype. Indians were characterized as supremely suited to be the guardians of the wilderness—and they should be set to work as forest rangers and game wardens; their "technical knowledge, accumulated during thousands of years of study and observation, could be of immense value in helping to save from destruction Canada's wilderness country and its inhabitants."[42] When Grey Owl met King George at Buckingham Palace, these were the ideas he pressed upon him. Grey Owl sought to end the marginalization of aboriginal people by giving them a key role to play in the development of the country.

While Grey Owl took advantage of the image of the Indian to advance his career as a writer, he in turn made an important contribution to the image. His plan for a corps of Native forest guardians may not have caught on, but through his books and public appearances he established the Indian in the public mind as a natural preservationist. Civilized, industrial man was "the parasite supreme of all the earth" he wrote.[43] He walked through the woods and only saw the profits to be made by cutting down the trees. On the other hand, Native people, living close to nature, learned a reverence and a responsibility for it. They were conservationists by instinct. The greening of the Indian begins with Grey Owl. To him belongs the credit for affirming, if not creating, the image of the Indian as the original environmentalist, an image which has gained strength in the years since he expressed it.

A case in point is Chief Seattle. "Whatever befalls the Earth befalls the sons of the Earth. Man did not weave the web of life; he is merely a strand in it. Whatever he does to the web, he does to himself." These words are part of a speech supposedly delivered in 1854 by Chief Seattle, or Seeathl, a leader of the Suquamish people of the Pacific Northwest. Seattle's speech has become one of the sacred texts of the new eco-consciousness. His words convey a deep respect for the natural world and a stark warning that the White Man cannot continue to despoil the world. The speech is moving in its simplicity and gains much of its credibility for having been spoken by a Native elder. It has been translated into several languages. Environmental groups in Europe and America have published versions of it. In 1987 the eco-activist David Suzuki quoted large portions of the speech in the *Globe and Mail*, calling it the expression of a Native world view "that offers a profoundly different vision of the human place in nature."[44] In 1990, the Canadian government included Seattle's words in its so-called Green Plan for an environmentally friendly country.

But lurking behind the popular image of Chief Seattle lies another, more mundane story. The Chief was real enough, all right, and he actually did give a speech: but it was not the speech which has since become The Speech. What has been given to us as the words of Chief Seattle has since been traced to Dr. Henry Smith, a physician who made notes of Seattle's address (probably based on a translation, since Seattle spoke little English) and filed them away. Thirty-three years later, in 1887, Smith published a newspaper article in which he included a reconstruction of part of what he had heard in 1854. Over the years, different versions of Smith's version have appeared. The most prominent was a script written in 1970-71 as the basis for an ecological film produced by the Southern Baptist Convention in the United States. The author of the script, Ted Perry, a non-Native, made no bones about the fact that while he used a version of Smith's version of Seattle's speech for inspiration, he came up with his own version which differed markedly from the original. In the end, it turns out that Chief Seattle's famous speech, cited so often as representing an authentic Native view of the world, was written by a White Man long after Seattle was dead.[45]

Just as Grey Owl's message was deemed to be more important than his masquerade, so the merit of Seattle's speech relies on the ideas it expresses, not who wrote it. But merit and celebrity are not the same thing. There is no question that the speech derives most of its popularity from its supposed Indian origins. Non-Natives are prone to romanticize Indians and the uncomplicated, mystical vision they are believed to possess. As the example of Seattle's speech indicates, this is just as true today as it was in Grey Owl's day.

V

The huge popularity of these three celebrity Indians—Pauline Johnson, Buffalo Child Long Lance, and Grey Owl—reveals a desire on the part of non-Native Canadians to understand and admire what they considered to be the virtues of Indian-ness. Each of the three expressed aspects of the Imaginary Indian. The poems of Pauline Johnson evoked for listeners the proud, independent Indian of history. Buffalo Child Long Lance touched a chord of pathos when he described the difficult transition the Indian was making from traditional society to the White Man's world. And Grey Owl reminded his audience that the Indian had a lot to teach the modern world about the necessity of preserving wild nature from the reckless forces of economic development. In each case, non-Natives believed they were listening to the very best in the Indian character, even when it turned out that the voice was not Native at all.

That said, the defining characteristic of the celebrity Indian is that he or she be selected by non-Natives. Other Native people were happy enough to have their concerns conveyed to White society, but if they had had the choice they would not necessarily have chosen these particular representatives. Of course, they did not have a choice.

Celebrity Indians were chosen by Whites. The example of Grey Owl suggests that it was not even necessary to be Native to be a celebrity Indian. The essential thing was to conform to the White stereotype of what an Indian was. After that, the rest was easy.

Celebrity Indians did not challenge the values of mainstream Canadian society. Pauline Johnson was an outspoken patriot who wished to see Native and non-Native merge in a common nationality. Long Lance, too, aspired to assimilate with the dominant culture. Even Grey Owl's anti-industrial message could be comfortably absorbed by the burgeoning wilderness preservation movement.

Celebrity Indians were hailed as spokespeople for their race, but they delivered a message that mainstream Canadian society was prepared to hear. If they had not, if they had tried to convey an overtly political message for instance, they would not have received a platform at all. The dominant society set the agenda and the terms of the discussion. At the same time when Pauline Johnson and Grey Owl attracted so much public acclaim, Native leaders who were attempting to achieve political gains for their people were meeting a blank wall of indifference.

CHAPTER SEVEN

Indians of Childhood

MUCH OF WHAT WE learn about Indians we learn as children. In games and pastimes, from story books and
school books, at summer camp, and more recently from
comic books, television and movies, children learn what an Indian is.
Long before I encountered Native people in my own life, I already
knew about Indians from watching Chief Thunderthud (the originator of the phrase "Kowa Bonga!") and Princess Wintersummer Au-
tumnspring on the *Howdy Doody Show,* and laughing at the antics of
Little Beaver on *Red Ryder,* the first television program I remember
seeing. Many of the images we hold as adults are obtained in childhood and never abandoned: the Imaginary Indian is very much an
Indian of childhood.

It is no surprise that as children we are fascinated by the Imaginary Indian. The Imaginary Indian is, after all, much of a child himself: unsophisticated, undisciplined, independent. Too high-spirited
and willful to perform the essential business of industrial society, the
Imaginary Indian is the perfect model for youngsters chafing against
the rules and duties of the adult world. Children love animals; so does
the Imaginary Indian. Children love to roam freely in the woods;
so does the Imaginary Indian. Children love secret ceremonies and
dressing up in costume; so does the Imaginary Indian. Children
yearn to perform brave deeds in combat; so does the Imaginary Indian. Children are in rebellion against the established order. So is the
Imaginary Indian.

I learned how to play Indian from movies and television. But where did children of an earlier generation learn? There were books of course, novels of juvenile adventure set in the northern woods and the great western plains, written by missionaries and hacks with as much knowledge of aboriginal people as they had of the peoples of remotest Africa. There was school, where young students absorbed the history of their country, including stories of the role played by Indians. Before World War I, there was the Wild West Show, where city youngsters got an exciting taste of cowboys and Indians. And in the early years of the twentieth century, there was a remarkable youth movement which took its inspiration from the image of the Noble Indian and tried to introduce children to the pleasures and values of wilderness life.

All these Indians—the Indians of fiction, of the Wild West Show, of schoolbooks and summer camps—were imaginary. Few children in Canada had any direct knowledge of Native people, who were pretty much confined to their reserves at the margins of society. Instead, White kids were exposed to images of the Indian created by various White writers and educators. These images were not all negative. On the contrary, many were very positive. But they were not authentic: they represented the concerns and prejudices of White adult society instead of actual Native Canadians.

II

"Yan was much like other twelve-year-old boys in having a keen interest in Indians and in wild life, but he differed from most in this, that he never got over it."[1] With these words, Ernest Thompson Seton began *Two Little Savages*, his phenomenally successful novel for boys. Published in 1903, the book tells the story of Yan, the sensitive nature lover oppressed by a tyrannical father and two detestable brothers, who escapes his heartless domestic world by going native. Yan and two friends decide: "Let's be Injuns and do everything like Injuns." Under the tutelage of a wise old trapper, the boys build a tipi in the woods where they camp out and have a series of escapades while learning to be "bushwise."

Part autobiography, part adventure story, *Two Little Savages* is primarily a practical handbook of woodlore for kids. At the time he wrote it, Seton was incubating his outdoor youth movement, the League of the Woodcraft Indians, a precursor to the Boy Scouts. He had planned originally to write an encyclopedia of Indian woodcraft, but was convinced by Rudyard Kipling that a work of fiction might reach a wider audience.[2] *Two Little Savages* retains much of Seton's educational intent. The novel is crammed with diagrams and instructions for erecting tipis, stuffing owls, sewing leather moccasins, rubbing sticks to make a fire, reading smoke signals, and many other woodcraft skills. It is the only work of fiction I know that includes an index.

Seton's books and the entire woodcraft movement were unique for their time because they promoted the Indian as an appropriate role model for North American youth. While many of his contemporaries believed in the conventional stereotype of the drunken, lazy, dissolute Indian, Seton actually proposed that children had much to learn from Native Americans. His preoccupation—some would say his obsession—with Indians eventually cost Seton the support of the public, but for several years he led the most popular youth movement in America.

When Ernest Thompson Seton originated his Woodcraft League for boys he was already a famous naturalist, lecturer, artist, and author of four books of illustrated animal stories. As a storyteller he was much in demand, dramatizing his animal tales with sound effects and lantern slides. As a scientist, he was official naturalist to the government of Manitoba and friend to many of the leading wildlife scientists

Ernest Thompson Seton in Indian dress, 1917.

in New York and Washington. It was this prestige as an interpreter of wild nature that made the success of his youth movement possible.

Seton was born in 1860 in a small seaport town in northern England.[3] His family name was actually Thompson; he later added the name Seton in the mistaken belief that he was connected to a prominent Scottish family. His father was a shipowner who fell on hard times and in 1866 moved his family to Ontario where young Ernest grew up, first on a backwoods farm near Lindsay, then in Toronto.

Seton's father was a dominant presence in his life. Outwardly a man of probity, he was a humourless disciplinarian in the home and Seton grew to detest him. On the evidence of the other children, his father was not the brutal skinflint Seton made him out to be. But Seton believed he was and nursed a persecution complex into full-blown hatred. Upon the death of his mother in 1897, Seton broke with his father completely, accusing him, unfairly it seems, of being a "worthless loafer, a petty swindler, a wife-beater and a child murderer." For the remaining five years of his father's life, the two men did not speak.

Seton was a hot-tempered, imaginative, intelligent boy who rebelled against his family's strict Presbyterianism. Whenever he could he escaped into the woods, where he developed the interest in wild creatures which became his life work. Like his character Yan, Seton built himself a secret hideaway in Toronto's Don Valley and skulked through the underbrush playing at being an Indian. And like Yan, Seton never got over his childhood fascination with what he conceived to be the free and independent life of the Native American.

As Seton's artistic talent blossomed, his father decided he should become a painter. Seton apprenticed to a portraitist in Toronto, attended the Ontario School of Art, and went to London to study at the Royal Academy. But despite all this formal training, Seton was drawn to the study of natural history and spent more time sketching wildlife than he did seeking commissions for portraits.

In 1882, Seton, now in his early twenties, joined two of his brothers in Manitoba, where they were homesteading, and began in his spare time to explore the prairie, study the wildlife, and make his first contacts with Native people. One day when he was out hunting near Carberry he met a Cree named Chaska. Seton was impressed by Chaska's skill as a tracker and hunter and the way he handled himself in the woods. This encounter had a profound influence on the way Seton later idealized Native people. But he recognized that he was not destined to be a frontiersman, and he returned to the East and a career as a writer and artist.

Seton's first published book, a collection of magazine articles entitled *Wild Animals I Have Known*, appeared in 1898, when he was nearly forty. With this and subsequent collections, Seton established the realistic animal story as a literary form. His lectures, undertaken to promote the books, drew enthusiastic crowds of people who were charmed by his tales of wild creatures, illustrated by his own drawings. He soon became the leading popularizer of natural history in North America.

If wildlife was Seton's first concern, the plight of the Indian came a close second. It was understandable that someone who cared so deeply about wild nature himself would feel an affinity for people who were so closely associated with the wilderness. On one occasion in Hollywood, Seton met a woman claiming to be a Mahatma from India. During this strange encounter, the woman told Seton that he had been a "Red Indian Chief" in a former life, "reincarnated to give the message of the Red Man to the White race."[4] Whether or not he took this message literally, Seton did feel the plight of the Indian strongly and lobbied actively to redress what he later called "an unbroken narrative of injustice, fraud, and robbery."[5]

But Seton's program transcended political reforms. Swept up in the progressive movement of the early twentieth century, he was a moral reformer who advocated a complete transformation of industrial society. In their quest for material success, North Americans had become selfish and acquisitive, he said. They had forgotten how to live in harmony with nature. They had to find a new model for social regeneration. Seton found this model in the tribal life of the "Red Man."

Seton summed up his views of Indian society in a book called *Gospel of the Redman*, published in 1936, when he was seventy-six years old. He argued that "the Indian is the apostle of outdoor life, his example and precept are what the world needs to-day above any other ethical teaching." Indian civilization was superior to White civilization, he concluded, because it was "fundamentally spiritual" and concerned with the well-being of the group instead of the individual. Seton characterized Indians as socialists "in the best and literal meaning of the word." They lived communally in villages, shared whatever they had with every member of the community, did not recognize private property or accumulate great wealth. According to Seton, Indian society was virtually free of vice until Whites arrived with their diseases, liquor, and greed.[6]

Seton's claim for the superiority of the aboriginal way of life was astonishing for its time. It was much more conventional to rank societies on an ascending scale, from primitive to civilized, with industrial society sitting securely at the top end. But Seton believed this comparison was based on false criteria. If one considered instead the quality of spiritual life and the degree of harmony with nature, then, he said, the Red Man was superior.

Long before Seton published these ideas in book form he was putting them into practice with children. He was a firm believer in the moral benefits of healthy outdoor activity for youngsters. In the spring of 1901 at his country estate outside New York City, he erected a makeshift Indian village and invited several of the neighbourhood boys to take part in a weekend camp-out. The "tribe" which emerged from this experience was the prototype for the Woodcraft Indians, a movement of outdoor education for boys. Seton described his woodcraft movement in lectures and in a regular column in the widely-read *Ladies' Home Journal.* The movement spread like wildfire; by 1910, the League of the Woodcraft Indians was the largest youth organization in North America.

Seton borrowed heavily from many different Native traditions as he elaborated the details of his woodcraft movement. Individual groups were called tribes; the leaders were chiefs, and members took Indian-like names. The organization had its own ten commandments which each boy was expected to obey: don't rebel, don't kindle a wild fire, protect the song-birds, don't make a dirty camp, don't bring firearms into camp, keep the game laws, no smoking, no firewater in camp, play fair, and word of honour is sacred.[7]

Group activities included canoeing, archery, stalking, and nature studies. Boys wore head bands with feathers and a "scalp," a tuft of black horsehair which could be taken in competition, much to the shame of its owner. Meetings focussed on Native crafts and rituals, plant identification, animal tracking, and wilderness survival skills. A favourite game was the deer hunt, in which young warriors armed with homemade bows tracked down a stuffed burlap bag made up to resemble a deer. Seton stressed self-government; boys learned to get along cooperatively in groups with minimal adult supervision. All of this was presented in book form in the many editions of *The Birch-bark Roll of the Woodcraft Indians*, the bible of the movement.

Seton's movement was not confined to boys. A parallel group for girls called itself the Camp Fire Girls. Inspired by Seton's ideas, the Camp Fire Girls adopted many elements of the Woodcraft Indians.

Historians are still arguing about the extent to which the Woodcraft Indians influenced the Boy Scout movement. Some agree with Seton that he was the true founder of the Scouts, and that Robert Baden-Powell plagiarized most of his ideas from *The Birch-bark Roll*. Others say that Seton was merely one of several people involved in the boys' movement at the time, and not the most important one.[8] But there is no question that Seton was a key figure in the early years of the Boy Scouts of America. He met Baden-Powell during a visit to England in 1906 and shared with the British war hero his experiences with the Woodcraft Indians. Two years later, when Baden-Powell published *Scouting for Boys*, Seton complained that the Englishman was hijacking his movement by stealing his ideas and using them with only slight modifications. Nonetheless, in 1910, when the scouting movement migrated across the Atlantic to the United States, Seton joined the executive committee as its first chairman. His own

Lord Baden-Powell donned an Indian headdress during his 1935 visit to
Canada. In fact, Baden-Powell was one of those who did not believe the
Indian was an appropriate role model for youngsters.

Woodcraft movement was not growing as fast as he wished and he
hoped to inject his ideas into the new organization.

The trouble was that Seton's colleagues in the Scouts did not share
his enthusiasm for Indians. They agreed with his publisher, who told
Seton that there were "too many Americans who think of Indians
either as dirty and loafing degenerates, or as savages, to make the
idea popular when they think of educating their children."[9] The

Boy Scouts were based on a military model, with uniforms and fairly strict discipline, elements that were anathema to Seton, who became increasingly uncomfortable with the Scouting movement. As World War I approached, Scout organizers grew even more militaristic, and they began to view Seton as a pacifist and a socialist—certainly not a suitable role model for the youth of America. In 1915, they drummed him out of the Scout movement, claiming he was "in harmony with the views of anarchists and radical socialists."[10]

Seton now focussed his energies on the Woodcraft League, which he had not allowed to be absorbed by the Boy Scouts. Far from being influenced by critics of his organization, he emphasized even more its Indian elements. During the 1920s, the League was not as popular as the Scouts. It suffered from financial problems and membership declined. In 1930, Seton moved to New Mexico where he and his secretary, Julia Buttree, with whom he was now living, built Seton Village just outside Santa Fe. Along with Seton's home, the Village contained a museum/craft shop, a small zoo, an Indian village, and The College of Indian Wisdom where Woodcraft leaders came to be trained in Native crafts and skills. By this time Julia was joining Seton on his lecture tours, appearing on stage with him dressed in Indian costume performing songs and ceremonies. The pair continued to tour the country almost to Seton's death in October, 1946, at the age of eighty-six.

III

Seton's influence was not confined to the Woodcraft Indians. The youth movement in general was an aspect of a broader "back to the land" movement which swept North America at the turn of the century. The railway-building boom, and later the construction of roads, made the back country accessible to city dwellers as it never had been before. At the same time, the frontier was closing. The backwoods and western plains were being settled by waves of newcomers, and Canadians began to express nostalgia for the wilderness. The country was transformed by an economic boom in the decades before World War I and many people had second thoughts about the social costs of industrial progress. Major cities, which grew at a disconcerting rate between the censuses of 1891 and 1921, were the focus of much of this discontent. Critics characterized the modern city—overcrowded, unhealthy, and ugly—as a prison from which residents increasingly wished to escape back to the countryside to soothe their jangled nerves and find solace in nature. Whether it was summer cottaging, bicycling, canoeing, or alpine climbing, outdoor activity of all kinds became fashionable in light of a widespread belief that urban life was contributing to the physical and mental decline of the Canadian population. One response was the "summering movement" which sought solace and restoration in the great outdoors."[11]

City dwellers escaped to resorts and cottages on the lakes and rivers of the north to seek refuge from the hustle and bustle of modern life. Canoeing and camping became much in vogue. In the United States, John Muir and his Sierra Club were agitating for the preservation of California's Sierra Nevada. In Canada the federal government was being encouraged to set aside parks and forests for recreational use and preservation. This new, more positive attitude to nature by implication meant a new, more positive attitude to the people most associated with it—the Indian. People began to believe that the Indian retained qualities that "modern man" had lost. If civilization was artificial, frenetic and soulless, the Indian seemed to live a more authentic existence, closer to nature and basic human values. "They seem ... reposefully more in touch with permanent things than the America that has succeeded them," was how the British poet Rupert Brooke put it during his 1913 tour of Canada.[12] Disillusioned with modern, industrial society, many Canadians followed the example of

Ernest Thompson Seton and began to seek in the Imaginary Indian a model by which they might better themselves.

One activity which took its lead from Seton was camping, "the simple life reduced to actual practice," as Seton put it—and especially youth camping.[13] Camping combined the healthful, character-building benefits of outdoor activity with a chance to experience vicariously life as the Indians lived it. Inspired by the works of Seton and Pauline Johnson, middle-class Canadian youngsters took to the woods in growing numbers to play at being Indian. Organized summer camps sprang up across the eastern forest belt beyond the cities. Often their leaders borrowed their ceremonies and woodcraft activities from the pages of *Two Little Savages* and *The Birch-bark Roll*. With names like Oconto, On-da-da-waks, Wapomeo, Ahmek, Keewaydin, and Tanamakoon, these camps offered urban children their first, and most probably their only, glimpse of Indian life. In the words of a British magazine writer: "the boy may become a true white Indian."[14]

One of the leaders of the camping movement was a Toronto YMCA official named Taylor Statten, who became director of the first Y summer camp for boys in 1905. Although the Y was a deeply religious organization, Statten was equally influenced by the ideas of Ernest Seton, and in the 1920s, when Statten founded his own Camp Ahmek in Algonquin Park, he invited Seton to show off his woodcraft skills. According to Statten's biographer, Seton "showed the campers how to make sweat lodges, how to perform Indian dances correctly, how to conduct the Council Ring, in short, how to live like Indians during the camping season."[15]

It was common for camp leaders to take Indian-like names: Statten was known as Gitchiahmek; his wife Ethel was Tonakela. He founded the Order of Gitchiahmek and with great ceremony initiated camp counsellors and older boys. Only those who stayed out on all-night vigils and performed other feats of endurance became "braves" in

Under the influence of Ernest Thompson Seton, Indian woodcraft skills were a major part of most camp curricula. These girls are practicing archery at an Ontario camp in the 1920s.

the Order. The high point of the camp was the weekly Council Ring, held at dusk in the shadow of a large rock. As the campers sat around the fire in a circle, Gitchiahmek appeared atop the rock dressed in full Indian costume. "The twentieth century slipped away in the darkness," as a camp veteran recalled it:

> and all evidences of modern civilization were not only absent, but somehow forgotten as the Chief intoned the tribal prayers and called for reports from his sachems and braves. The fire lit up and danced over the encircling faces of blanket-wrapped figures ... And then the finale— perhaps after a fire-lighting or water-boiling contest, or after the Eagle Dance and other ancient games, and after the scouts' reports—the finale came with the lone figure atop the Council Rock and the singing voice drifting off into the still night.[16]

Camp Ahmek and other camps like it sought to develop character and to train future leaders. Campers learned self-reliance, responsibility, and Christian fellowship. The Imaginary Indian created by Ernest Thompson Seton was perfectly suited to this project. Seton and the camp leaders were well aware that they were presenting an idealized image of the Indian. They were not really interested in teaching youngsters about actual Native people. They wanted an Indian, as Seton wrote, "with all that is bad and cruel left out." Seton believed that such an Indian had existed before contact with the White Man. This was the Indian youngsters met at summer camp—proud, honourable, a child of the wilderness, master of woodcraft skills.

Through his books, lectures, and youth activities, Ernest Thompson Seton may have been more responsible than anyone else for creating the Imaginary Indian in the first decades of the twentieth century. By the end of his life, his claims on behalf of aboriginal civilization had become so extreme as to leave most of his public behind. ("The Civilization of the Whiteman is a failure," he wrote in the midst of the Great Depression; "it is visibly crumbling around us. It has failed at every crucial test." Indians, on the other hand, were "the most heroic race the world has ever seen, the most physically perfect race the world has ever seen, the most spiritual Civilization the world has ever seen." [17]) Nonetheless, his conviction that the values of an Indian mode of existence had direct relevance for modern society was shared by many youth workers, especially in Canada where hundreds of thousands of youngsters read his books, absorbed his woodcraft lore, and dreamed, however briefly, of living the free, bushwise life of the "little savage."

Seton may have been too extreme for his own time, but one hears many echoes of his Woodcraft League in the culture today. The men's movement, for example, exhorting men to discover the Wild

Man within and to go drumming and dancing in the woods on expeditions that sound suspiciously like Seton camp-outs, recalls *Gospel of the Red Man*. And what is the hit 1990 movie *Dances With Wolves* but a rewrite of *Two Little Savages*, with Kevin Costner in the role of Yan, heading off to the frontier to play Indian with his friends the Sioux? Seton gave expression to a persistent theme in North American culture, a desire on the part of Whites to go Native, a desire which is not, it seems, always confined to childish play. Like Yan, many of us have not got over a "keen interest in Indians and in wild life."

IV

But summer did not last forever. In the autumn, boys and girls returned from summer camp to the classroom, and there, in their textbooks, they learned about another Indian, an Indian distinctly different from the summer camp variety. No less imaginary than Gitchiahmek, schoolbook Indians nevertheless were invested with a more authentic aura if only because they were attached to real places and events—the great battles of the French-English war, the stealthy attacks on the villages of the St. Lawrence, the fur-trading posts of the far Northwest. The Indian who appeared in the textbooks was so divergent from the wise, woodcraft Indian that youngsters must have been at a loss to reconcile them. The two images represent, in the context of childhood, the ambivalent, almost schizophrenic attitude Canadians have always exhibited toward Native people.

As it entered its third decade of confederation, Canada was a discontented country. In every region the provinces were restive. Quebecers believed the hanging of Louis Riel was a plot devised by Ontario Orangemen. In Ontario, Premier Oliver Mowat argued obstinately for his version of decentralized federalism. Nova Scotia Premier W.S. Fielding flirted with secession, while westerners fumed at the arrogant policies of the CPR. It seemed that some wag's description of Canada as a group of fishing rods tied loosely at the handles had never been more accurate.

Among intellectuals and teachers, this sense of discontent, of failed promise, was reflected in a concern that youngsters in school were not getting a full understanding of their country's history. Education officials in all the provinces agreed that schools needed a new textbook which would convey an appreciation of what united the country rather than what divided it. In 1893, they proclaimed the Dominion History Competition, under the terms of which writers were given two years to submit manuscripts of new history texts, one of which would be chosen for use in classrooms from sea to sea. The winner would also receive a cash prize of $2,000.

When the competition closed on Dominion Day, 1895, the judges had received fifteen entries. Among them was a lengthy submission from Charles G.D. Roberts, then a professor at King's College in Windsor, Nova Scotia, and soon to be Canada's leading man of letters. Roberts thought his text was "the best work that I can do in prose," but it wasn't good enough for the judges. They chose instead *The History of the Dominion of Canada* by W.H.P. Clement, a B.C. supreme court judge.[18]

Judge Clement's book has since been (quite justly) described as "an incredibly dull and fact-ridden volume."[19] But at the time of its publication, prestigious educators thought that its contents were exactly what Canadian school children needed to know about the history of their country. It should come as no surprise that Native people were not considered of much interest to Judge Clement, who devoted one five-page chapter to "The Indian Tribes of Canada." Almost all of the information in the chapter relates to the geographical location of the different tribes. The Indian's "character and habits" are summarized in eighteen lines:

Master of woodcraft, he was seen at his best when hunting.
Upon the war-path he was cruel, tomahawking, scalping
and torturing with fiendish ingenuity. A stoic fortitude
when himself tortured was about his only heroic quality.
In his own village among his own clansmen he spent his
time in gambling, story-telling, or taking part in some
rude feast. In his domestic life the Indian was not without
virtues, and his squaw and papooses were treated with
somewhat rough and careless kindness. To his tribe he was
usually faithful, though to his foes false and crafty. Indian
religion was purest superstition ... [20]

Throughout the rest of the book, Clement seldom mentions
Indians; but when he does, he invariably describes them as savage,
dusky, fiendish, wily, or filthy. In Eastern Canada he presents them as
antagonistic to early European settlers, as an obstacle which had to
be overcome before the colony could flourish. On the Pacific Coast,
where "the men and women were so encrusted with paint and dirt
that their colour could not with certainty be determined," the Indians put up much less resistance because, writes Clement, "they were
fairly and kindly treated by the traders."[21] About the Indian in contemporary Canada, he is absolutely silent. A schoolchild would have
to be forgiven for thinking they had all disappeared.

Despite the award, Clement's wasn't the only history textbook in
use in schools at the turn of the century. Another was Charles Roberts'
unsuccessful entry in the Dominion competition (he had gone ahead
and got it published anyway),[22] which proved so successful with teachers that it was revised and reissued in 1915. Roberts' version of Canadian history was equally blind to Native people. His book includes no
introduction to Native societies, and no acknowledgement that anyone
was living in America before the explorers arrived. History begins with
the arrival of Europeans; thereafter Indians are given only a bit part to

Iroquois allant a la Decouverte

This typical image of the savage Iroquois warrior was reproduced reguarly in school history books.

play in the unfolding drama. Roberts presents them either as naive, superstitious pagans or treacherous warriors. All the horrors of "primitive" warfare are related with close attention to the bloody details, but Roberts does not pause to provide reasons for the Indians' behaviour. The student is left to conclude that they had none.

In their presentation of Native people, the history texts by Roberts and Clement were typical of the schoolbooks used by Canadian children in the early decades of the twentieth century. In general these books did not say much about the aboriginals—one author ended his brief discussion of the subject by stating that "much more might be said, but it would be tedious to do so"[23]—and what they did say was usually negative. Authors had a patriotic agenda which did not include the Indian. They wanted to inspire their young readers with dramatic stories of heroism and accomplishment. They wanted to depict, in Stephen Leacock's words, "the struggle of civilization against savagery."[24] Indians were useful only as victims or enemies.

Take the story of Adam Dollard des Ormeaux, one of the textbook heroes of early Canada. In 1660, he left his home in Montreal with a small party of Frenchmen and some Huron allies, to head off an Iroquois war party said to be descending on the colony. As the story goes, Dollard and his followers dug in at a small fort at the Long Sault on the Ottawa River where, vastly outnumbered, they held off the enemy for several days before being overwhelmed and slaughtered. Impressed by the bravery shown by Dollard and his companions, the Iroquois are said then to have reconsidered their plan to attack Montreal, deciding instead to go back to their own country.

Based on this account, Dollard became a national hero, credited with saving New France—and by extension Canada—from certain destruction at the hands of the Indians. Monuments have been raised to his memory; commemorative stamps have been issued. Each May, from the 1920s to the 1960s, Quebec celebrated Dollard des Ormeaux Day. The skirmish at the Long Sault has been called a "Canadian Thermopylae."

Unhappily perhaps, for Dollard anyway, modern historians have had to revise the textbook version of his story, with the result that Dollard is no longer the selfless patriot he was cracked up to be. The more likely story now seems to be that Dollard and his friends were looking for Indians to rob of their furs when they stumbled on the Iroquois quite by accident. Dollard, who was new to the colony, was probably not even in charge; it is more likely that one of the Huron was. The Iroquois were probably satisfied at having defeated the party of Hurons (their old enemies) and not the French at all, which would explain why they turned back after the encounter. Far from saving New France, the Dollard incident probably served to provoke the Iroquois into redoubling their attacks the next season.

Whatever the facts of the Dollard affair, generations of school children learned that he was a martyr to the survival of Canada. And, as one historian has written, "martyrs must have murderers"—in this case, Indians.[25] Indians are the villains of this story, as they are in so many of the stories told to students. In the process of creating national heroes for their young readers, the textbooks have to demonize the Indian.

Indians prowl the pages of these schoolbooks like wild animals prowling the forest. Much is made of their highly-developed senses. "They had bright, black eyes that could see ever so far, and ears that could hear clearly sounds that you would never notice."[26] Their always crowded, dirty lodges are no better than animal dens. Their ferocity, too, is compared to that of wild beasts. The Iroquois in particular are frequently compared to wolves ripping at the throat of New France. They stand for everything wild and ferocious about the new continent.

Textbook Indians are constantly in conflict. Students learned that the Red Man considered all other activities insignificant compared to warfare. "But to go to war was the most important part of an Indian's life; he cared for nothing else."[27] Whatever virtues Indians possess are the virtues of the warrior: strength, bravery, cunning, and great physical endurance. Students were asked to marvel at the Indians' ability to slip silently through the forest and to undergo the most horrible tortures without flinching.

On the other hand, the textbook Indian has all the vices of the warrior as well. Habitually described as vengeful, bloodthirsty, and cruel, Indian warriors are never to be mistaken for soldiers: whereas Europeans fight fairly, in the open and with a sense of honour, their Indian antagonists, motivated by blood lust, attack from ambush and can't be trusted to behave like gentlemen on the field of combat. "War is not a pretty thing at any time," Agnes Laut, a popular writer for children, remarks in her 1909 history, "but war that lets loose the bloodhounds of Indian ferocity leaves the blackest scar of all."[28] Like many of her colleagues, Laut did not shy away from recording grisly details of the suffering inflicted on innocent settlers by the "painted redskins." She tells the story of the young Pierre Radisson's abduc-

This illustration from an 1867 edition of John Richardson's novel, *Wacousta*, depicts the Indian as a savage, demonic figure.

tion at great length, lingering over the torture scenes ("the nails were torn from his fingers, the flesh burnt from the soles of his feet"[29]).

This ferocious image of the Indian was strongest in Quebec where the bloody history of relations between Native and colonist had immediate relevance. The historian Benjamin Sulte spoke confidently for all Quebecers when he wrote that "each of us has had an ancestor kidnapped, burned and eaten by the Iroquois." By the 1880s, when Sulte made his comment, the Indian wars had been over for 200 years, but stories of torture and murder were deeply engrained in the consciousness of Quebecers. Most of the writers of schoolbooks were Catholic nationalists who believed Native resistance to the early colonists, and to the Jesuit missionary efforts, to be an affront to the French-Canadian nation and the one true faith. The Indian, "Le Sauvage," was seen and portrayed as embodying everything that struck at the survival of French culture in North America.[30] And so the textbook Indian emerges as even more cruel and depraved in French than in English.

One of the most influential sources for the textbook Indian was a series of histories written by the American historian Francis Parkman. Beginning in 1851 with *The Conspiracy of Pontiac*, Parkman produced eight long books recounting the struggle between France and England for control of North America, a work he referred to as "the history of the American forest." His romantic approach to the past and his forceful narrative style won Parkman a huge audience for his books, in the United States and in Canada, and his views "completely dominated" the interpretation of the history of New France for several decades.[31] Seldom has a single writer, and never has another American, influenced so completely the way Canadians viewed their past.

Parkman was surely the Job of American letters. Beset by ill health and personal tragedy, he managed to accomplish his life's work only by an incredible exertion of will.[32] Born in 1823, he lived to be seventy years old but, except for the years of his youth, he was never free of pain and mental turmoil. The source of his troubles was apparently defective eyesight, perhaps exacerbated by a mild form of manic depression. At times his eyes caused him such torment that he had to live for days on end inside a darkened room, unable to read or even to speak. Arthritis attacked his knees and he could only walk with the aid of canes. When things were at their worst, his head was wracked with pain and his brain became a whirl of confused impressions; he couldn't concentrate, and didn't sleep for nights on end. At one point a doctor gave him six months to live: Parkman laughed. He wrote a friend sardonically: "I have known my enemy longer than he, and learned that its mission was not death, but only torment."

The 1850s was a particularly bleak period for Parkman. During most of the decade he was too debilitated to work. Then, as he appeared to be improving, his young son died. Hardly had he recovered from this blow than his wife died soon after giving birth to another child. No one believed he would keep his sanity let alone resume his writing career. Yet, after years of almost permanent invalidism, the cloud of misery which had enveloped his life lifted and Parkman was healthy enough to resume and to finish his monumental history.

Parkman's view of the military conflict between France and England, which was finally resolved with Wolfe's victory over Montcalm on the Plains of Abraham, was summed up in his famous phrase: "A happier calamity never befell a people than the conquest of Canada by the British arms." New France, according to Parkman, was a backward society, feudal, priest-ridden, and militaristic. As a romantic, Parkman found the heroic events of New France's history irresistible and he rendered them in colourful prose unequalled by any writer since. But ultimately his purpose was to celebrate the victory of English democracy and Protestant religion and the freedom and progress he believed they guaranteed.

Native people were caught in the middle of this titanic struggle between tyranny and liberty: to Parkman, the Indians, and the forest wilderness they inhabited, were victims of the inexorable march of western civilization; and Native cultures were fated by their backwardness to disappear. In his opinion, the Iroquois were the most highly developed of the Native tribes. He admired their sagacity, their form of government, the complexity of their social organization. Yet even they, he concluded, were incapable of true civilization, by which he meant a settled way of life governed by law, science, and Christianity. Indians, he wrote, could not overcome their ferocious cruelty and barbarism: their superstitious belief in spirits and monsters left them in a state of perpetual fear and intellectual bondage. Parkman believed that Indian society was resistant to all change. The people would not, because they could not, give up their accustomed ways. As a result, they were doomed.[33]

The image of the Indian found in Parkman's books was actually something new. Earlier in the century, historians of Canada treated Native people with much more respect, giving them credit for being rational human beings with an accurate sense of their own self-interest. Ethnohistorian Bruce Trigger argues that as long as aboriginals were important in the life of the country—as traders and military allies—they received reasonably fair treatment at the hands of historians. Only after about 1840, when Native people had ceased to play much of a role in Canadian society, did historians begin to marginalize and demonize them.[34]

By the end of the nineteenth century and on into the twentieth, Francis Parkman's view of the Indians prevailed in most Canadian history books, and in school books in particular. Many of the dramatic events of New France were lifted from the pages of his books and retold for children. While students learned about the selfless heroism of Dollard des Ormeaux, Madeleine de Verchères, Isaac Brock, and the Jesuit missionaries, they also learned about the ferocity and duplicity of the Indians. The textbook Indian is clearly inferior to the European colonists and, a la Parkman, blind to the advantages of adopting the White Man's ways.

Textbooks from 1840 on depict the first 300 years of Canadian history as an extended battle for existence. As long as warfare dominates the story, the Indians have a role to play, no matter how secondary or how sanguinary. While French and English, and later, Americans, contested for control of the continent, Native people are crucial either as allies or enemies. In this context, the textbooks make room for the occasional Good Indian. The Good Indian is one who stands shoulder to shoulder with Canadians in their struggle for independence: Joseph Brant and Tecumseh are the two most common examples. Unlike the Iroquois, Brant and Tecumseh are loyal friends and allies and the texts present them as the finest examples of their race.

Indians tend to disappear from these textbook histories once the War of 1812 has been covered. With the war successfully completed, Canada embarked on an era of peace and students took up the issues of responsible government and confederation. There is no place for the Indian in these matters. Even when they describe the opening of the West, most authors grant Indians only a cameo role in the second Riel rebellion. The western treaties and life on the reserves as subjects are all but ignored. The textbook Indian is very much a figure of the past, frozen in time like a butterfly in amber. Textbooks implied, if they did not state outright, that the important business of civilization went on without them. History was something that happened only to White people.

V

In the world of childhood, there were two Indians. One was the Indian of campouts and woodcraft lore and wilderness adventure. This was the Indian presented by Ernest Thompson Seton, an Indian to respect and admire. The other was the schoolbook Indian, a threat to the Canadian nation, an Indian to fear and to pity.

Seton's Indian had important lessons to teach children about self-reliance and living in harmony with nature, whereas the schoolbook Indian was fundamentally at odds with modern society. The Imaginary Indian of childhood was thus a Janus-like figure, its two faces looking in opposite directions to indicate the confusion non-Natives felt about its real identity. For many Canadians, this confusion was never to be resolved. As adults, they continue to carry contradictory images of the Indian around in their heads.

PART THREE

<><><><><><><><><><><><><><>

Appropriating the Image

ONE DAY, FOR REASONS now forgotten, I found myself wondering why General Motors had chosen to name one of their cars *Pontiac*. It seemed a strange choice, on the face of it: as most North Americans learn in school, Pontiac was a leader of the Ottawa people who forged a grand alliance of tribes to drive the English from the interior of America. From 1763 to 1765, he led the Native people in assaults on several forts. "And as for these English," he reportedly told his followers, "these dogs dressed in red, who have come to rob you of your hunting grounds, and drive away the game, you must lift the hatchet against them. Wipe them from the face of the earth ..." Hardly the kind of sentiment designed to win favour in the boardrooms of corporate America.

Curious, I wrote to General Motors, and their public relations department sent me a package of information celebrating the career of Pontiac, described therein as "the greatest Indian Chief of all time," and an "outstanding figure in the history of the American Indian. No individual of that race ever attained the distinction and power that Pontiac did."

Yes, but didn't he also lead a rebellion against White civilization, the very civilization epitomized by the automobile? General Motors was blind to the anomaly. In 1925, when the Pontiac was introduced, there can be little doubt that GM simply wanted to identify a new product with speed, power, and the force of nature, attributes long associated with Indians. Pontiac was a well-known Indian; his name would lend the car exactly the image the company was seeking—let the historians worry about the details.

One of the earliest advertisements for the Pontiac features not
the chief but the Indian Princess.

The point is not that General Motors presented a false image of
Pontiac. That may or may not be. The point is that the company appropriated an actual historical character and turned him into a com-
mercial icon of the industrial age. A figure who once led an unprecedented resistance against White civilization is now a symbol of that
civilization. An important part of Native history is at once trivialized
and domesticated.

Pontiac is not an isolated example. He represents, in fact, a final
stage in the creation of the Imaginary Indian. Not only are Indian
images used to represent what non-Natives think about Indians, they
are appropriated by non-Natives as meaningful symbols of their own
culture.

CHAPTER EIGHT

Marketing the Imaginary Indian

I N 1929, WHEN BUFFALO Child Long Lance was living in New York, the B.F. Goodrich Company introduced a new type of canvas running shoe. The "Chief Long Lance Shoe" was modelled on an Indian moccasin and endorsed by Long Lance in an extensive advertising campaign. "In our primitive life, nothing was more important than our feet," Long Lance is quoted as saying in one magazine advertisement. "I wonder if the white race would not be sturdier if they took better care of their feet in childhood—by wearing shoes that allow free exercise of the foot and leg muscles." As part of the publicity for the new sneakers, Goodrich published a booklet, *How to Talk in Indian Sign Language*, featuring photographs of a bare-chested Long Lance, in breechcloth and headband, manipulating his hands.[1]

B.F. Goodrich wished to associate its shoes with speed, strength, and durability. There was no better way to do this than to associate them with the Indian, known for his ability to run like the wind for hours at a time. Of course, shoes were not the first products to be marketed with the help of the Indian image. The association of Indians and products was a venerable one, going back at least to the travelling medicine shows of the late eighteenth century, in which potions and elixirs were peddled on the strength of their connection with Indian healing practices. The first decades of the twentieth century saw the appearance of dozens and dozens of products which tried to find favour with consumers by identifying with the Indian: Pocahontas perfume, Red Indian motor oil, Iroquois beer, Squaw Brand canned vegetables—the list goes on and on. For some products, the Indian was used as an all-purpose symbol of Canada. For others the Indian image was used to associate a product with the out-of-doors, or with strength and courage, or with the simple innocence of nature.

This tradition continued in the naming of sports teams after Indian groups—the Braves, the Redskins, the Indians. It represented an attempt to link the team with the courage, ferocity, strength, and agility of the Indian. For the same reasons, audiences at sporting events occasionally utilized the Imaginary Indian. In 1916, for example, students at the University of British Columbia came up with the following chant:

> Kitsilano, Capilano, Siwash, Squaw,
> Kla-How-ya, Tillicum, Skookum, Wah,
> Hiyu Mamook! Muck-a-Muck-a, Zip!
> B.C. Varsity. Rip! Rip! Rip!
> V-A-R-S-I-T-Y. Varsity.

Later the university adopted the Thunderbird as the name for its athletic teams.[2] More recently, the Atlanta Braves baseball team had an Indian mascot named Chief Noc-a-homa who inhabited a tipi just beyond the outfield fence. When Native groups complained, the team retired the Chief, but during the 1991 World Series, Braves' fans angered aboriginal Americans once again by using fake tomahawks and the so-called "tomahawk chop" to urge on the team.

The irony of seeking victory by invoking the totemic power of a socially oppressed people was apparently not recognized. But a grasp of irony has never been the strong suit of White society when it wishes to appropriate elements of Native culture.

Advertising relies on a simple message to make a point. It deals in stereotypes. Once it began using images of Native people, advertising created a whole new context for the Imaginary Indian. Suddenly images of the Indian were appearing on the pages of mass-circulation magazines, on billboards, on the shelves at the local supermarket. The Imaginary Indian became one of the icons of consumer society. The result was a reduction of aboriginal cultures to a series of slogans, a set of simplistic and patronizing attitudes. Take, for example, this jingle used by General Motors to promote the Pontiac in 1927:

> Heap Big Injun,
> Pontiac a warrior brave was he,
> One day he met Miss Sleeping Fawn
> and fell in love you see,
> Now, Sleeping Fawn was up to date,
> No birch canoe will do,
> You get a car and take me for a riding when you woo,
> Pontiac, Pontiac, Heap Big Injun Brave ...[3]

Many of the images of Indians which appeared in advertisements were intended to be positive. They reveal a widespread admiration for certain qualities which the public associated with "Indianness": bravery, physical prowess, natural virtue. Of course, these were qualities Indians were thought to have possessed in the distant past, before contact with the White Man. Advertisements did not feature Indians in suits or dresses; they did not highlight life on the reserve or on the other side of the tracks. Instead they showed the classic Indian head in feather headdress or the Indian princess in beaded doeskin. Advertising reinforced the belief that the best Indian was the historical Indian. It used the Indian as a symbol to appeal to modern consumers who admired values they associated with pre-industrial society.

II

The marketing of the Imaginary Indian reached its peak not with a

Hector Crawler, a Stoney chief, promotes the "Big Chief" banjo in this publicity photo for the Ludwig Banjo Company, ca. 1925. It is not clear why the chief is wearing gloves to play the banjo.

product but an experience, the experience of railway travel. More than any other single aspect of White civilization, the railway transformed the world of the Indian, especially in Western Canada. It was the railway which conveyed the hundreds of thousands of new settlers into the West. It was the railway which kept these settlers supplied with everything they needed to establish the new grain economy. And it was the railway which transported the products of the new economy to market. Ironic, then, that the railway should lead the way in marketing the image of the Indian to sell its services to travellers.

The settlement of the West did not happen all at once. The Canadian Pacific Railway was completed in 1885, but the flood of immigrants into the new land did not begin for another decade. Meanwhile, the CPR had to find some way of paying for itself. Tourism was one answer. Cornelius Van Horne, the CPR's first general manager, determined to attract travellers by offering them first-class accommodation on his transcontinental trains.[4] Sleeping cars were fitted out with oversize berths, richly upholstered seats, mahogany and satinwood panelling, polished brass fittings, and bathrooms in every car. Elegant dining cars offered sumptuous meals and imported wines at tables set with white linen and gleaming silver. But comfort was not enough: travellers had to be offered spectacle. And here the CPR capitalized on one of its greatest assets—the magnificent beauty of the western landscape. Company officials recognized that the West could be sold as one great tourist attraction. The Rocky Mountains especially offered travellers some of the most spectacular scenery in the world. "1001 Switzerlands Rolled Into One" was how Van Horne described them.

The railway's publicity department began churning out posters, books, and pamphlets extolling the natural wonders of Canada's West. No less an authority than the governor-general, the Marquis of Lorne, was enlisted in the cause. "Nowhere can finer scenery be enjoyed from the window of a car than upon this line," Lorne enthused in an article published by the CPR as its first promotional effort.[5] Some of the country's leading painters and photographers received free passes on the trains to go west and record the scenery. The CPR then used these scenes in its publicity material, or sold them along the route as postcards, viewbooks, and individual prints.

At about the same time in the United States, the Santa Fe Railway began using artists to create a marketable image of the American southwest which would appeal to travellers.[6] Several painters concentrated on producing scenes of the Pueblo Indians which were reproduced on the railway company's calendar and distributed all over America. The "Santa Fe Indian" became a well-known symbol of the railway, and of the exotic, picturesque desert southwest. In Canada, on the other hand, artists remained mesmerized by the mountains to the exclusion of anything else. Lucius O'Brien, John Fraser, Thomas Mower Martin, and F.M. Bell-Smith were just a few of the members of the "Railway School" of painters who made lush, dramatic portraits of towering peaks. They did not see the same artistic potential in the Indians of the West as their American counterparts did in the Southwest. Photographers, however, tended to pay more attention to the Indian. William Notman, Alexander Henderson, Oliver Buell, and scores of less well-known photographers aimed their primitive equipment at the Native villages beside the CPR mainline, capturing images of the Native people going about their daily activities. These photographs sold briskly to passengers wanting mementoes of their trip.[7] At Banff, reported the English writer Douglas Sladen in his account of a cross-Canada train ride in 1894, "you can hire a fly, for all the world like a Brighton fly, with a pair of horses, to drive you over excellent gravelled roads to the Devil's Lake, or to very near the top of the big mountain. The American cockney spends all day driving about in these flies, and all night in buying ten-by-eight

One of the Indian photographs which the CPR made available for sale to travellers.

photographs."[8] Photographs were reproduced and distributed widely as part of the company's propaganda. In this form, they were the first encounter many eastern Canadians would have with the Indians of the frontier.

Following the example of their southern counterparts, the CPR gradually realized that the Indians were a surefire tourist attraction. "The Indians and the bears were splendid stage properties to have at a station where both the east and west bound trains ... stop for lunch," remarked Sladen.[9] It was not entirely by accident then, that in 1894, when floods washed out the track, the company sent local guide and outfitter Tom Wilson down to the Stoney reserve at Morley to invite the Indians back to Banff to entertain the marooned travellers. The Indians performed traditional dances and competed in a number of rodeo events for prizes put up by the railway company. The whole affair turned out to be so popular that the CPR and local businesses decided to make Banff Indian Days an annual summer event.[10] The railway sponsored a similar pageant in Desbarats, Ontario, each summer with actors in Native costume performing scenes from a version of Longfellow's popular long poem, "Hiawatha."[11]

Travel on the CPR boomed in the years before World War I. In 1913, fifteen and a half million passengers rode the train. Encouraged by the railway's publicity machine, many of them went west to discover the much-heralded beauty of plains and mountains. Tourists were excited at the possibility of seeing wild Indians in their natural setting from the safety and convenience of a railcar. It was every bit as exotic as visiting the depths of Africa or some distant island in the Pacific.

Reality did not always measure up, however, as the British traveller Edward Roper discovered on his cross-Canada excursion in 1890. Pausing at Maple Creek, Saskatchewan, Roper observed a group of Blackfoot lingering around the railway station. "Many of them were partly civilized in dress, though ragged and dirty, and there was very little of the picturesque about them. Some few had good faces, but the ideal Red Man was not there." Later, at Gleichen, Alberta, Roper was pleased to have a chance to see some less "civilized" Natives, who impressed him with their paint and feathers and decorated clothing. These were much closer to the wild Indians of his imagination and he admired their animated good looks and clean appearance. Roper enjoyed throwing coins and oranges from the back of the train to watch young Natives scramble in the dust for them.[12] In B.C., he was surprised to find Indians occupying prominent places in White society. "I conclude that there must be something really good in a race which can, if only here and there, produce such specimens." However, he was impressed mainly by the indifference with which Canadians seemed to view the Indians. "The Canadians," he told his readers, "seemed to regard them as a race of animals which were neither

Posters for Banff Indian Days encourage visitors to come and witness Indians in their traditional setting.

benefit nor harm to anyone, mentioning that they were surely dying out, and that when they were all gone it would be a good thing."[13] Of course, the fact that the Indians were vanishing added an urgency to the tourists' quest for novelty. If they didn't see them soon, they might never see them.

III

Once the West was settled, the Indians lost some of their appeal as advertising devices. Western Canada was no longer promoted as a wild frontier. Tourists came west for the scenery and the hiking and the skiing, not to see the primitive Red Man. Still, there remained among travellers a fascination with Indians and their exotic culture and railways continued to capitalize on it whenever they could. One such opportunity arose in the 1920s in northern British Columbia.

An Indian parade down the main street of Banff was a feature of Banff Indian Days, sponsored by the CPR as a tourist attraction.

For several decades, collectors had been stripping coastal villages of native artifacts and selling them to museums around the world. Most highly prized were the giant totem poles which over time had come to symbolize the people of the Northwest Coast. By 1920, hardly any of the huge monuments remained in their village settings, and those that did were in a sorry state of natural decay. A large cache of about seventy poles stood in the Indian villages along the Skeena River. During World War I, the construction of the Grand Trunk Pacific Railway through the river valley to Prince Rupert placed these villages right on the mainline of a transcontinental railway. As a result, the poles became a major tourist attraction. One Montreal newspaper calculated that they were the most photographed spot in Canada after Niagara Falls.[14]

Canadian National Railways, the publicly-owned corporation which took over the Grand Trunk after the war, recognized the value of the poles and took a leading role in their preservation, along with the Indian Department, the Parks Branch, and the Victoria Memorial Museum in Ottawa. The expense of the project was justified mainly as a stimulus to tourism and therefore to the business of the CNR, though several of the officials involved were serious ethnologists who had more scientific reasons for preserving the poles. The Skeena Valley line was advertised as the railway to totem-pole land and thought was given to the creation of a major tourist resort. The initiative for the project came from government and railway officials, not the local Gitksan people who owned the poles. The Natives were not very interested in marketing their culture for tourists, and some of their chiefs asked the government to stop meddling with the poles. Harlan Smith, an official with the museum, reported that the Gitksan asked why a government which a few years earlier had banned the erection of new poles now wanted to preserve old ones. The Natives believed that their monuments were being used to put rail fares into the pockets of the CNR and wondered why they should cooperate. When the project finished in 1930, only about one-third of the Skeena Valley poles were restored. Still, the result was a benefit to the railway which highlighted the totems in its publicity material.

During the summer of 1926, the artists A.Y. Jackson and Edwin Holgate visited the Skeena to sketch the poles and the Native villages. Both men believed they were witnessing the remains of a culture in decline. Jackson later wrote that "the big powerful tribes ... have dwindled to a mere shadow of their former greatness."[15] Wanting to

The ubiquitous totem pole, looking a little hastily carved, turns up in this scene from *The Cariboo Trail*, a 1950 Hollywood feature starring Randolph Scott (*fourth from left*).

take advantage of public interest in the poles, and in West Coast Natives generally, the CNR installed a "Totem Pole Room" for dining and dancing in the Chateau Laurier, its hotel in Ottawa, and commissioned Holgate to design it. The finished product, which opened in 1929, featured columns done up to resemble totem poles, large murals, and Native masks and designs festooning the walls.[16]

The marketing of the Skeena Valley poles as a tourist attraction by the CNR was part of a curious phenomenon—the appropriation of the totem pole as an unofficial symbol of British Columbia. The trend began in the 1920s, when various public bodies became alarmed at the rapid disappearance of poles from Native villages into the hands of museums and collectors, mainly outside Canada. As the number of poles dwindled, their value as works of art rose in public estimation. White British Columbians, and Canadians generally, decided that they were an important national treasure, a visible link with the country's first peoples and a part of its heritage which had to be preserved.

In Vancouver, the Art, Historical and Scientific Association was at the forefront of this movement. Founded in 1889, the AHS created the original Vancouver Museum to hold its growing collection of historical art and artifacts, including "a representative collection of native relics and handicrafts." Later, the AHS conceived the idea of erecting a model Indian village in Stanley Park "to give to the present and succeeding generations an adequate conception of the work and social life of the aborigines before the advent of the white man." The village did not materialize, and the association began collecting totem poles instead. The congregation of poles which now attracts the attention of so many visitors at Brockton Point in the park originated with these early efforts of the AHS.[17]

Since the 1920s, totem poles have appeared at a large number of public buildings, hotels, parks, and shopping plazas in British Columbia. Almost every provincial milestone has been celebrated with the raising of a pole. Immediately following World War II, the BC Electric Company, owners of public transit systems on the Lower Mainland and Vancouver Island, altered the insignia on its vehicles to feature a large, spread-winged thunderbird, familiar from the top of so many totems. A tall Haida pole welcomes people entering Canada at the Peace Arch border crossing south of Vancouver. In 1958, when B.C. celebrated its centennial, the province presented Queen Elizabeth with a Kwakiutl pole which now stands in Windsor Great Park in England. In 1966, to celebrate the centennial of the union of the colonies of British Columbia and Vancouver Island, the province inaugurated the "Route of the Totems," a series of poles erected along highways and at ferry terminals from Victoria to Prince Rupert. In the mid-1980s, Duncan, a small town on Vancouver Island, declared itself the "City of Totem Poles" and commissioned a group of poles as a way of encouraging travellers to visit.[18] While Native people venerate totem poles for social and historical reasons, many non-Natives apparently share a more superstitious belief that poles have the power to make people stop and spend their money.

The totem pole is just one aspect of Native culture that has been adopted by non-Native Canadians as a symbol of their own. In 1991, the federal government unveiled a huge sculpture at the entrance to the new Canadian embassy building in Washington, D.C. The "Spirit of Haida G'waii" is a five-ton bronze statue depicting a canoe spilling over with Haida myth figures, carved by the renowned West Coast artist, Bill Reid, who is part Haida himself. Reid and his work are acclaimed worldwide. He ranks among the top monumental artists in Canada. However, it must be assumed that a sculpture in such a prestigious public location is intended to be not only a work of art but more than that, a symbol for Canada itself. The choice of a giant Haida canoe is an interesting attempt by the government to absorb Haida mythology into a more general mythology of relevance to all Canadians.

These attempts are ubiquitous. Recently I opened an American magazine to discover a government advertisement encouraging tourists to visit Canada.[19] A bold headline ran across two pages: "Only in God's Country could you meet such interesting souls." A stunning photograph shows two figures, presumably Native people, seated on a sandy beach. They are both wearing large raven's head masks, brightly painted, with long beaks. In the background, a third figure, carrying a ceremonial drum and wrapped in what appears to be a Chilkoot blanket, emerges from the mist at the water's edge. Offshore, islands melt into a blue haze.

The text, which begins by informing readers that "our native peoples have been entertaining visitors for centuries," incorporates

Becoming an Indian was an honour enjoyed by many prominent Canadians, among them the writer Charles G.D. Roberts. In 1928, when he was president of the Canadian Authors' Association, Roberts was made a chief of the Sarcee in a ceremony at a reservation near Calgary. Roberts received a bonnet of eagle feathers and a new name, Chief Great Scribe.

a version of a creation myth. Raven beats his wings and brings the world into being. "The most revered of spirits and master of ceremonies, the Raven embodies what this land is today," continues the text. "Magic. For here the supernatural abides in all that is living." The advertisement is promoting Canada but refers specifically to British Columbia, where apparently everyone is a pantheist and the "Animal People" are "our link to another realm."

Needless to say, this is not a British Columbia I recognize, and I grew up there. Nor is it a British Columbia which any visitor should have any reasonable expectation of encountering. The Animal People do not show themselves to tourists. This British Columbia is the fabulation of an advertising copy-writer with a vivid Imaginary Indian.

The Indians in the advertisement are familiar enough. They are spiritual, mysterious Indians. They are a part of the land, like the animals, in touch with the unseen forces of nature. They appeal to the widespread conviction on the part of non-Natives that Native people experience the natural world in a way that is qualitatively different from the rest of us. As well, the Indians in the advertisement belong to history. Dressed in traditional costumes and placed in a context that evokes the past, they are not Indians as they appear to us in modern life. They are thoroughly exotic and otherworldly.

The advertisement is only indirectly interested in the Indian, however. It is more interested in making the Indian a symbol for Canada. It is telling potential visitors that Canada is an extraordinary, even supernatural, place where they are going to have unusual experiences. Like the Indians in the photograph, Canada is presented as embodying a sense of the mystery of the natural world. Indians are used to represent not a place that is modern and familiar, but rather a place that exists outside of time in another reality. There is really no difference between this advertisement and the photographs of Plains people used by the CPR to attract customers west a hundred years ago: Canada is still Indian country.

IV

Many aspects of Native culture have been appropriated over the years and turned into commodities to help sell products in the marketplace. These products range from running shoes to cars to the country itself. Indian heroes like Pontiac, Indian artifacts like totem poles, Indian attitudes like the stoicism of the cigar-store Indian have all been invoked. Products are linked to the Indian in the expectation that some supposedly Native virtues will rub off. Indians themselves become commodities in the marketplace. The advertising image is based on stereotypes of the Imaginary Indian already abroad in the culture. In turn, advertising reinforces the stereotype by feeding it back into the mainstream culture in a self-repeating loop.

It may seem unimportant that images of Indians have appeared in tourist brochures and on tins of canned vegetables, coins, and hood ornaments. But the phenomenon is not a trivial one. Many writers have observed that non-Natives have experienced a persistent sense of alienation in North America ever since the first Europeans arrived here. "Americans are really aliens in North America," says Vine Deloria, the American Sioux writer, "and try as they might they seem incapable of adjusting to the continent." In their search for ways to feel at home, Deloria continues, the newcomers have looked to the first inhabitants of the continent: "Indians, the original possessors of the land, seem to haunt the collective unconscious of the white man, and to the degree that one can identify the conflicting images of the Indian which stalk the white man's waking perception of the world one can outline the deeper problems of identity and alienation that trouble him."[20] One response to this dilemma is to "go Native," to become an Indian, or at least to take on Indian identities, either directly, as Archie Belaney did when he turned into Grey Owl, or spuriously, by appropriating elements of Indianness and making them representative of mainstream society.

Since the beginning of the country, non-Native Canadians have wanted Indians to transform themselves into Whites, to assimilate into the mainstream. But there has also been a strong impulse among Whites, less consciously expressed perhaps, to transform themselves into Indians. Grey Owl simply acted out the fantasy. Each time they respond to a sales pitch which features an Indian image, each time they chant an Indian slogan from their box seats, each time they dress up in feathers for a costume party or take pride in the unveiling of yet another totem pole as a symbol of the country, non-Native Canadians are trying in a way to become indigenous people themselves and to resolve their lingering sense of not belonging where they need to belong. By appropriating elements of Native culture, non-Natives have tried to establish a relationship with the country that pre-dates their arrival and validates their occupation of the land.

PART FOUR

◇◇◇◇◇◇◇◇◇◇◇◇◇◇◇◇

Implementing the Image

THROUGHOUT THE nineteenth century, a single idea dominated the study of North American prehistory. According to the experts, an ancient race of gifted people once occupied most of the continental interior from the Great Lakes to the Gulf of Mexico. These people raised gigantic mounds of dirt, sometimes in the shape of strange figures, sometimes as vast conical hillocks, sometimes as long embankments. The configuration of the mounds indicated a complex and advanced civilization at work. Inside the mounds, excavators found the remains of entombed bodies and metal artifacts, which convinced an impressionable public that a prehistoric empire once existed in America which must have rivalled the Aztecs and the ancient Greeks in splendor and accomplishments.[1]

The discovery of the mounds, and by extension, a lost race of Mound Builders, touched off a long and tangled debate. Who were the Mound Builders, and where had they come from? There was no shortage of answers to these questions: they were said to be the Lost Tribes of Israel which somehow had migrated to America from Palestine long before Christ; or they were a group of Welsh-speaking Indians; or they were Hindus who had crossed the Bering Strait from India not long after the Great Flood; they were Romans; they were Persians; they were survivors of the lost city of Atlantis. Whoever they were, they had to have come to America long before Columbus, and theorists believed that after flourishing for several generations they had moved south into Mexico where they became the Toltecs, forerunners of the Aztec people.

None of the experts debating these questions ever proposed the obvious: that the Mound Builders might have been the ancestors of contemporary Native people. Conventional wisdom of the nineteenth century simply disallowed such a notion: Indians, in conventional wisdom, represented too low a level of civilization, bereft of the organizational skills and technical know-how required to erect the mounds. Prevailing theory held the Indians to be interlopers, barbarian hordes descended out of the north like Attila—to sack the ancient cities of the Mound Builders, thereby precipitating a kind of Dark Ages in the New World—a Dark Ages which would not end until the first European settlers arrived. This, in spite of the records of the early French and Spanish, who encountered contemporary Natchez living in a Mound culture in what is now the northeastern US.

It was not until the early years of the twentieth century that modern archaeology unravelled some of the riddle of the great mounds and exploded the myth of an ancient, vanished race. The mounds, it turned out, were built by Native North Americans, predecessors of the people who inhabited the continent when Europeans arrived. The myth of the Mound Builders flourished for so long because the image of the Imaginary Indian was strong enough to prevail over common sense: White Americans, incapable of comparing Native cultures to their own, could only compare the culture of the Imaginary Indian to their own. So it would follow logically from such a view that the mounds were more likely to have been built by migrating Hindus in the time of Noah, than that they might be the product of cultures indigenous to the continent.

II

Images have consequences in the real world: ideas have results. The Imaginary Indian does not exist in a void. In their relations with Native people over the years, non-Native Canadians have put the image of the Indian into practice. They have assumed that the Imaginary

Indian was real, as real as people once thought the ancient Mound Builders were. And they have devised public policy based on that assumption.

But if the Indian is imaginary, could government policy be any more realistic than the wildest theories about the Mound Builders?

CHAPTER NINE

The Bureaucrat's Indian

IN THE SUMMER of 1906, a trio of Edwardian intellectuals set out from Ottawa on an expedition into the Canadian hinterland. Their leader was Duncan Campbell Scott, poet and Indian administrator, who can be pictured in pith helmet and mosquito net, trailing a finger languidly in the stream while reading aloud from the *Oxford Book of Poetry* as his Native canoemen bent their broad backs to the paddle. Seated next to him is his friend Pelham Edgar, the literary critic. "Duncan and I sit side by side in the big bark canoe," Edgar wrote, "and we gloat over things—cloud effects, peeps of vistas through the islands as they shift past us, and lights and shadows on the water ..." Joining these two aesthetes is the painter Edmund Morris, who had come along to sketch portraits of the Native people. Morris "fitted in with our party to perfection," recalled Edgar, "and his artist eye served to sharpen our own perceptions of significant aspects of things we might never have noted." [2] Drifting lazily across the black waters of northern lakes, camping at night beneath the star-speckled sky, the three comrades fished, painted, wrote poems, and philosophized around the crackling fire:

> You will recall, of all those magic nights,
> One when we floated on the sunset lights,
> In all the mirrored crimson from the flare;
> Not knowing whether we were lead by air
> Or by secret impulse of the lake. [3]

Duncan Campbell Scott, the Indian commissioner, being paddled through the Ontario wilderness during the 1906 treaty expedition.

Occasionally, duty called, and Scott and his friends were reminded that they were not visiting the north country purely for their own pleasure. The previous year, the Canadian government had initiated treaty proceedings with the Ojibway and Cree of northern Ontario.[4] In his non-literary mode, Scott was an official in the Indian Affairs Department and he had been appointed one of the commissioners to negotiate the treaty (known as Treaty 9). Scott had passed the previous summer dispensing treaty payments and, finding the conditions salubrious, elected to take his friend Edgar with him when he returned to complete the job. He was further delighted to welcome Morris, whom the Ontario government had asked to paint portraits of the Native leaders he encountered.

Each of these Edwardian intellectuals had a different response to their summer excursion. Edgar seems to have treated it as something of a lark. He spent most of his time admiring the scenery and fishing. "The Indians had two long names for me," he recalled, "one of which translated means 'The man who always asks where the trout are,' and the other 'The man who always fishes and never catches anything.'" He observed the aboriginals mainly as exotic curiosities and concluded that on the whole "the Province of Ontario treats its Indian population with a fairness that amounts to generosity."[5]

The summer affected Edmund Morris more deeply. He was appalled that in a civilized country such as Canada, Natives were reduced to living in poverty the equal of which he had not seen before. Diseases like influenza, tuberculosis, and measles were killing off the people at a great rate. Morris himself visited homes where he saw youngsters wasting away in their beds. Fur-bearing animals were disappearing in the face of over-trapping by White interlopers, leaving the Natives destitute. A treaty payment of $8 per person was hardly going to improve conditions for these northern people. Morris returned to the city thinking (naively, as we have seen elsewhere in these pages) that he could put his art at their service.[6]

Duncan Scott, as a twenty-six-year veteran of the Indian department, had had much more exposure to Native people than either of his travelling companions, who were both seeing them for the first time. Scott had already formulated the image of the Indian he would hold for the rest of his career, an image he shared with the readers of *Scribners' Magazine* in an article he wrote after returning from the Treaty 9 expedition.[7]

"In the early days the Indians were a real menace to the colonization of Canada," Scott explained. If they had banded together, they might have annihilated the colonies "as easily as a child wipes pictures from his slate." The Indian of the not-too-distant past was "full of force and heat … ready to break out at any moment in savage dances, in wild and desperate orgies in which ancient superstitions were involved with European ideas but dimly understood and intensified by cunning imaginations inflamed with rum." Only the cleverest diplomacy, Scott believed, managed to keep the peace in those dangerous days.

Scott's lurid description of the savage Red Man contrasts sharply with the peaceable Cree and Ojibway his treaty party encountered in northern Ontario. He attributed this "transformation" to "the effect of education and contact with a few of the better elements of our civilization," notably the Christian missionaries (and never to the nature of the people themselves). At the same time, he maintained, Indians were still children in terms of their intellectual development: they could not possibly grasp the complex legal and constitutional issues involved in treaty-making. As a result, negotiations for Treaty 9 were kept simple and the implications of the treaty left unexplored. "The simpler facts had to be stated, and the parental idea developed that the King is the great father of the Indians, watchful over their interests and ever compassionate." Scott closed his account of the Treaty 9 expedition with a warning and a prediction. Do not think, he told his readers, that civilizing the Indian is the work of one generation, or even two. It might take as long as four centuries before Indians merged with Whites and ceased to exist as a distinct people. But "making an end" of the Indian was the objective of government policy and it was going to happen.

To the modern reader, Scott's words have a sinister ring, sounding as they do like a kind of Final Solution. But in his day they were the soothing words of conventional wisdom. Assimilation—the "euthanasia of savage communities," as a senior British colonial official put it—was the avowed aim of government Indian policy.[8] Indians were a problem—a problem that would be solved by its own disappearance. To accomplish this objective, the federal government devised its own Imaginary Indian, the Official Indian of law and regulation. From 1913, when he became senior bureaucrat in the Indian Department, to 1932, when he retired, Duncan Campbell Scott was the leading apologist for government policy and the leading expositor of the Official Indian.

II

The broad outline of Canadian Indian policy in the early twentieth century was an inheritance from the past. In the eighteenth and early nineteenth centuries, Britain needed Native people in its armed struggle for control of the continent. Accordingly, they received all the respect due to military allies. Following the War of 1812, however, when conflict with the United States ended and settlers began encroaching on the wilderness, British colonial officials who minded Canadian affairs recognized that a new relationship had to be worked out with Native people. No longer needed as military allies, the aboriginals had lost their value to the White intruders—and were now perceived to be a social and economic problem rather than a diplomatic one. Officials began to think in terms of civilizing the Indians so that they might assume a role in mainstream Canadian society. To this end, reserves were created as places where Indians would be taught to behave like Whites. Subsequent legislation codified the policy of civilization in a tangle of laws and regulations that would have the effect of erecting a prison wall of red tape around Canada's Native population.

The fundamental expression of the Official Indian became the Indian Act. First promulgated in 1876, amended often since then, the Indian Act consolidated and strengthened the control the federal government exercised over its aboriginal citizens. The aim of the Act, as of all Indian legislation, was to assimilate Native people into the Canadian mainstream.[9] Assimilation as a solution to the "Indian problem" was considered preferable to its only perceived alternative: wholesale extermination. There is nothing to indicate that extermination was ever acceptable to Canadians. Not only was it morally repugnant, it was also impractical. The American example showed how costly it was, in terms of money and lives, to wage war against the aboriginals. The last thing the Canadian government wanted to do was initiate a full-scale Indian conflict. It chose instead to go about the elimination of the Indian problem by eliminating the Indian way of life: through education and training, the Red Man would attain civilization. Most White Canadians believed that Indians were doomed to disappear anyway. Assimilation was a policy intended to preserve Indians as individuals by destroying them as a people.

The Indian Act defined an Indian as "any male person of Indian blood reputed to belong to a particular band," his wife, and children. The Act excluded certain individuals from Indian status. The most notorious exclusion was Native women who married non-Native men. These women were considered no longer to be Indians and lost any privileges under the terms of the Act, a situation which remained unchanged until 1985. Indian became a legislated concept as well as a racial one, maintained solely through political institutions to which Native people, who had no vote until 1960, had no access.

Special status—Indian status—was conceived as a stopgap measure by White legislators who expected Indians gradually to abandon their Native identity in order to enjoy the privilege of full Canadian citizenship—a process formally known as enfranchisement. As soon as Natives met certain basic requirements of literacy, education, and moral character, they would be expected to apply for enfranchisement. In return for giving up legal and treaty rights, the enfranchisee would receive a portion of reserve lands and funds and cease to be an Indian, at least in law. The government expected that in time most Indians would opt for enfranchisement, which was conceived as a reward for good behaviour. In fact, the vast majority of Native people chose not to be rewarded in this way: in the sixty-three years between 1857, when enfranchisement was first legislated, and 1920, only 250 individuals took advantage of the opportunity to shed their Native identity. [10]

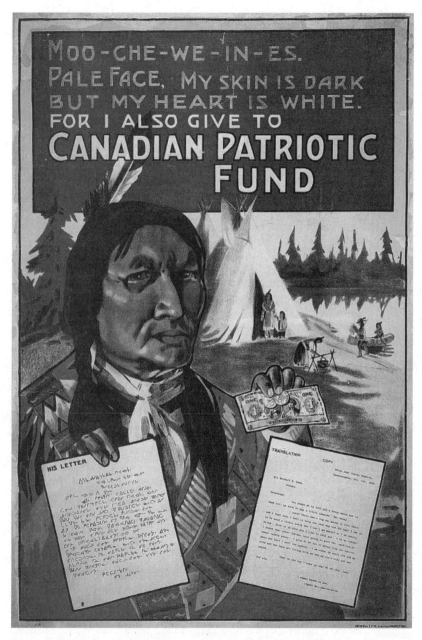

This image of the loyal Indian rallying to the cause during World War I is reminiscent of an earlier period when Indians were valued as allies in the colonial wars.

The Indian Act treated Native people as minors incapable of looking after their own interests and in need of the protection of the state.
"The Indian is a ward of the Government still," Arthur Meighen, then
minister of the interior, told Parliament in 1918. "The presumption
of the law is that he has not the capacity to decide what is for his ultimate benefit in the same degree as his guardian, the Government of
Canada."[11] Indians did not possess the rights and privileges of citizenship; they couldn't vote, they couldn't buy liquor, and they couldn't
obtain land under the homestead system. The government expected
that Indians would abuse these rights if they had them, that they had
to be protected from themselves and from predatory Whites who
would take advantage of them. By the same token, status Indians did
not have to pay federal taxes (if they were able to find employment)
and were "protected from debt" (a condition that usually meant they
could not secure loans from financial institutions). They were people
apart from mainstream Canadian society. But the ultimate aim of Indian policy was not a system of apartheid. Segregationist, apartheid-
like laws were sometimes imposed, but their purpose was tactical:
they were intended to serve the long-term policy of assimilation.

If the government wanted to civilize the Indian, what constituted
civilization in the official mind? There were several qualities which
bureaucrats sought to impress on their Native charges. One was a
respect for private property. The fact that Native people seemed to
lack a sense of private ownership was widely regarded as a sign of
their backwardness. Tribalism, or tribal communism as some people
called it, was blamed for stifling the development of initiative and
personal responsibility. In the hope of eradicating tribalism, the 1876
Act divided reserves into lots. Band members could qualify for location tickets which, after they proved themselves as farmers, gave
them title (but not necessarily ownership) to their own piece of land.

Meanwhile, the reserve itself was an integral part of the civilizing process. Reserves were originally intended as safe havens where Native people could live isolated from the baleful influence of their White neighbours. From the Native point of view, reserves secured a land base for their traditional life ways. But in the nineteenth century, officials increasingly thought of reserves as social laboratories where Indians could be educated, Christianized, and prepared for assimilation.

Agriculture was an important weapon in the war on Native culture. As game resources disappeared, farming seemed to be the only alternative way for Natives to make a living. More than that, at a time when industrialism was in its infancy, farming was seen as the profession best suited to a virtuous, civilized person: tilling the soil was an ennobling activity which fostered an orderly home life, industrious work habits, and a healthy respect for private property. Farming would cause Natives to settle in one place and end the roving ways so typical of a hunting lifestyle and so detrimental to the sober, reliable routines on which White society prided itself.

Another component of civilization was Christianity. Few Whites had any sympathy for or understanding of Native religious ideas, which were dismissed as pagan superstitions. Religious training was left to missionaries, but the government did its part by banning Native traditional religious and ceremonial practices—for example, the potlatch on the West Coast and the sun dance on the Prairies.

Democratic self-government was also imposed on Native people. The ability to manage elected institutions was believed to be another hallmark of civilized society. Band members were required to elect chiefs and councillors who exercised limited authority over local matters. Indian Department officials retained the power to interfere in the political affairs of the band. The attempt to teach the Indians democracy was part and parcel of the assimilationist agenda. The elected councils were intended to replace traditional forms of Native government over which federal officials lacked control.

Fred Dieter *(left)* and Joseph Ironquill, two members of the File Hills colony. The colony was an experiment in social engineering, aimed at transforming Natives into respectable, hard-working farmers.

A property-owning, voting, hard-working, Christian farmer, abstemious in his habits and respectful of his public duties—that was the end product of government Indian policy. "Instead of having a horde of savages in the North-West, as we had a few years ago," Clifford Sifton, the minister of the interior, told Parliament in 1902, "we shall soon have an orderly, fairly educated population, capable of sustaining themselves." [12] The message the minister intended to deliver was that the Indian had gone from painted savage to yeoman farmer in one generation.

In reality it was not that simple. As time passed, officials grew impatient at the slow pace of assimilation. Native people seemed reluctant to embrace the benefits of White civilization. They resisted many of the measures the government imposed on them. As the American historian Brian Dippie put it, civilization seemed to be a gift more appreciated by the donor than the recipient.[13] Officials concluded that Indians were by nature lazy, intellectually backward, and resistant to change. It seemed to be the only explanation: to blame the Indian for not becoming a White man fast enough. As a result, the government passed a series of amendments to the Indian Act in an attempt to speed up the process of assimilation. Regulations became increasingly coercive. Officials received authority to spend money belonging to an Indian band without the members' permission. They could impose the elected system of government on bands, and depose elected leaders of whom they did not approve. At the end of the century, a series of industrial and residential schools removed Native children from their families so that they could be acculturated more easily. A draconian pass system was enacted by which individual Natives could not leave their reserves without the permission of an agent. A system of permits made it difficult for Native people to sell their produce on the open market. While the government said it wanted Natives to become self-sufficient farmers, it erected a series of legal obstacles which made it very difficult for aboriginal farmers to compete with their White neighbours. Frustration at the slow pace of assimilation reached its peak in 1920, when the government took upon itself the legal power to enfranchise an Indian against his or her will; in other words, Indians could be involuntarily stripped of their status. This legislation raised such opposition that it was rescinded two years later, but it was re-enacted in the 1930s. It was a sign of just how desperate the government was to rid itself of the Indian problem by ridding itself of the Indian.

Looking for a success story to reassure themselves and the public that Indian "civilization" was possible, government officials found one in the File Hills colony of southern Saskatchewan.[14] File Hills was the brainchild of William Morris Graham, the resident Indian

Young Indians at the File Hills colony were encouraged to join the brass band as an alternative to their traditional pursuits.

agent. Since joining the Indian Department in 1885, Graham had identified what he considered to be a weakness in the policy of assimilation. Once Native students completed their studies at a residential school, he noted, they usually returned to their parents on the reserve where they quickly fell back into their traditional way of life (white officials derisively described this process as going "back to the blanket"). Graham proposed establishing a model agricultural colony where specially selected graduates could be isolated from family influences and taught to become independent farmers. In 1901, the first five colonists were settled on tracts of land at File Hills and received houses and loans with which to purchase furnishings and farm implements. From this modest beginning, the colony grew and prospered until by 1915 it consisted of thirty-six families cultivating over 3,000 acres of land.

The File Hills colony was an experiment in social control. Graham monitored every aspect of daily life. "Hardly a day passes that some officer of the department does not visit them," he reported. Young male colonists were encouraged to marry only their fellow graduates from residential school. Houses were neatly whitewashed and surrounded with flower beds and vegetable gardens. Graham frowned on too much visiting back and forth for fear that it would reinforce the old, "tribal ways" and distract colonists from their work. Native languages were prohibited, as was any type of traditional gathering or dancing. Substitute activities were provided: a brass band, a sewing circle, lectures by the Farmers' Institute, a baseball league.

File Hills attracted a great deal of admiring attention. The Indian Department used it as a showpiece, an example of what it was possible to do with the Indians in the right circumstances. Distinguished visitors trooped through the colony and journalists singled it out as a highly successful experiment. In 1914, a senior American official called it "an illustration of Indian administration which approaches nearest to the perfect ideal." [15] In truth, however, File Hills was maintained more for its public relations value than as a practical solution to the problems of Indian administration. No other colonies like it were created. In fact, the Liberal government of Wilfrid Laurier showed more interest in finding ways to strip reserves of land so that it might become available to non-Native homesteaders. [16]

Nonetheless, File Hills provided a great boost to the career of William Morris Graham. "To him belongs the very proud distinction of being the first man to solve the problem of making the Indian take kindly and successfully to farming," crowed the *Manitoba Free Press* in 1921. [17] His apparent success at File Hills won Graham a promotion in 1904, and he went on to become Indian Commissioner for the prairie provinces and would perhaps have succeeded Duncan Scott as the most senior bureaucrat in the department had not a liquor scandal hastened his retirement in 1932. Indeed, Graham's career was a clear indication that the way to succeed in the Indian service was to show initiative in subverting the rights of the Indians. As well as orig-

inating the File Hills experiment, he led attempts to eradicate traditional Native dancing and eagerly expropriated Native land, with or
without Native permission, whenever he thought Whites could put
it to better use.

Graham's great rival, and nemesis, was Duncan Campbell Scott.
Both men spent their entire working lives in the Indian Department,
Scott in Ottawa and Graham in the western provinces. About the
only thing the two men shared was a faith in the assimilationist trend
of government policy. Otherwise they circled each other warily, invariably touching off sparks when they came into contact. Graham,
ambitious and slightly paranoid, possessed the field worker's natural
conviction that headquarters did not understand the situation on the
ground. Quick to take offence, he believed that Scott was plotting
against him. "Mr. Graham cannot be written to as we would write
to other inspectors," admitted Scott, "but our directions must be expressed with as much care as if we were diplomatists addressing a
foreign power."[18] Unfortunately for Graham, Scott outranked him in
the department and would not be bullied into letting him get his own
way. On one occasion, when Graham let it be known he would resign
if he did not get more help in his office, Scott simply called his bluff.
"Mr. Graham is labouring under the delusion that he is indispens-
able," he wrote to a colleague. Graham remained in the service, but
his antipathy towards Scott increased over the years, culminating in
what he considered to be the conspiracy to deny him the position of
deputy superintendent of the Indian Department when Scott left it.

Perhaps what galled Graham the most was that while he yearned
for the top post, Scott, who held it, did not seem to take it seriously enough. "His work in the civil service interested him," recalled
Scott's friend E.K. Brown, "but the centre of his life was not in his
office, where he seldom came early, and never stayed late. After he retired his conversation did not run on the Indian department."[19] Away

from the office, the thin, austere poet presided over a wide-ranging cultural circle in Ottawa. He was a leading member of the drama league, the music society, and the poetry club, and secretary of the Royal Society. His renown as a writer far outstripped his reputation as a civil servant. At the same time as he was working his way up the bureaucratic ladder, he had managed to publish several books of poetry, a collection of stories, and a study of John Graves Simcoe, as well as co-editing a major series of twenty historical biographies *(The Makers of Canada)*. When the British poet Rupert Brooke passed through town in 1913, he visited Scott, calling him "the only poet in Canada." All this was a long way from day-to-day administration of the Indian Department.[20]

Nonetheless, Scott's position as the senior official in charge of Indian policy from 1913 to 1932 provided him with an important platform from which to project an image of the Official Indian. In speeches, articles, and appearances before parliamentary committees, he expressed views which clearly supported government initiatives. Scott believed that Canada had always carried out its obligations to its Native population. He acknowledged that contact between Natives and the earliest White settlers had created problems. But these were solved, he said, with the help of the missionary, the Mountie, and the Indian agent. When alcohol and disease threatened to destroy the aboriginals, wrote Scott, "the Government determined that the race should be saved."[21] As a result of intervention by the Indian Department, he explained, Native people received training in farming and stock raising and began to enter the mainstream of Canadian society. "The department has made these Indians self-supporting in two generations," Scott boasted: "a remarkable transition."[22] Some Natives still clung obstinately to the old ways, he admitted, but firm guidance and education at the residential schools were winning the fight to eradicate the last vestiges of "primitive" traditions. In a 1931 speech reprinted as a pamphlet, Scott concluded that "the Government will in time reach the end of its responsibility as the Indians progress into civilization and finally disappear as a separate and distinct people, not by race extinction but by gradual assimilation with their fellow citizens."[23]

The process of assimilation was not as benignly evolutionary as Scott liked to think it was. In retirement, he painted himself as a disinterested public servant carrying out official policy to the best of his ability. "I had for about twenty years oversight of their [the Indians] development and I was never unsympathetic to aboriginal ideals," he wrote E.K. Brown in 1941, "but there was the law which I did not originate and which I never tried to amend in the direction of severity."[24] Actually, Scott had a great deal of latitude when it came to enforcing regulations under the Indian Act and to recommending changes to the Act, and he often took "the direction of severity." For instance, no sooner was he put in charge of the Indian Department than he proposed changes to the Act which made it an offence punishable by imprisonment for an Indian to attend traditional ceremonies or to wear "aboriginal costume" in public shows or exhibitions. "The purpose of the amendment to the Act," he explained to R.B. Bennett, then a Calgary lawyer, "was to prevent the Indians from being exploited as a savage or semi-savage race, when the whole administrative force of the Department is endeavouring to civilize them ..."[25]

Two other incidents reveal Scott's active involvement in policy making. In 1920, it was his initiative that led to attempts to force Indians to give up their special legal status, whether or not they wanted to do so. Appearing before the parliamentary committee which was considering the appropriate amendment to the Act, Scott made his famous statement of the policy he was following as deputy superintendent: "Our object is to continue until there is not a single Indian in Canada that has not been absorbed into the body politic and there is no Indian question, and no Indian Department, that is the whole object of this Bill." [26] Scott attempted to stage-manage the committee hearings so that Native people who opposed the changes would not be heard. In the end the amendment passed but, because of Native opposition, compulsory enfranchisement was not carried out to any degree.

The second case related to the activities of Native political organizations. Scott hated these organizations, principally because they were not under the thumb of his department. He arranged for police spies to infiltrate their meetings. Then, in 1927, he concocted another amendment to the Indian Act which made it illegal for the Indians to hire lawyers or advisors to help them with their grievances. Scott claimed these counsellors were radical agitators, or unscrupulous troublemakers taking advantage of the Indians to line their own pockets. So Native people, at Scott's direction, were denied the right to employ legal and political help with their claims against the government. [27]

If this was all we knew of Scott, a patronizing bully, smugly confident of the superiority of White civilization, then we could pigeon-hole him as a dutiful, insensitive bureaucrat. But Scott also wrote poems about Indians, poems which were highly regarded in his day for their sympathetic understanding of Indian character, poems which reveal another set of attitudes and project a different image of the Indian. While in his official capacity he promoted the destruction of Native culture, as a poet he chose often to lament it.

In a general way, Scott's poems depict the reduction of the Indian from warrior to ward of the state. [28] They are filled with images of savagery, stoicism, and death. In "Watkwenies," an elderly woman recalls her long knife dripping with enemy blood and hears "the war cry of the triumphant Iroquois." In "The Forsaken," another Indian woman bites off a piece of her own flesh to bait a fish hook to feed her starving child, then later, when she is "old and useless" is abandoned by that same son to freeze to death. In "At Gull Lake: August, 1810," a jealous chieftain disfigures the face of one of his wives with hot coals. In Scott's Indian poems, the Natives are played out, doomed, "their vaunted prowess is all gone."

But Scott's poems also convey a kind of lurid respect for the Indians, for their wild independence, their dignity, their "savage past." Scenes of death and destruction are tinged with melancholy. Take, for example, "The Onondaga Maiden," published in 1898:

> She stands full-throated and with careless pose,
> This woman of a weird and waning race,
> The tragic savage lurking in her face,
> Where all her pagan passion burns and glows;
> Her blood is mingled with her ancient foes,
> And thrills with war and wildness in her veins;
> Her rebel lips are dabbled with the stains
> Of feuds and forays and her father's woes.

Or this image of a Plains chieftain from "Lines in Memory of Edmund Morris":

> Think of the death of Akoose, fleet of foot,
> Who, in his prime, a herd of antelope
> From sunrise, without rest, a hundred miles
> Drove through rank prairie, loping like a wolf,
> Tired them and slew them, ere the sun went down.

Scott's poems were not read by a wide enough public to have had much impact on the way Canadians thought about Native people. His work as a public servant was far more influential in that regard. What his poems illustrate, however, is the contradictory attitudes he, and so many of his compatriots, held towards Indians. On the one hand he denigrated their culture and endorsed policies intended to annihilate it. On the other hand, he lamented the passing of the "weird and waning race." Scott believed that, as noble and picturesque as they were historically, Indians were misfits in the modern world. For their own good they had to be dragged, kicking and screaming if necessary, into a new future. As E.K. Brown said of his friend: "The poet in him and the civil servant agreed in believing that the future of the Indians, if it were not to be extinction or degredation, depended on their being brought more and more nearly to the status of the white population." [29]

III

For many decades, government Indian policy was premised on an image of the Indian as inferior. Officials repeatedly described Indians as children. Like children, Indians could not be given full responsibility to make their own decisions about their own lives. This was what the Indian Act and the Indian Department were for. "I do not think we need waste any time in sympathy for the Indian," Arthur Meighen once told Parliament, "for I am pretty sure his interests will be looked after by the Commissioner." [30]

When children disobeyed, they had to be corrected. By the same logic, the life of the Indian was hedged around with hundreds of regulations, ranging from the serious to the petty, designed to win compliance with the government's assimilationist agenda. Most of the laws which robbed Native people of their independence were justified as measures taken to protect them from predatory Whites. In Western Canada, these laws served a secondary purpose of protecting Whites from a perceived Indian threat, especially in the mid-1880s, when the possibility of a Native uprising was taken seriously. At this time, while assimilation remained the long-term goal, pacification was the immediate objective.

Government policy encouraged the public to see Indians as incapable of occupying any but the lowest place in society. After all, children could not presume to take on the responsibilities of adults. "I have no hesitation in saying—we may as well be frank—that the Indian cannot go out from school, making his own way and compete with the white man," Clifford Sifton, the Liberal minister responsible for Indian affairs from 1896 to 1905, told Parliament. "He has not the physical, mental or moral get-up to enable him to compete. He cannot do it."[31] The logical conclusion to be drawn was that Native people were incapable of doing most jobs in society. The education provided at residential school was designed to prepare the Indian for work as a farmer or labourer. Duncan Scott boasted near the end of his career that, asked to describe a Canadian Indian, he could as easily mention a medical doctor as a "solitary hunter making the rounds of his traps in the remote north country."[32] But this was mere sophistry. Nothing in the system of Indian administration headed by Scott encouraged a young Native to aspire to a professional occupation.

Indians were considered unprogressive, wedded to a way of life which they stubbornly refused to abandon. When plans to transform Native people into successful farmers failed, which they did for a variety of reasons, not least because government policies almost guaranteed it, Canadians blamed the Indians themselves. It was part of the image of the Indian that he was by nature a hunter and a fighter, not a farmer. Conventional wisdom had it that the Indian was lazy, unstable, incapable of settling down to an orderly existence. "Restlessness was inherent in the Indian disposition," wrote George Stanley in his 1936 history, *The Birth of Western Canada*. "His dislike of uncongenial labour was proverbial."[33] A nomadic hunter by experience and inclination, the Indian was considered poor material for the plow and the punch clock. Conveniently ignored was the fact that many Native people were keen to take up agriculture but were thwarted by government

Hayter Reed, a senior official in the Indian Department, with a young companion, dressed for the Governor General's ball in Ottawa, 1896. Autocratic and intolerant, Reed was hated by Natives, who called him Iron Heart because for economic reasons he stopped rations to starving people. He was also the originator of the notorious pass system for western reserves. At the Ottawa ball, where he organized several guests to dress as Indians, he caused a sensation by delivering a speech to the Governor General "in the Indian language," with the poet Wilfred Campbell interpreting.

policies confining them to unsuitable land and restricting their use of modern farming methods.[34]

Most Canadians believed that Indians were capable of acquiring civilization. Of course there were exceptions—racists who believed in the indelible inferiority of aboriginals—but most people believed in the possibility of cultural evolution: that is, that Indians could "grow up" to attain a level of equality with their White co-citizens—not in one generation certainly, but within two or three. Education and exposure to White society would have their effect. "When the crisis is past, and the influences of the Christian religion have fully exerted their power," promised the missionary and Indian authority John Maclean, "and these have been accepted and experienced by the red men, the descendants of the ancient lords of Canada will become recognized as agents fitted for aiding in the development of the country, and giving unity to our race."[35] But not as long as they remained Indian. It was the *sine qua non* of government policy that Indians had to abandon their identity as Indians before they could become full Canadians. In other words, Indians had to be destroyed so they could be saved.

At the heart of government Indian policy lay a second paradox.[36] The stated aim of the policy was to assimilate Indians into the mainstream of Canadian society, but the means chosen to implement this policy was segregation. Native people were kept distinct and separate on their reserves, their behaviour closely controlled by a host of special laws and regulations. They received privileges which aroused White resentment while they were refused the most fundamental rights available to other Canadians. Interaction between White and Native was discouraged when it was not banned outright. Whites were encouraged to view Natives as different and inferior. And then, as the final insult, when the policy of assimilation did not work, Indians received the blame for it: they did not seem to be holding up their end of the "bargain." Non-Natives tended, at least implicitly, to view their relationship with Native people as a contract. In return for special status, the Indians were supposed to have agreed to abandon their Indianness. When the Indians did not appear to be following through on this agreement, non-Natives began to think that Natives were getting something for nothing, an opinion which persists to the present day. Officials concluded that Indians were by nature too ignorant, too indolent, too tradition-bound to make the leap into the modern world.

Naturally, policy makers thought they were doing the right thing. Assimilation seemed to them the only possible future for the Indian, and in order for assimilation to work, Indians had to be protected from all the negative aspects of White society which conspired to destroy them. The official mind held Native society to be totally unsuited to the modern world, which would rapidly wipe it out. Duncan Campbell Scott and his colleagues argued that government was the great benefactor of the Indian. Without the wise intervention of the Indian Department, the Indian would disappear entirely. It was for the Indians' own good that officials treated them like children, at least until they had acquired the skills and habits appropriate to modern society. Too bad if the Indians did not understand, but that could not be allowed to affect the assimilationist enterprise.

Assimilation continued to be a cornerstone of Canadian Indian policy for many years. As recently as 1969, it was the explicit objective of the Trudeau government's infamous White Paper, which proposed an end to Indian status, the abolition of the Department of Indian Affairs, and the repeal of the Indian Act. Indians were overnight to become citizens like any others. Trudeau himself believed firmly in treating everyone equally, and opposed the idea of special status for Natives within Canada as vehemently as he opposed it for Quebec within Confederation. "It's inconceivable I think that in a given society, one section of the society have a treaty with the other section of the society," he said in a famous speech in 1969. "We must all be equal under the laws and we must not sign treaties amongst ourselves ..."[37]

The uproar sparked by the White Paper went a long way towards finally discrediting assimilation as an acceptable foundation for Indian policy. Since that time, non-Natives have had to learn that Native people want to retain their distinctive identities, living in partnership with White society, equal but separate. Events since 1969 have transformed official Indian policy. But what have they done to the Imaginary Indian?

CHAPTER TEN

Guns and Feathers

THE LAST TWO DECADES have seen a revolution in public thinking about the Indian. Raised on *Howdy Doody* and *The Lone Ranger*, I have seen the Native peoples of the North defend their way of life against southern megaprojects which threaten their land. I have watched Elijah Harper change the constitutional direction of the country with a wave of his feather, and I have seen the tanks roll at Oka. It is a long way from Chief Thunderthud to the Mohawk Warriors.

In 1968, during the discussions leading up to his government's controversial White Paper on Indian policy, Prime Minister Pierre Trudeau wrote: "In terms of *realpolitik*, French and English are equal in Canada because each of these linguistic groups has the power to break the country. And this power cannot yet be claimed by the Iroquois, the Eskimos, or the Ukrainians."[1] In Canada, Trudeau was saying, political power depends on your ability to destroy the country: if you do not have that ability, you do not have real power. No one thought for a moment in 1968 that Native people had the ability, so why should they enjoy the power?

Now the country is twenty-five years older and we have learned how wrong we were. With the Meech Lake constitutional debacle, and the armed standoff at Oka, Native people proved that they, too, could break the country. If this is what it took—confrontation, roadblocks, constitutional impasse, threats of secession—Natives proved as adept at it as any White politician. The result? Now, suddenly, they enjoy unprecedented political power. Their representatives sit with the prime minister and the provincial premiers. Aboriginals are now recognized as one of the founding peoples of Canada. Constitutional talks are incomplete without Native people present.

All of this came about because Native people refused to live within the stereotypes White people fashioned for them. They would not disappear; they would not be obedient children and assimilate; they would not go away. But even as these events unfold before us, it is clear that our response to them, as non-Natives, is still conditioned by the image of the Imaginary Indian.

There is a simple test which people who study stereotyping like to perform. Ask a child to draw a picture of an Indian. Even though they can see Native people in ordinary clothes on the television news almost every night, youngsters invariably draw the Wild West Indian, in feathers and buckskin, usually holding a weapon. But then take the test yourself. When I did I discovered the first image that occurred to me was a photograph I remembered from the early 1970s of a young Ojibway man taking part in a roadblock at Kenora, Ontario, sitting on the hood of a car cradling a rifle. (Of course, for most of us this image was updated by the powerful photographs of Mohawks and soldiers confronting each other across the barricades at Oka.) And the second image that occurred to me was of Elijah Harper, seated at his desk in the Manitoba legislature, calmly twitching his eagle feather and bringing the process of constitutional change in the country to an abrupt halt. The warrior versus the wise elder; it turns out that the images of Indians we are offered today are not much different from what they have always been.

II

When two cultures meet, especially cultures as different as those of western Europe and indigenous North America, they inevitably interpret each other in terms of stereotypes. At its best, in a situation of equality, this might be seen as a phase in a longer process of familiarization. But if one side in the encounter enjoys advantages of wealth or power or technology, then it will usually try to impose its stereotypes on the other. This is what occurred in the case of the North American encounter between European and aboriginal. We have been living with the consequences ever since.

Over the years the Indian of stereotype, the Imaginary Indian, has had many identities. When the first Europeans arrived in New France, they held fairly positive opinions about the aboriginals they encountered, and upon whom they relied for protection. They admired aspects of Native character and society and they believed that Indians, while "primitive," had the capacity to become "civilized." As Native people showed antagonism to the ambitions of the colonizers, however, relations between the two groups deteriorated. Euro-Canadians began to demonize the Indian, especially the Iroquois. No longer were Indians noble savages extending the hand of friendship. Instead they became the ignoble savage, the wicked, bloodthirsty redskin of so many history books and cheap novels. In the mid-nineteenth century, this stereotype justified the pacification of the Plains Indians in preparation for the arrival of White settlers. In the nineteenth century as well, racial theories which described the Indian as biologically inferior became popular. Non-Natives argued that Indians were a deficient people condemned to disappear in the face of a superior civilization. Once Canada was settled from sea to sea, Indians were pushed to the margins of society and largely ignored.

Non-Native Canadians have tended to view Indians as the enemies of promise. In the White version of history, Indians stood in the way of Canada realizing its true potential. In colonial times they were a constant threat to the survival of White society, appearing suddenly out of the forest to pillage and slaughter defenceless settlers. Indians represented to the White imagination everything that was evil and alien about the new continent. They seemed to represent a threat to the "national dream" of a transcontinental nation. Once the dream became reality, Indians, no longer a threat, were characterized as a problem and marginalized on reserves. Non-Natives infantilized Indians, imagining them to be children incapable of taking on the responsibilities of the adult world and so condemned to a state of dependence. The solution was assimilation, an end to the Indian problem.

Our imaginings about the Indian have also gone to the other extreme. We have a long history of romanticizing Indians, discovering in their character and culture many fine qualities we think are lacking in our own. From the Noble Savage of years ago to the Mystic Shamans and Original Environmentalists of today, we continue to create idealized images of Indians which may have as little connection to reality as the demonic ones.

Our responses to Native peoples reveal more than racism, fear, and misunderstanding. It is more complicated than that. Our thinking about Indians relates to our thinking about ourselves as North Americans. Despite the stories we tell ourselves about "discovering" an empty continent, stories told mainly to console ourselves for getting here second, we have to admit that we were latecomers. Native people claim the land by virtue of it being their home. For Whites, the issue has been more problematic.

Sometimes we thought it was simply a matter of conquering the Indians, taking their territory, and absorbing them out of existence. Then America would be ours. Sometimes we thought just the opposite, that we had to become Indians in order to be at home here. This myth of transformation lies at the heart of Canadian culture: Canadians need to transform themselves into Indians. In this sense,

Grey Owl was the archetypal Canadian, shedding his European past and transforming himself into an Indian in order to connect through the wilderness with the New World. This is the impulse behind the appropriation by White society of so many aspects of Native culture, trivial as this cultural poaching often seems to be. It also explains the persistent desire by non-Natives to "play Indian," whether by dressing up in feathers and moccasins at summer camp, or by erecting another totem pole as a representative symbol of Canada, or by roaring an Indian chant from the bleachers at a baseball game. This behaviour, repeated over and over, reveals a profound need on the part of non-Natives to connect to North America by associating with one of its most durable symbols, the Imaginary Indian.

There is an ambivalence at the heart of our understanding of what Canadian civilization is all about. On the one hand, the national dream has always been about not being Indian. Since the days of the earliest colonists, non-Natives have struggled to impose their culture on the continent. Indians were always thought of as the Other, threatening to overwhelm this enterprise. Noble or ignoble, it didn't really matter. There was no place for the "savage" in the world the newcomers were building. Canadian history, as Stephen Leacock said, was the struggle of civilization against savagery. There was never any question on which side Indians stood.

On the other hand, as a study of the Imaginary Indian reveals, Euro-Canadian civilization has always had second thoughts. We have always been uncomfortable with our treatment of the Native peoples. But more than that, we have also suspected that we could never be at home in America because we were not Indians, not indigenous to the place. Newcomers did not often admit this anxiety, but Native people recognized it. "The white man does not understand the Indian for the reason he does not understand America," said the Sioux Chief Standing Bear. "The roots of the tree of his life have not yet grasped the rock and soil. The white man is still troubled with primitive fears; he still has in his consciousness the perils of this frontier continent ..."[2] As we have seen, one way non-Natives choose to resolve this anxiety is to somehow become Indian.

In the jargon of the day, Canadians are conflicted in their attitudes toward Indians. And we will continue to be so long as the Indian remains imaginary. Non-Native Canadians can hardly hope to work out a successful relationship with Native people who exist largely in fantasy. Chief Thunderthud did not prepare us to be equal partners with Native people. The fantasies we told ourselves about the Indian are not really adequate to the task of understanding the reality of Native people. The distance between the two, between fantasy and reality, is the distance between Indian and Native. It is also the distance non-Native Canadians must travel before we can come to terms with the Imaginary Indian, which means coming to terms with ourselves as North Americans.

AFTERWORD TO THE SECOND EDITION

In February 2010 British Columbia hosted the Olympic Winter Games at venues around Vancouver and at the mountain resort community of Whistler. Along with the sixteen days of sports competitions, the 21st Winter Olympiad turned out to be a gold mine for the student of the Imaginary Indian. Well before the events themselves got underway, the Organizing Committee unveiled the Games' mascots, which were supposedly based on "traditional First Nations creatures." These doll-like creations (which were, of course, reproduced as plush toys) included Miga, a sea bear which was part orca, part Kermode bear; Quatchi, an earmuff-wearing Sasquatch; and Sumi, a "guardian spirit" blending elements of an orca, a thunderbird, and a black bear. Even if Olympic mascots are intended primarily to engage and entertain children, this particular cuddly trio could not help but reveal one of the favourite stereotypes that Canadians have long held about Aboriginal people: that they enjoy a special, spiritual relationship to nature. Nor could the choice of mascots avoid reducing Aboriginal culture to an infantile parody of complex cultural ideas and practices.

Once they began, the Games provided an unprecedented opportunity for members of the four host First Nations—the Lil'wat, the Musqueam, the Squamish, and the Tsleil-Waututh—to showcase their cultures. For its part, the Olympic Organizing Committee went out of its way to include Aboriginals in key events. At the opening ceremonies, for example, First Nations participants featured prominently. One of the highlights of the show was the appearance of four welcome figures rising from the floor of the main stage (looking awfully phallic but everyone seemed to agree not to notice). The stage, which was decorated with Aboriginal designs, spilled over with Native people in traditional dress from across Canada who were given the honour of welcoming the parade of Olympic athletes into the stadium. The three-hour show was filled with First Nations iconography: legends, totem poles, shamans, feather headdresses, and so on. The noble and spiritual Indian was everywhere on display and a foreign observer might have been forgiven for thinking that Canadians still wore skin clothing and worshipped giant bears.

In their involvement of the First Nations in the planning and presentation of the Games, the Vancouver Winter Olympics suggest that much has changed in the presentation of the Imaginary Indian in the past twenty years. No one would dream nowadays of staging a large, national event like the Olympics without including Aboriginal people and likewise no one would dream of presenting them in contexts that were derogatory or which they did not approve. At the same time, the actual content of the images that emerged from the Games suggests that not so much has changed. Non-Aboriginals still seem to be most comfortable when they can infantilize and spiritualize Aboriginal people, treating them as historic figures of legend and myth rather than citizens of the twenty-first century.

*

In 1991, while I was writing *The Imaginary Indian*, the Canadian government announced the appointment of a Royal Commission on Aboriginal Peoples. As the commissioners themselves noted, their commission was created at "a time of anger and upheaval." The standoff at Oka, Quebec, was fresh in everyone's mind and roadblocks and protests were becoming almost an everyday occurrence across Canada.

In August 1995, while the Royal Commission worked on its report, a group of First Nations activists and sympathizers occupied a piece of land next to Gustafsen Lake in the interior of British Columbia, claiming it had spiritual significance and asserting ownership. This tense confrontation ended in gunfire and the arrest and conviction of several activists. Later that same summer an Ontario Provincial Police assault team swarmed a Native occupation at Ipperwash Provincial Park in southwestern Ontario, killing one man, Dudley George, and wounding two others.[1] (A member of the OPP would later be found guilty of criminal negligence in the death of George and a public inquiry traced responsibility for the ill-fated police raid all the way to the office of then-Premier Mike Harris.) The Royal Commission, then, became the government's response to this heightened sense of crisis in the country.

The Commission released its report in November 1996. Its fundamental conclusion was that the policy of assimilation that had guided government policy for generations was a mistake. There should be a new partnership between Aboriginal and non-Aboriginal, said the report, based on the recognition that Aboriginal peoples are nations. They were nations when they made alliances with the colonial powers, argued the Commission; they were nations when they signed treaties with the Canadian government; and they remain nations with a right to govern themselves as part of Canada. The Commission's report detailed a familiar litany of poverty and inequality. Infant mortality rates among Aboriginals were double the national rate. Life expectancy was lower, while the rates of suicide and infectious diseases were higher. Many reserve communities lacked clean drinking water and adequate housing. Half of all Aboriginal children lived in poverty. And so on. The answer, argued the Commission, was increased self-government. Aboriginals needed the freedom and resources to fashion their own institutions that would find their own solutions to the problems that plagued their communities. The refusal of the Canadian government to commit to this approach was "blocking the way forward."

The report of the Royal Commission was generally well received by the Aboriginal community and by liberal and left-wing opinion makers in the country. It was less well received by many people who had come to question what political scientist Tom Flanagan called "the aboriginal orthodoxy." In his book-length response to the Royal Commission's report, *First Nations? Second Thoughts* (2000), Flanagan argued that at the heart of this orthodoxy was the belief that separateness offered the best opportunity for Aboriginals to improve their lives. In his view, this idea, which had been endorsed by the Royal Commission, was profoundly misguided. What Aboriginals should aspire to, Flanagan wrote, was more involvement with Canadian institutions, not less. Years of living apart had done nothing but leave Canada's First Nations marginalized and impoverished. According to this argument, the challenges facing Aboriginals can best be met by unleashing market forces that require greater integration with mainstream Canadian society. "Call it assimilation, call it integration, call it adaptation, call it whatever you want," Flanagan concluded, "it has to happen."[2] Naturally enough, when Flanagan became a key advisor to the Canadian Alliance, later Conservative Party, Aboriginal leaders were concerned that Flanagan's views were shared by his boss, Stephen Harper, a future prime minister. And it wasn't just Aboriginal leaders. In an article in the October 2004 issue of *The Walrus* magazine, journalist Marci McDonald suggested that a coterie of right-wing academics from Calgary, to which Flanagan belonged, wanted to impose a rigidly conservative agenda on the country, including a rejection of Aboriginal rights. Deploying terms like "godfather" and "modern-day Rasputin" to describe Flanagan's influence, McDonald painted him as a dangerous, right-wing extremist (and a self-interested one who accepted healthy consulting fees from the government to refute Aboriginal treaty claims).

More recently Flanagan co-authored another book, *Beyond the Indian Act* (2010), in which he set out a plan to give First Nations people ownership of their own property so as to be able to participate more fully in the mainstream economy. This plea for "red capitalism" has been promoted by other commentators, notably in the pages of the *National Post* newspaper in a series of articles that appeared early in 2008. Titled "Rethinking the Reserve," the series included interviews with several experts, both Aboriginal and non-Aboriginal, who thought that First Nations must take steps to become independent of their traditional dependency on government. The series painted reserves as nests of patronage and mismanagement and traced their problems to a leadership that was using the millions of public dollars they received to enrich themselves, their friends, and their families. It also argued that the biggest obstacle to Aboriginal economic development was "the inability of First Nations to exercise real control over their land, free of government paternalism" and argued that Aboriginal people should be able to own their own land the same as other Canadians and be free of government restrictions so they could use the land as capital to kick-start Native economic recovery.[3] In other words, Aboriginals needed to get out from under the government paternalism that was stifling their development in myriad ways. In the process, it was assumed they would become more like other Canadians.

Tom Flanagan and the *National Post* were representative voices from the political right, but criticism of the Royal Commission was not confined to the right side of the spectrum. A pair of leftist scholars from Alberta, Frances Widdowson and Albert Howard, joined the debate in 2008 with a controversial book attacking what they called the "Aboriginal Industry." In *Disrobing the Aboriginal Industry*,

Widdowson and Howard claimed that a set of consultants, lawyers, academics, accountants, and do-gooders—some venal, some merely misguided—comprise an "industry" with a vested interest in obscuring the gap that exists between Aboriginals and the modern world and in keeping the former in a disadvantaged situation. Put bluntly, Widdowson and Howard argued that it is in the self-interest of the "industry" to prolong the problems it is supposed to be resolving. The two main initiatives promoted by the "Aboriginal Industry," said Widdowson and Howard, are land claims and self-government, and like Flanagan, they believed both are unlikely to solve the problems facing modern Aboriginal people. Once again, integration was presented as the best option for Aboriginal people, not the self-determination championed by the Royal Commission.

The critiques advanced by Flanagan and Widdowson and Howard are part of what might be called the New Assimilationism. Twenty years ago, when I wrote *The Imaginary Indian*, it seemed to me that very few people believed any more that assimilation was an acceptable answer to the problems facing Aboriginal people. The last time assimilation was formal government policy was on June 25, 1969 when Prime Minister Pierre Trudeau and his Indian Affairs minister Jean Chrétien presented their White Paper on Indian policy revealing their plans to dismantle the department of Indian affairs, repeal the Indian Act, and integrate Aboriginal people into mainstream Canadian society. The Indian would disappear, to be replaced by a modern Aboriginal with the same rights and responsibilities as any other citizen. But Indians did not want to disappear, as the outcry that greeted Trudeau's plan showed, and the government backed down. Yet it turns out that assimilation, which had been a mainstay of government policy since the country began, did not disappear either; it merely went underground and has re-emerged since in the works of Flanagan and others who believe that without further integration

Aboriginal people are condemned to remaining on the margins of Canadian society with all the poverty, dysfunction, and dependency that implies.

One of the main criticisms of Trudeau's White Paper was the manner in which he tried to implement it. He more or less sprang it on an unsuspecting Aboriginal population without any consultation. On the day Trudeau announced the White Paper in the House of Commons, Aboriginal leadership was as stunned as anyone else to learn the government's intention. Almost as much as the policy itself, it was the arrogance of the government that angered so many Aboriginals, fuelling the backlash against the White Paper and contributing to an invigoration of Aboriginal nationalism. The New Assimilationism suffers from the same arrogance. To be sure, a few Aboriginal leaders across the country have come out in support of the privatization of reserves and the overhaul of band government. But the views of the majority seem to be better expressed by the Royal Commission than by the New Assimilationists. After generations of struggling to preserve their cultures, their land, and their rights, it is not surprising that Aboriginal people are suspicious of the siren song of "integration," or "whatever you want to call it."

Despite the vigour of this debate between assimilation and self-government sparked by the Royal Commission on Aboriginal Peoples, it has been overshadowed by a more troubling issue: the residential schools. The federal government, which ran the schools in partnership with the Anglican, Catholic, Presbyterian, and United churches, began phasing them out in the 1960s, but the true horror of what went on in some of them only began to emerge with clarity in the 1980s. Many of the schools were incubators of disease, especially tuberculosis, where Native children basically went to die. At others, youngsters were abused sexually and psychologically. The whole enterprise, which was intended to prepare Aboriginal children for a life

in mainstream white society, has been labelled a form a cultural geno-
cide. The Royal Commission blamed the schools for the high rates of
suicide, substance abuse, and family dysfunction in Aboriginal communities. Individual staff members at different schools were charged
and convicted of gross indecency and sexual assault, revelations that
forced the churches formally to apologize for the role they played.
During the early 1990s the federal government resisted calls for a
public inquiry into the schools, even when one came from its own
Royal Commission, and refused to consider an apology or any sort of
compensation. But as the baneful legacy of the schools became better understood, pressure on the government intensified until January
1998 when Jane Stewart, then minister of Indian Affairs, presented
a "Statement of Reconciliation" in which she stated that "the Government of Canada acknowledges the role it played in the development and administration of these schools." The minister went on:
"To those of you who suffered this tragedy at residential schools, we
are deeply sorry."

The government's apology was by no means the end of the story.
In May 2006, after months of negotiation with Aboriginal groups,
the federal government announced the Indian Residential Schools
Settlement Agreement, which provided for cash payments to former
students, a new process for dealing with cases of abuse, a fund to support various commemorative projects, and the creation of a truth and
reconciliation commission intended to help all Canadians understand
the legacy of the schools. And then, in June 2008, Prime Minister
Stephen Harper apologized again. We now recognize, he told the
House of Commons, "that the consequences of the Indian residential schools policy were profoundly negative and that this policy has
had a lasting and damaging impact on aboriginal culture, heritage
and language." In his remarks, Harper explicitly stated that assimilation was "wrong ... and has no place in our country," seemingly

an endorsement for the Royal Commission's view that assimilation means not the salvation but the destruction of Aboriginal people.

The residential schools are a complex issue. Horrible things went on at the schools for which there can be no excuse. There is no reason to doubt that they precipitated a cycle of abuse that has beset Aboriginal communities ever since. At the same time, there were parents who wanted their children to attend the schools, and there are former students who attest to the value of the education they received. It is the purpose of the Truth and Reconciliation Commission to acknowledge the impact of the residential school experience and to find ways of dealing with its ongoing legacy. I hope the Commission will provide a way of understanding this terrible story that does not cast the Indian once again in the familiar and stereotypical role of passive victim.

*

Along with these political developments during the past twenty years, another important change has been the emergence of First Nations voices to speak for themselves. In 1992, when I concluded *The Imaginary Indian*, I wrote that the most effective way to transcend the stereotypes was to listen to what Aboriginal people themselves were saying rather than imposing our own ideas on them. At the time there were not many of these voices to listen to. Lee Maracle, Tomson Highway, Maria Campbell, and Jeannette Armstrong were some of the Canadian Aboriginal writers who had started to get published, but it was still fairly rare for Aboriginal people to write about their own experiences and have access to the media that could distribute them. That was left to sympathetic whites or Imaginary Indians such as Grey Owl. Today, by contrast, there are many writers and artists who are expressing, from the inside out, what it is to be Aboriginal and Canadian and their audience has widened considerably. This is not the place for a catalogue, but I am thinking of people like the Ojibway playwright and journalist Drew Hayden Taylor, Richard Wagamese, the Ojibway novelist, or Tom King, novelist, essayist, and originator of the slyly hilarious "Dead Dog Café Comedy Hour" ("Stay calm. Be brave. Wait for the signs.") that ran on CBC Radio from 1997 to 2000. In 2003 King became the first Aboriginal invited to give the annual Massey Lectures that are broadcast each year by CBC Radio, joining the likes of Jane Jacobs, Martin Luther King Jr., Willy Brandt, and Claude Lévi-Strauss on the roster of previous lecturers. All of these writers, and many others, speak from within the Native experience to tell the rest of us just how empty, insulting, laughable and dangerous the Imaginary Indian has been.

At the same time a number of young Aboriginal artists in Canada have received wide exposure. Unlike older artists who have worked within traditional styles such as Norval Morrisseau and the Wood-lands school or Bill Reid and Robert Davidson in British Columbia, younger Native artists are angrier, more political and more innovative. Take, for example, British Columbia's Lawrence Paul Yuxweluptun, who paints robotic, science fiction-like figures in brightly coloured landscapes inscribed with the formlines of the Northwest Coast style but blasted by the white man's industrial development. The Group of Seven are famous for erasing Aboriginals from their version of the Canadian wilderness. An artist like Yuxweluptun doesn't just re-establish the Aboriginal presence; he reclaims the wilderness itself and reconfigures it as homeland. His vision of the land is a far cry from the "Super, Natural British Columbia" of the government tour-ist brochure. As the critic Charlotte Townsend-Gault put it, "[Yux-weluptun] is painting not landscape but land claims."[4] "My home, my native land," Yuxweluptun has written. "Land is power, power is land. This is what I try to paint."[5] Another example is Brian Jungen, also from British Columbia. Less overtly political perhaps than Yuxweluptun, Jungen is an artist who takes objects from everyday life (plastic chairs, beer coolers, running shoes, food trays) and reconfigures them as objects that refer to aspects of Aboriginal culture. So that, for instance, a running shoe becomes a mask, patio furniture becomes the skeleton of a whale, a baseball bat becomes a carved totem figure. In Jungen's work, it is the objects of mainstream Canadian culture that have become exotic and are on display just like the artifacts of Native culture. Both these artists are playing with the images of the Imaginary Indian, exposing them, turning them on their head, revealing not just their vacuity but the harm they have done.

*

In 2007 Thomas King produced a short film titled "I'm Not the Indian You Had In Mind" in which he challenges many of the familiar stereotypes non-Aboriginals have had, and still have, about Aboriginal people. I presume the title of the film is based on an incident King recalled in his 2003 CBC Massey Lecture series, published as *The Truth About Stories*. As a young man, King, who was working on a tramp steamer bound for New Zealand, met a German cook who had been raised on the stories of Karl May, a late-nineteenth-century German novelist who wrote books about Indians, even though he had never seen one, and the American West, even though he had never been there. When King tells the cook that he himself is a North American Indian, the cook regards him sceptically and says, "You're not the Indian I had in mind."[6]

There is a bit of that German cook in every Canadian. We are raised on images of the Indian—romantic and negative—picked up from television and Hollywood movies. As a result, modern First Nations people are not the Indians we have in mind. The opening ceremony at the Winter Olympics suggests that these images still have a strong hold on us. At the same time, other voices, the voices of the

Aboriginal people themselves, are contesting the conventional narratives about Canada. They are rejecting their role as fantasy figures in the Canadian imagination. The Imaginary Indian survives, but he/she is becoming increasingly unrecognizable as Canadians are being educated by their Aboriginal fellow citizens to a new understanding of white-Aboriginal relations and therefore to a new understanding of the history of the country.

ENDNOTES

CHAPTER ONE: INTRODUCTION

1. Charles Mair, *Through the Mackenzie Basin* (Toronto: William Briggs, 1908), p. 54.
2. Robert F. Berkhofer, Jr., *The White Man's Indian: Images of the American Indian from Columbus to the Present* (New York: Random House, 1978), p. 3.
3. Reasons for Judgement, *Delgamuukw v. Her Majesty the Queen*, March 8,1991, p. 13.

CHAPTER TWO: THE VANISHING CANADIAN

1. Paul Kane, *Wanderings of an Artist* in J. Russell Harper, ed., *Paul Kane's Frontier* (Toronto: University of Toronto Press, 1971), p. 51.
2. Ibid., p. 59.
3. Ibid., p. 51.
4. Ibid., p. 14.
5. Ibid., p. 68.
6. Ibid., p. 74.
7. Ibid., p. 98.
8. Cited in ibid., p. 28.
9. Barry Lord, *The History of Painting in Canada* (Toronto: NC Press, 1974) p. 95.
10. Cited in Harper, p. 41.
11. John Maclean, *The Indians of Canada: Their Manners and Customs* (Toronto: William Briggs, 1889), p. 339.
12. The details of Verner's biography are from Joan Murray, *The Last Buffalo: The Story of Frederick Arthur Verner, Painter of the Canadian West* (Toronto: Pagurian Press, 1984).
13. A.Y. Jackson, *A Painter's Country* (Toronto: Clarke, Irwin and Co., 1958), p. 191.
14. Cited in Murray, p. 97.
15. Biographical details are from Jean S. McGill, *Edmund Morris, Frontier Artist* (Toronto: Dundurn Press, 1984).

16. Cited in McGill, p. 110.

17. Toronto *Globe*, 10 April 1909.

18. Cited in Geoffrey Simmins and Michael Parke-Taylor, *Edmund Morris: "Kyaiyii"* 1871-1913 (Regina: Norman Mackenzie Art Gallery, 1984), p. 51.

19. 21 July 1909, cited in Simmins and Parke-Taylor, p. 47.

20. These have been transcribed by Mary Fitz-Gibbon and published as *The Diaries of Edmund Montague Morris: Western Journeys* 1907–1910 (Toronto: Royal Ontario Museum, 1985).

21. Introduction to ibid., p. 6.

22. Simmins and Parke-Taylor, p. 10.

23. Ibid.

24. PAC, Emily Carr Papers, MG30 D215, vol. 10, "Lecture on Totems" April 1913, p. 52.

25. Ibid., p. 53.

26. Maria Tippett, *Emily Carr: A Biography* (Toronto: Oxford University Press, 1979), p. 29. Doris Shadbolt, *Emily Carr* (Vancouver: Douglas and McIntyre, 1990), p. 87; also useful is Paula Blanchard, *The Life of Emily Carr* (Vancouver: Douglas and McIntyre, 1987).

27. "Lecture on Totems," pp. 40–41.

28. Ottawa *Citizen*, 2 Dec. 1927.

29. Toronto *Daily Star*, 9 Jan. 1928.

30. Emily Carr, *Klee Wyck* (Toronto: Clarke, Irwin and Co., 1941), p. 19.

31. Cited in Brian W. Dippie, *The Vanishing American: White Attitudes and US Indian Policy* (Middletown, Conn.: Wesleyan University Press, 1982), p. 212-214.

32. Ibid., p. 209.

33. Christopher M. Lyman, *The Vanishing Race and Other Illusions* (New York: Pantheon Books, 1982), p. 113.

34. See Bill Holm and George Irving Quimby, *Edward S. Curtis in the Land of the War Canoes* (Vancouver: Douglas and McIntyre, 1980).

35. A.D. Coleman and T.C. McLuhan, *Portraits from North American Indian Life* (Toronto: newpress, 1972), p. vi.

36. Douglas Sladen, *On the Cars and Off* (London: Ward, Lock and Bowden Ltd., 1895).

37. Susan Sontag, *On Photography* (New York: Farrar, Straus & Giroux, 1977) p. 4.

CHAPTER THREE: WRITING OFF THE INDIAN

1. Earl of Southesk, *Saskatchewan and the Rocky Mountains* (Edmonton: Hurtig, 1969; first published 1873), pp. 28, 35, 154.
2. Ibid., p. 34.
3. Viscount Milton and W.B. Cheadle, *The North-West Passage by Land* (London: Cassell, Petter and Galpin, 1865), p. 9.
4. Ibid., p. 41.
5. William Francis Butler, *The Great Lone Land* (London: Sampson, Low, Marston, Low and Searle, 1872), pp. xv, 242.
6. Ibid., p. 243, 250
7. Ibid., p. 268.
8. George M. Grant, *Ocean to Ocean* (Edmonton: Hurtig, 1967; first published 1873), pp. 48, 93, 106, 178.
9. For a detailed analysis of the work of these three men, see Sarah Carter, "The Missionaries' Indian: The Publications of John McDougall, John Maclean and Egerton Ryerson Young," *Prairie Forum*, v. 9, n. i (Spring 1984), pp. 27-44.
10. John McDougall, *On Western Trails in the Early Seventies* (Toronto: William Briggs, 1911), p. 38.
11. Maclean, *Indians of Canada*, pp. 82, 322.
12. Egerton Ryerson Young, *By Canoe and Dog Train Among the Cree and Saulteaux Indians* (New York: Eaton and Mains, 1890), p. 78.
13. McDougall, *On Western Trails*, p. 25.
14. John McDougall, *Saddle, Sled and Snowshoe: Pioneering on the Saskatchewan in the Sixties* (Toronto: William Briggs, 1896), p. 252.
15. E.R. Young, *Stories from Indian Wigwams and Northern Campfires* (London: Charles H. Kelly, 1894), p. 38.
16. Stephen Leacock, *The Dawn of Canadian History* (Toronto: Glasgow, Brook and Co., 1921), p. 44.
17. Stephen Leacock, *Canada, The Foundation of its Future* (Montreal: The House of Seagram, 1941), p. 19.
18. Marius Barbeau, "Our Indians –Their Disappearance" *Queen's Quarterly* (1931), pp. 695, 701, 707.
19. Diamond Jenness, *The Indians of Canada* (Toronto: University of Toronto Press, 1977; first published 1932), pp. 261, 264.

CHAPTER FOUR: RED COATS AND REDSKINS

1. R.G. MacBeth, *Policing the Plains* (Toronto, 1931), p. 29.

2. The most important include Col. S.B. Steele, *Forty Years in Canada* (New York: Dodd, Mead and Co., 1915); Cecil Denny, *The Law Marches West* (Toronto: J.M. Dent and Sons Ltd., 1939); E.J. Chambers, *The Royal North-West Mounted Police: A Corps History* (Montreal: Mortimer Press, 1906); John G. Donkin, *Trooper and Redskin in the Far North-West* (London: Sampson Low, Marston, Searle and Rivington, 1889); and A.L. Haydon, *The Riders of the Plains: A Record of the Royal North-West Mounted Police of Canada, 1873-1910* (Toronto: Copp Clark Co., 1912).

3. Steele, pp. 53, 57-58.

4. MacBeth, p. 22.

5. Denny, p. 1.

6. Ibid., p. 2.

7. MacBeth, p. 43.

8. William F. Butler, *The Great Lone Land* (London: Sampson Low, Marston, Low and Searle, 1872), p. 200.

9. Haydon, p. 69.

10. MacBeth, p. 61.

11. Denny, p. 202.

12. Haydon, p. 156.

13. See, for example, John Tobias, "Canada's Subjugation of the Plains Cree, 1879-1885" in *The Canadian Historical Review* LXIV, 4 (Dec 1983): 519–548; Gerald Friesen, *The Canadian Prairies: A History* (Toronto: University of Toronto Press, 1984), p. 153.

14. Chambers, p. 77.

15. I am indebted to my friend David Lee, an historian with the Historic Parks Branch of Environment Canada, for sharing his research with me; W.A. Fraser, "Soldier Police of the Canadian Northwest," *The Canadian Magazine*, vol. xiv, no. 4 (Feb. 1900), pp. 362-374.

16. Chambers, p. 117-118; for a modern treatment of this incident see John Jennings, "The North West Mounted Police and Indian Policy after the 1885 Rebellion" in F. Laurie Barron and James B. Waldran, eds., *1885 and After* (Regina: Canadian Plains Research Centre, 1986), p. 232 ff.

17. MacBeth, p. 41.

18. Denny, p. 72.

19. Jennings, p. 228.

20. Chambers, p. 150.

21. MacBeth, p. 92.

22. Details of the Sitting Bull episode are in Grant MacEwen, *Sitting Bull: My Years in Canada* (Edmonton: Hurtig Publishers, 1973) and C. Frank Turner, *Across the Medicine Line* (Toronto: McClelland and Stewart, 1973).

23. MacBeth, p. 88.

24. Ibid., p. 66.

25. This version is in Haydon, p. 85.

26. Dick Harrison, *Unnamed Country: The Struggle for a Canadian Prairie Fiction* (Edmonton: University of Alberta Press, 1977), p. 156.

27. Cited in R.G. Moyles and Doug Owram, *Imperial Dreams and Colonial Realities: British Views of Canada* 1880–1914 (Toronto: University of Toronto Press, 1988), p. 45.

28. Ray Allen Billington, *Land of Savagery, Land of Promise: The European Image of the American Frontier in the Nineteenth Century* (New York: W.W. Norton and Co., 1981), p. 35 ff.

29. Charles Gordon, *Postscript to Adventure: The Autobiography of Ralph Connor* (Toronto: McClelland and Stewart, 1975), p. 148; first published 1938.

30. Ralph Connor, *Corporal Cameron of the North West Mounted Police* (Toronto: The Westminster Co. Ltd., 1912), p. 308.

31. Ibid., p. 382.

32. Ibid.

33. Ibid., p. 387.

34. Ralph Connor, *The Patrol of the Sun Dance Trail* (Toronto: The Westminster Co. Ltd., 1914), p. 12.

35. Ibid., p. 94.

36. Ibid., p. 193.

37. Ibid., p. 257.

38. Connor, *Postscript to Adventure*, p. 150.

39. Peter Morris, *Embattled Shadows: A History of Canadian Cinema, 1895-1939* (Montreal: McGill-Queen's University Press, 1978), pp. 110-112.

40. Pierre Berton, *Hollywood's Canada* (Toronto: McClelland and Stewart, 1975), p. 111.

41. Ibid., p. 126.

42. Ibid., p. 165.

43. MacBeth, p. 40.

CHAPTER FIVE: PERFORMING INDIANS

1. Toronto *Globe*, Aug. 22, 1885.

2. Ibid, Aug. 24, 1883.

3. Ibid.

4. Sarah J. Blackstone, *Buckskins, Bullets and Business: A History of Buffalo Bill's Wild West* (New York: Greenwood Press, 1986), p. 69.

5. Toronto *Globe*, op. cit.

6. Ibid.

7. This discussion of the wild west show depends on Blackstone; and Don Russell, *The Wild West or, A History of the Wild West Shows* (Fort Worth: Amon Carter Museum, 1970).

8. Toronto *Globe*, 24 Aug. 1885.

9. Ibid.

10. John C. Ewers, "The Emergence of the Plains Indian as the Symbol of the North American Indian," in Arlene B. Hirschfelder, ed., *American Indian Stereotypes in the World of Children* (Metuchen, N.J.: The Scarecrow Press, 1982), pp. 16-32.

11. Douglas Cole, *Captured Heritage: The Scramble for Northwest Coast Artifacts* (Vancouver: Douglas & McIntyre, 1985), p. 71.

12. Blackstone, p. 88.

13. John G. Neihardt, *Black Elk Speaks* (New York: William Morrow and Co., 1932), p. 219.

14. Calgary *Herald*, 1 July 1908.

15. Ibid.

16. Keith Regular, "On Public Display," *Alberta History*, vol. 34, no. 1 (Winter 1986), pp. 1–10.

17. E. Brian Titley, *A Narrow Vision: Duncan Campbell Scott and the Administration of Indian Affairs in Canada* (Vancouver: University of British Columbia Press, 1986), p. 172.

18. Sarah Carter, *Lost Harvest: Prairie Indian Reserve Farmers and Government Policy* (Montreal: McGill-Queen's University Press, 1990), p. 232.

19. Ibid., pp. 174-75.

20. Douglas Cole and Ira Chaikin, *An Iron Hand Upon The People* (Vancouver: Douglas and McIntyre, 1990), p. 133.

21. Titley, pp. 164-65.

22. For a detailed discussion, see Titley, pp. 162 ff.

23. Regular, p. 6.

24. James H. Gray, *A Brand of its Own: The 100 Year History of the Calgary Exhibition and Stampede* (Saskatoon: Western Producer Prairie Books, 1985), pp. 80-81.

25. Douglas Cole, *Captured Heritage*, p. 279.

CHAPTER SIX: CELEBRITY INDIANS AND PLASTIC SHAMANS

1. The story of *The Education of Little Tree* is in *The New York Times*, 4, 30 Oct. 1991.
2. This description is taken from Betty Keller's biography *Pauline: A Biography of Pauline Johnson* (Vancouver: Douglas and McIntyre, 1981), pp. 56-58, which is the source of most of the biographical material in this chapter.
3. Toronto *Globe*, 18 Jan. 1892.
4. Ibid., 20 Feb. 1892.
5. Cited in Keller, p. 71.
6. Ibid., p. 73.
7. Walter McRaye, *Town Hall Tonite* (Toronto: The Ryerson Press, 1929, p. 171.
8. E.T. Seton, "Introduction" to Pauline Johnson, *The Shagganappi* (Toronto: William Briggs, 1913), p. 7.
9. Mrs. W. Garland Foster, *The Mohawk Princess* (Vancouver: Lions' Gate Publishing Co., 1931), p. 63.
10. Cited in Keller, p. 72.
11. Seton, p. 6.
12. Ibid., p. 5.
13. Toronto *Globe*, 14 Oct. 1886.
14. Foster, p. 96.
15. Charles Mair, "Pauline Johnson: An Appreciation," *Canadian Magazine* (July 1913), p. 282.
16. *Globe*, 18 Jan. 1892.
17. Ibid., 22 May 1892.
18. Pauline Johnson, "A Pagan in St. Paul's Cathedral," *The Moccasin Maker* (Toronto: The Ryerson Press, 1913), p. 139.
19. Rayna Green, "The Pocahontas Perplex: the Image of Indian Women in American Culture," *The Massachusetts Review*, v. XVI, n. 4 (Autumn 1975).
20. *Globe*, 22 May 1892.
21. Chief Buffalo Child Long Lance, *Long Lance* (New York: Cosmopolitan Book Company, 1928), p. 7.
22. Ibid., pp. 277-78.
23. The details of Long Lance's life are from Donald B. Smith, *Long Lance: The True Story of an Imposter* (Toronto:Macmillan of Canada, 1982).
24. *Maclean's*, 15 May 1926.
25. Ibid., 15 Feb. 1923.
26. Ibid., 15 May 1926.
27. Toronto *Star*, 11 Dec. 1924.
28. For details of Grey Owl's life I have relied on Lovat Dickson, *Wilderness*

Man: The Strange Story of Grey Owl (Toronto: The Macmillan Co. of Canada, 1973), and Donald B. Smith, *From the Land of Shadows: The Making of Grey Owl* (Saskatoon: Western Producer Prairie Books, 1990).

29. May 22, 1932.

30. Cited in Dickson, p. 214.

31. Ibid., p. 5.

32. Ibid., p. 233.

33. Cited in Smith, p. 166.

34. Grey Owl, *Pilgrims of the Wild* (Toronto: Macmillan, 1934), p. 53.

35. Smith, p. 85.

36. Cited in ibid., p. 157.

37. Lovat Dickson, ed., *The Green Leaf: A Tribute to Grey Owl* (London: Lovat Dickson Ltd., 1938), p. 30.

38. Grey Owl, *Tales of an Empty Cabin* (Toronto: Macmillan, 1936), p. 326.

39. Ibid., p. vi.

40. Dickson, *The Wilderness Man*, p. 239.

41. Dickson, *The Green Leaf*, p. 68.

42. Cited in Smith, p. 164.

43. *Tales of An Empty Cabin*, p. 331.

44. *Globe and Mail*, 17 Oct. 1987.

45. Rudolf Kaiser, "'A Fifth Gospel, Almost': Chief Seattle's Speech(es): American Origins and European Reception," *Indians and Europe*, Christian F. Feest, ed. (Aachen: Edition Herodot, Raderverlag, 1987): pp. 505-526.

CHAPTER SEVEN: INDIANS OF CHILDHOOD

1. Ernest Thompson Seton, *Two Little Savages* (New York: Grosset and Dunlap, 1903), p. 10.

2. Julia M. Seton, *By a Thousand Fires* (New York: Doubleday, 1967), p. 245.

3. I have relied for biographical details on H. Allen Anderson, *The Chief: Ernest Thompson Seton and the Changing West* (College Station, Texas: Texas A&M University Press, 1986) and Betty Keller, *Black Wolf: The Life of Ernest Thompson Seton* (Vancouver: Douglas & McIntyre, 1984).

4. E.T. Seton and Julia M. Seton, *Gospel of the Redman* (Santa Fe, New Mexico: Seton Village, 1963), p. vi. Originally published in 1936 by Doubleday.

5. New York *Herald*, Nov. 22, 1912.

6. *Gospel of the Redman*, pp. xiv, 1, 26.

7. E.T. Seton, *The Birch-bark Roll of the Woodcraft Indians* (New York: Doubleday, Page and Co., 1906), p. 12.

8. Tim Jeal, *The Boy-Man: The Life of Lord Baden-Powell* (New York: William Morrow & Co., 1990), pp. 376–379.

9. Quoted in Anderson, p. 156.

10. Quoted in Keller, p. 177.

11. George Altmeyer, 'Three Ideas of Nature in Canada, 1893-1914," *Journal of Canadian Studies*, v. XI, n. 3 (August 1976), pp. 21–36. See also Douglas Cole, "Artists, Patrons and Public: An Enquiry into the Success of the Group of Seven," *Journal of Canadian Studies*, v. 13, n. 2 (Summer 1978): pp. 69–73.

12. Sandra Martin and Roger Hall, *Rupert Brooke in Canada* (Toronto: PMA Books, 1978), p. 120.

13. *The Birch-bark Roll*, p. i.

14. Quoted in Bruce W. Hodgins and Jamie Benidickson, *The Temagami Experience* (Toronto: University of Toronto Press, 1989), p. 114.

15. CA.M. Edwards, *Taylor Statten: A Biography* (Toronto: The Ryerson Press, 1960), p. 88.

16. Ibid., p. 97.

17. *Gospel*, pp. 103, 107.

18. John Coldwell Adams, *Sir Charles God Damn: The Life of Sir Charles G.D. Roberts* (Toronto: University of Toronto Press, 1986), p. 60.

19. Kenneth Windsor, "Historical Writing in Canada (to 1920)" in Carl F. Klinck, *Literary History of Canada* (Toronto: University of Toronto Press, 1965), p. 220.

20. W.H.P. Clement, *The History of the Dominion of Canada* (Toronto: William Briggs, 1897), p. 13.

21. Ibid., p. 138.

22. Charles G.D. Roberts, *A History of Canada for High Schools and Academies* (Toronto: Macmillan of Canada, 1897).

23. Henry H. Miles, *The Child's History of Canada* (Montreal: William Dawson, ninth edition, [1870] 1910), p. 22.

24. Stephen Leacock, *Canada, The Foundation of its Future* (Montreal: The House of Seagram, 1941), p. 69.

25. James W. St.G. Walker, "The Indian in Canadian Historical Writing" in Canadian Historical Association *Papers*, 1971, p. 36.

26. E.L. Marsh, *Where the Buffalo Roamed* (Toronto: The Macmillan Co. of Canada, 1923), p. 2.

27. J.N. Mcllwraith, *The Children's Study of Canada* (London: Fisher Unwin, 1899), p. 6.

28. Agnes Laut, *Canada: The Empire of the North* (Toronto: William Briggs, 1909), p. 171.

29. Ibid., p. 96.

30. Donald B. Smith, *Le Sauvage: The Native People in Quebec historical writing on the Heroic Period (1534–1663)* (Ottawa: National Museum of Man, Mercury Series, 1974).

31. Windsor, "Historical Writing," p. 232.

32. Biographical details are from Mason Wade, *Francis Parkman: Heroic Historian* (New York: Viking Press, [1942] 1972).

33. Parkman's views of the Indian are summarized in Francis Parkman, *The Jesuits in North America* (Boston: Little Brown & Co., 1963), pp. 3–87. Originally published 1867.

34. Bruce Trigger, "The Historians' Indian: Native Americans in Canadian Historical Writing from Charlevoix to the Present," *Canadian Historical Review*, LXVII, 3 (Sept. 1986), pp. 316–321.

CHAPTER EIGHT: MARKETING THE IMAGINARY INDIAN

1. Donald B. Smith, *Long Lance: The True Story of an Imposter* (Toronto: Macmillan, 1982), pp. 180–181.

2. I am grateful to my friend Jim Taylor for this reference.

3. Quoted in Deborah Doxtator, *Fluffs and Feathers: An Exhibit on the Symbols of Indianness* (Brantford: Woodland Cultural Centre, 1988), p. 46.

4. E.J. Hart, *The Selling of Canada* (Banff: Altitude Publishing, 1983), p. l2 ff.

5. Cited in ibid., p. 23.

6. T.C. McLuhan, *Dream Tracks: The Railroad and the American Indian, 1890-1930* (New York: Harry N. Abrams Inc., 1985).

7. Margery Tanner Hadley, "Photography, Tourism and the CPR," L'A. Rosenvall and S.M. Evans, eds., *Essays on the Historical Geography of the Canadian West* (Calgary: University of Calgary Press, 1987), p. 58.

8. Douglas Sladen, *On the Cars and Off* (London: Ward, Lock and Bowden Ltd., 1895).

9. Ibid., p. 306.

10. Hart, p. 59.

11. Leslie Monkman, *A Native Heritage* (Toronto: University of Toronto Press, 1981), p. 129.

12. Edward Roper, *By Track and Trail: A Journey Through Canada* (London: W.H. Allen and Co., 1891), pp. 118, 120.

13. Ibid., pp. 118, 244

14. This discussion was based on David Darling and Douglas Cole, "Totem

Pole Restoration on the Skeena, 1925–30," *BC Studies*, n. 47 (Autumn 1980), pp. 29–48.

15. A.Y. Jackson, *A Painter's Country* (Toronto: Clarke, Irwin and Co., 1958), p. 111.

16. Dennis Reid, *Edwin Holgate* (Ottawa: National Gallery of Canada, 1976), pp. 14–15.

17. John C. Goodfellow, *The Totem Poles in Stanley Park* (Vancouver: Art, Historical and Scientific Association of Vancouver, n.d.).

18. Hilary Stewart, *Totem Poles* (Vancouver: Douglas and McIntyre, 1990).

19. "The Sophisticated Traveller," *The New York Times Magazine*, part 2 (May 17,1992), pp. 2-3.

20. Vine Deloria, "American Fantasy," forward to Gretchen M. Bataille and Charles L.P. Silet, eds., *The Pretend Indians: Images of Native Americans in the Movies* (Ames, Iowa: Iowa State University Press, 1980), p. x.

PART FOUR: IMPLEMENTING THE IMAGE

1. The story of the Mound Builders is in Robert Silverberg, *Mound Builders of Ancient America: The Archaeology of a Myth* (Greenwich, Conn.: New York Graphic Society Ltd., 1968).

CHAPTER NINE: THE BUREAUCRAT'S INDIAN

1. Pelham Edgar, *Across My Path* (Toronto: The Ryerson Press, 1952), p. 59.

2. Ibid., p. 65.

3. "The Fragment of a Letter" in Raymond Souster and Douglas Lochhead, eds., *Powassan's Drum: Poems of Duncan Campbell Scott* (Ottawa: Tecumseh Press, 1985), p. 177.

4. The treaty is discussed in James Morrison, *Treaty Nine* (1905-06): *The James Bay Treaty* (Ottawa: Treaties and Historical Research Branch, Indian and Northern Affairs Canada, 1986); and James Morrison, "The Poet and the Indians," *The Beaver* (Aug.–Sept., 1988), pp. 4–16.

5. Edgar, pp. 59, 63.

6. Jean S. McGill, *Edmund Morris, Frontier Artist* (Toronto: Dundurn Press, 1984), p. 64.

7. Duncan Campbell Scott, "The Last of the Indian Treaties" in *The Circle of Affection* (Toronto: McClelland and Stewart, 1947), pp. 109–122. (Originally published *Scribners Magazine*, Dec. 1906.)

8. Cited in J.R. Miller, *Skyscrapers Hide the Heavens: A History of Indian-White Relations in Canada* (Toronto: University of Toronto Press, 1989), p. 100.

9. For a discussion of the Indian Act and its predecessors, see John Leslie

and Ron Maguire, eds., *The Historical Development of the Indian Act* (Ottawa: Treaties and Historical Research Branch, 1979); John L. Tobias, "Protection, Civilization, Assimilation: An Outline History of Canada's Indian Policy," Ian A.L. Getty and Antoine S. Lussier, eds., *As Long As the Sun Shines and Water Flows: A Reader in Canadian Native Studies* (Vancouver: University of British Columbia Press, 1983), pp. 38–55; John S. Milloy, "The Early Indian Acts," Getty and Lussier, pp. 56–64; and Miller, *Skyscrapers*, pp. 109–115.

10. Miller, p. 190.

11. House of Commons Debates, 1918, vol.11, 23 April, p. 1049.

12. Cited in E. Brian Titley, *A Narrow Vision: Duncan Campbell Scott and the Administration of Indian Affairs in Canada* (Vancouver: UBC Press, 1986), p. 19.

13. Brian W. Dippie, *The Vanishing American: White Attitudes and U.S. Indian Policy* (Middletown, Conn.: Wesleyan University Press, 1982), p. 61.

14. For the File Hills colony, see Sarah Carter, "Demonstrating Success: The File Hills Colony," *Prairie Forum* (Fall 1991), pp. 157-183; and E. Brian Titley," W.M. Graham: Indian Agent Extraordinaire," *Prairie Forum*, vol. 8, no. 1 (1983), pp. 25–41.

15. Cited in Titley, "W.M. Graham," p. 28.

16. Sarah Carter, *Lost Harvests: Prairie Indian Reserve Farmers and Government Policy* (Montreal: McGill-Queen's University Press, 1990), p. 244 ff.

17. *Manitoba Tree Press*, 1 Jan. 1921.

18. Cited in Titley, *A Narrow Vision*, p. 186.

19. E.K. Brown, "Duncan Campbell Scott: A Memoir," David Staines, ed., *Responses and Evaluations: Essays on Canada* (Toronto: McClelland and Stewart, 1977), p. 134.

20. For Scott's literary career, see Titley, *A Narrow Vision*, pp. 23-36; Robert L. McDougall, ed., *The Poet and the Critic: A Literary Correspondence Between D.C. Scott and E.K. Brown* (Ottawa: Carleton University Press, 1983); and Sandra Gwyn, *The Private Capital* (Toronto: McClelland and Stewart, 1984), pp. 436-466.

21. Duncan Campbell Scott, *The Administration of Indian Affairs in Canada* (Ottawa: The Canadian Institute of International Affairs, 1931), p. 2.

22. Ibid., p. 10.

23. Ibid., p. 27; see also Duncan Campbell Scott, "Indian Affairs, 1867-1912," Adam Shortt and Arthur G. Doughty, eds., *Canada and Its Provinces*, vol. 7 (Toronto: T.& A. Constable, 1913), pp. 593-626.

24. McDougall, *The Poet and the Critic*, p. 26.

25. Cited in Titley, *A Narrow Vision*, p. 176.
26. Cited in John L. Taylor, *Canadian Indian Policy During the Inter-War Years*, 1918-1939 (Ottawa: Treaties and Historical Research Branch, 1984), p. 147.
27. Ibid., p. 181.
28. All citations are from Glen Clever, ed., *Selected Poetry of Duncan Campbell Scott* (Ottawa: The Tecumseh Press, 1974).
29. Cited in E. Palmer Patterson, "The Poet and the Indian: Indian Themes in the Poetry of Duncan Campbell Scott and John Collier," *Ontario History*, vol. LIX (1967), p. 73.
30. Cited in Titley, *A Narrow Vision*, p. 41.
31. David J. Hall, "Clifford Sifton and Canadian Indian Administration 1896-1905," Ian A.L. Getty and Antoine Lussier, eds., *As Long as the Sun Shines and Water Flows*, p. 126.
32. Scott, *The Administration of Indian Affairs*, p. 25.
33. George F.G. Stanley, *The Birth of Western Canada*, 1936. 2nd ed. (Toronto: University of Toronto Press, 1961), p. 239.
34. Sarah Carter, "Two Acres and a Cow: 'Peasant' Farming for the Indians of the Northwest, 1889-97," *Canadian Historical Review*, LXX, 1 (March 1989), p. 28; see also her excellent *Lost Harvests: Prairie Indian Reserve Farmers and Government Policy*.
35. John Maclean, *The Indians of Canada* (Toronto: William Briggs, 1889), p. 135.
36. Tobias, "Protection, Civilization, Assimilation," p. 42.
37. Cited in Sally Weaver, *Making Canadian Indian Policy: The Hidden Agenda*, 1968-70 (Toronto: University of Toronto Press, 1981), p. 179.

CHAPTER TEN: GUNS AND FEATHERS

1. Weaver, *Making Canadian Indian Policy*, p. 55.
2. Cited in Drinnon, *Facing West*, p. 230.

AFTERWORD TO THE SECOND EDITION

1. See Peter Edwards, *One Dead Indian: The Premier, the Police, and the Ipperwash Crisis* (Toronto: Stoddart Publishing, 2001).
2. Tom Flanagan, *First Nations? Second Thoughts* (Montreal: McGill-Queen's University Press, 2000; second edition 2008), p. 196.
3. *National Post*, Feb. 14, 2008.
4. Charlotte Townsend-Gault, Scott Watson, and Lawrence Paul

Yuxweluptun, eds. *Lawrence Paul Yuxweluptun: Born to Live and Die on Your Colonialist Reservations* (Catalogue for an exhibition at the Morris and Helen Belkin Art Gallery, University of British Columbia, June 20–Sept. 16, 1995, Vancouver, BC), p. 7.

5. Ibid., p. 1.

6. Thomas King, *The Truth About Stories* (Toronto: House of Anansi, 2003), p.48.

PHOTO CREDITS

p. 65 Reproduced with permission of Library and Archives Canada, Ottawa, Ontario (C37113).

p. 86 Reproduced with permission of Library and Archives Canada, Ottawa, Ontario (C66055).

p. 106 Reproduced with permission of the Buffalo Bill Historical Centre, Cody, Wyoming; Gift of The Coe Foundation (1.69.108).

p. 112 Reproduced with permission of the Glenbow Archives, Calgary, Alberta (NA 1473-16).

p. 115 Reproduced with permission of the Glenbow Archives, Calgary, Alberta (NA 274-6).

p. 121 Wikipedia Commons. http://en.wikipedia.org/wiki/File:RCA_Indian_Head_test_pattern.JPG

p. 127 Reproduced with permission of the Brant Historical Society, Brantford, Ontario (S635/946.10.48).

p. 127 Reproduced with permission of the Vancouver Public Library, Vancouver, B.C. (9429).

p. 133 Reproduced with permission of the Toronto Public Library, Toronto, Ontario (CSM S. Solman, Alfred. Ontario. 1906).

p. 141 Reproduced with permission of the Glenbow Archives, Calgary, Alberta (NA 177-1).

p. 146 Reproduced with permission of the City of Toronto Archives, Toronto, Ontario (Fonds 1266, Item 41837).

p. 147 Reproduced with permission of Library and Archives Canada, Ottawa, Ontario (PA 147585).

p. 150 Reproduced with permission of the Archives of Ontario, Toronto, Ontario (ACC 9164 S 14482).

p. 160 Reproduced with permission of Library and Archives Canada, Ottawa, Ontario (PA 185770).

p. 165 Reproduced by kind permission of The Scout Association Trustees, London, England.

p. 169 Reproduced with permission of Ontario Camping Association Papers, Trent University Archives, Peterborough, Ontario (72-007/1/3).

p. 174 Reproduced with permission of Library and Archives Canada, Ottawa, Ontario (C3165).

p. 177 Reproduced with permission of Rare Books and Special Collections, McGill University Library, Montreal, Quebec (Lande 2136).

p. 185 Reproduced with permission of the Toronto Public Library, Toronto, Ontario. (CSM B. Bell, Nelson H. Pontiac. c1927. Copyright by Pontiac Division of General Motors Products of Canada Limited, Oshawa).

p. 189 Reproduced with permission of the Whyte Museum of the Canadian Rockies, Banff, Alberta (V469).

p. 192 Reproduced with permission of the Glenbow Archives, Calgary, Alberta (NA 4035-87).

p. 194 Reproduced with permission of the Whyte Museum of the Canadian Rockies, Banff, Alberta (M20).

p. 194 Reproduced with permission of the Whyte Museum of the Canadian Rockies, Banff, Alberta.

p. 195 Reproduced with permission of the Whyte Museum of the Canadian Rockies, Banff, Alberta.

p. 197 Reproduced with permission of the George Eastman House, Motion Picture Department Collection, Rochester, N.Y. (42464).

p. 200 Reproduced with permission of the Queen's University Archives, Kingston, Ontario (Box 3 File 73 Coll. 2036).

p. 210 Reproduced with permission of Library and Archives Canada, Ottawa, Ontario (PA 59516).

p. 215 Reproduced with permission of the Toronto Public Library, Toronto, Ontario (1914–18. Patriotic Fund. Item 1).

p. 218 Reproduced with permission of the Saskatchewan Archives Board, Regina, Sask. (R-A21-1).

p. 220 Reproduced with permission of the Glenbow Archives, Calgary, Alberta (NA 3454-36).

p. 229 Reproduced with permission of Library and Archives Canada, Ottawa, Ontario (PA 139841).

SOURCES CONSULTED

Adams, Howard. *Prison of Grass: Canada from the Native Point of View*. Toronto: New Press, 1975.

Adams, John Coldwell. *Sir Charles God Damn: The Life of Sir Charles G.D. Roberts*. Toronto: University of Toronto Press, 1986.

Altmeyer, George. "Three Ideas of Nature in Canada, 1893–1914." *Journal of Canadian Studies*, v. XI, n. 3 (August 1976): 21–36.

Anderson, H. Allen. *The Chief Ernest Thompson Seton and the Changing West*. College Station, Texas: Texas A&M University Press, 1986.

Atwood, Margaret. *Survival*. Toronto: Anansi, 1972.

Barbeau, Marius. "Our Indians—Their Disappearance." *Queen's Quarterly* (1931): 691–707.

Barron, F. Laurie. "The Indian Pass System in the Canadian West, 1882–1935." *Prairie Forum*, v. 13, n. i (Spring 1988): 25–42.

Barron, F. Laurie and James B. Waldran, eds. *1885 and After*. Regina: Canadian Plains Research Centre, 1986.

Bataille, Gretchen M. and Charles L.P. Silet. *The Pretend Indians: Images of Native Americans in the Movies*. Ames, Iowa: Iowa State University Press, 1980. With a forward by Vine Deloria.

Berkhofer, Robert F. Jr. *The White Man's Indian*. New York: Random House, 1979.

Berton, Pierre. *Hollywood's Canada*. Toronto: McClelland and Stewart, 1975.

Billington, Ray Allen. *Land of Savagery, Land of Promise: The European Image of the American Frontier in the Nineteenth Century*. New York: W.W. Norton and Co., 1981.

Blackstone, Sarah J. *Buckskins, Bullets and Business: A History of Buffalo Bill's Wild West*. New York: Greenwood Press, 1986.

Blanchard, David. "For Your Entertainment Pleasure – Princess White Deer and Chief Running Deer – Last 'Hereditary' Chief of the Mohawk: Northern Mohawk Rodeos and Showmanship." *Journal of Canadian Culture*, v. I, n. 2 (Fall 1984).

Blanchard, Paula. *The Life of Emily Carr.* Vancouver: Douglas and McIntyre, 1987.

Brown, E.K. *Responses and Evaluations: Essays on Canada.* David Staines, ed. Toronto: McClelland and Stewart, 1977.

Brown, Jennifer S.H. "Mission Indian Progress and Dependency: Ambiguous Images from Canadian Methodist Lantern Slides." *Arctic Anthropology* v. 18, n. 2 (1981): 17–27.

Bryce, George. *A Short History of the Canadian People*, rev. ed. Toronto: The Ryerson Press, 1915. 1st ed. 1887.

Butler, William Francis. *The Great Lone Land.* 1872. Reprint. Edmonton: M.G. Hurtig, 1968.

Caine, W.S. *A Trip Round the World in* 1887–8. London: George Routledge and Sons, Ltd., 1892.

Carr, Emily. *Klee Wyck.* Toronto: Irwin Publishing, 1941.

———. "Lecture on Totems"April 1913. Emily Carr Papers. MG 30 D215, v. 10. Public Archives of Canada, Ottawa.

Carter, Sarah. "Demonstrating Success: The File Hills Farm Colony." *Prairie Forum* (Fall 1991): 157–183.

———. *Lost Harvests: Prairie Indian Reserve Farmers and Government Policy.* Montreal: McGill-Queen's University Press, 1990.

———. "The Missionaries' Indian: The Publications of John McDougall, John Maclean and Egerton Ryerson Young." *Prairie Forum*, v. 9, n. i (Spring 1984): 27–44.

———. "Two Acres and a Cow: 'Peasant' Farming for the Indians of the Northwest, 1889–97." *Canadian Historical Review*, v. LXX, n. i: 27–52.

Chamberlin, J.E. *The Harrowing of Eden.* New York: The Seabury Press, 1975.

Chambers, Capt. Ernest J. *The Royal North-West Mounted Police: A Corps History.* Montreal: Mortimer Press, 1906.

Churchill, Ward. *Fantasies of the Master Race: Literature, Cinema and the Colonization of American Indians*, M. Annette Jaimes, ed. Monroe, Maine: Common Courage Press, 1992.

Clement, W.H.P. *The History of the Dominion of Canada.* Toronto: William Briggs, 1897.

Clever, Glen, ed. *Selected Poetry of Duncan Campbell Scott.* Ottawa: The Tecumseh Press, 1974.

Cole, Douglas. "Artists, Patrons and Public: An Enquiry into the Success of the Group of Seven." *Journal of Canadian Studies*, v. 13, n. 2 (Summer 1978): 69-78.

——. *Captured Heritage: The Scramble for Northwest Coast Artifacts.* Vancouver: Douglas and McIntyre, 1985.

Cole, Douglas and Ira Chaikin. *An Iron Hand Upon the People.* Vancouver: Douglas and McIntyre, 1990.

Coleman, A.D. and T.C. McLuhan. *Portraits from North American Indian Life.* Toronto: newpress, 1972.

Connor, Ralph. *Corporal Cameron of the North West Mounted Police.* Toronto: The Westminster Co. Ltd., 1912.

——. *Postscript to Adventure.* Toronto: McClelland and Stewart, 1975.

——. *The Patrol of the Sun Dance Trail.* Toronto: The Westminster Co. Ltd., 1914.

Darling, David and Douglas Cole. "Totem Pole Restoration on the Skeena, 1925–30: An Early Exercise in Heritage Conservation." *BC Studies,* n. 47 (Autumn 1980): 29–48.

Denny, Sir Cecil. *The Law Marches West.* Toronto: J.M. Dent and Sons Ltd., 1939.

Dickson, Lovat. *The Green Leaf: A Tribute to Grey Owl.* London: Lovat Dickson Ltd., 1938.

——. *Wilderness Man, The Strange Story of Grey Owl.* Toronto: The Macmillan Co. of Canada, 1973.

Dippie, Brian W. *The Vanishing American: White Attitudes and US Indian Policy.* Middleton, Conn.: Wesleyan University Press, 1982.

Donkin, John G. *Trooper and Redskin in the Far North-West.* London: Sampson, Low, Marston, Searle and Rivington, 1889.

Doughty, Howard. *Francis Parkman.* New York: The Macmillan Co., 1962.

Doxtator, Deborah. *Fluffs and Feathers: An Exhibit on the Symbols of Indianness.* Brantford, Ont.: Woodland Cultural Centre, 1988.

Drinnon, Richard. *Facing West: The Metaphysics of Indian Hating and Empire Building.* Minneapolis: University of Minnesota Press, 1980.

Edgar, Pelham. *Across My Path.* Toronto: The Ryerson Press, 1952.

Edwards, C.A.M. *Taylor Statten: A Biography.* Toronto: The Ryerson Press, 1960.

Ewers, John C. "The Emergence of the Plains Indian as the Symbol of the North American Indian." In *American Indian Stereotypes in the World of Children,* Arlene B. Hirschfelder, ed. Metuchen, N.J.: The Scarecrow Press, 1982.

Foster, Mrs. W. Garland. *The Mohawk Princess.* Vancouver: Lions' Gate Publishing Co., 1931.

Fraser, W.A. "Soldier Police of the Canadian Northwest." *The Canadian Magazine*, v. XIV, n. 4 (Feb. 1900): 362–374.

Friar, Ralph and Natasha Friar. *The Only Good Indian: The Hollywood Gospel.* New York: Drama Book Specialists, 1972.

Friesen, Gerald. *The Canadian Prairies: A History.* Toronto: University of Toronto Press, 1984.

Getty, Ian A.L. and Antoine S. Lussier, eds. *As Long as the Sun Shines and Water Flows: A Reader in Canadian Native Studies.* Vancouver: UBC Press, 1983.

Godsell, Philip H. *Red Hunters of the Snows.* Toronto: The Ryerson Press, 1938.

Goldie, Terry. *Fear and Temptation: The Image of the Indigene in Canadian, Australian and New Zealand Literature.* Montreal: McGill-Queen's University Press, 1989.

Goodfellow, Rev. John C. *The Totem Poles in Stanley Park.* Vancouver: Art, Historical and Scientific Association of Vancouver, [1925].

Grant, George M. *Ocean to Ocean.* 1873. Reprint. Edmonton: M.G. Hurtig, 1967.

Gray, James H. *A Brand of its Own: The 100 Year History of the Calgary Exhibition and Stampede.* Saskatoon: Western Producer Prairie Books, 1985.

Green, Rayna. :The Pocahontas Perplex: The Image of Indian Women in American Culture." *The Massachusetts Review*, v. XVI, n. 4 (Autumn, 1973): 698–714.

Gresko, Jacqueline. "White Rites and Indian Rites: Indian Education and Native Responses in the West, 1870-1910." In *Western Canada Past and Present*, A.W. Rasporich, ed. Calgary: McClelland and Stewart, 1975.

Grey Owl [Archie Belaney]. *Pilgrims of the Wild.* Toronto: Macmillan, 1934.

——. *Tales of an Empty Cabin.* New York: Dodd, Mead and Co., 1936.

Gunn, S.W.A. *Totem Poles in Stanley Park.* Vancouver: W.E.G. MacDonald, 1965.

Gwynn, Sandra. *The Private Capital: Ambition and Love in the Age of Macdonald and Laurier.* Toronto: McClelland and Stewart, 1984.

Hadley, Margery Tanner. "Photography, Tourism and the CPR: Western Canada 1884-1914." In *Essays on the Historical Geography of the Canadian West*, L.A. Rosenvall and S.M. Evans, eds. Calgary: University of Calgary, 1987.

Harper, J. Russell. *Paul Kane's Frontier.* Toronto: University of Toronto Press, 1971.

Harrison, Dick. "Mountie Fiction: A Reader's Guide." *RCMP Quarterly* (Sept. 1975): 39–46.

——. *Unnamed Country: The Struggle for a Canadian Prairie Fiction.* Edmonton: University of Alberta Press, 1977.

Hart, E.J. *The Selling of Canada: The CPR and the Beginnings of Canadian Tourism.* Banff: Altitude Publishing, 1983.

Haycock, Ronald. *The Image of the Indian: Canadian Indian as Subject and Concept in a Sampling of Popular Magazines, 1900–1970.* Waterloo: Waterloo Lutheran University Press, 1971.

Haydon, A.L. *The Riders of the Plains: A Record of the Royal North-West Mounted Police of Canada, 1873–1910.* Toronto: Copp Clark Co., 1912.

Hirschfelder, Arlene B., ed. *American Indian Stereotypes in the World of Children.* Metuchen, N.J.: The Scarecrow Press, 1982.

Hodgins, Bruce W. and Jamie Benidickson. *The Temagami Experience.* Toronto: University of Toronto Press, 1989.

Holm, Bill and George Irving Quimby. *Edward S. Curtis in the Land of the War Canoes.* Vancouver: Douglas and McIntyre, 1980.

Honour, Hugh. *The New Golden Land: European Images of America from the Discoveries to the Present Time.* New York: Pantheon Books, 1975.

Hopkins, J. Castell. *The Story of Our Country: A History of Canada for 400 Years.* Toronto: John C. Winston, 1912.

Horrall, S. W. "Sir John A. Macdonald and the Mounted Police Force for the Northwest Territories." *Canadian Historical Review,* v. 53 n. 2 (June 1972): 179–200.

Jackson, A.Y. *A Painter's Country.* Toronto: Clarke, Irwin and Co., 1958.

Jaenen, Cornelius J. *Friend and Foe: Aspects of French-Amerindian Cultural Contact in the Sixteenth and Seventeenth Centuries.* Toronto: McClelland and Stewart, 1976.

Jeal, Tim. *The Boy-Man: The Life of Lord Baden-Powell.* New York: William Morrow and Co., 1990.

Jenness, Diamond. *The Indians of Canada.* 7th ed. Toronto: University of Toronto Press; 1st ed. 1932.

Jennings, John. "The North-West Mounted Police and Indian Policy After the 1885 Rebellion." In *1885 and After,* F. Laurie Barron and James B. Waldran, eds. Regina: Canadian Plains Research Centre, 1986.

Johnson, E. Pauline. *The Moccasin Maker.* Introduction by A. LaVonne Brown Ruoff. Tucson: University of Arizona Press, 1987. 1st ed. 1913.

——. *The Shagganappi.* Toronto: William Briggs, 1913.

Kaiser, Rudolf. "'A Fifth Gospel, Almost': Chief Seattle's Speech(es): American Origins and European Reception." Christian F. Feest, ed. *Indians and Europe.* Aachen: Edition Herodot, Raderverlag, 1987.

Kane, Paul. *Wanderings of an Artist.* In *Paul Kane's Frontier,* J.R. Harper. Toronto: University of Toronto Press, 1971. 1st ed. 1859.

Keller, Betty. *Black Wolf: The Life of Ernest Thompson Seton.* Vancouver: Douglas and McIntyre, 1984.

——. *Pauline: A Biography of Pauline Johnson.* Vancouver: Douglas and McIntyre, 1981.

King, Thomas, Cheryl Calver and Helen Hoy, eds. *The Native in Literature.* Toronto: ECW Press, 1987.

Laut, Agnes C. *Canada: The Empire of the North.* Toronto: William Briggs, 1909.

Leacock, Stephen. *Canada, The Foundation of its Future.* Montreal: The House of Seagram, 1941.

——. *The Dawn of Canadian History,* v. I. Toronto: Glasgow, Brook and Co., 1921.

Leslie, John and Ron Maguire, eds. *The Historical Development of the Indian Act.* 2nd ed. Ottawa: Treaties and Historical Research Centre, Indian and Northern Affairs Canada, 1979.

Long Lance, Chief Buffalo Child. "Before the Red Coats Came." *Maclean's Magazine,* 15 Feb. 1923: 12–13,48–50.

——. "I Wanted to Live Like the White Man." *Maclean's Magazine,* 15 May 1926: 16, 60.

——. *Long Lance.* New York: Cosmopolitan Book Corp., 1928.

Lord, Barry. *The History of Painting in Canada.* Toronto: NC Press, 1974.

Lyman, Christopher M. *The Vanishing Race and Other Illusions.* New York: Pantheon Books, 1982.

Mair, Charles. *Through the Mackenzie Basin.* Toronto: William Briggs, 1908.

——. "Pauline Johnson: An Appreciation." Introduction to *The Moccasin Maker,* Pauline Johnson. Toronto: William Briggs, 1913.

——. "Pauline Johnson: An Appreciation." *The Canadian Magazine,* v. XLI, n. 3 (July 1913): 281–283.

MacBeth, R.G. *Policing the Plains.* Toronto, 1931.

McCourt, Edward. *Remember Butler: The Story of Sir William Butler.* Toronto: McClelland and Stewart, 1967.

McDougall, John. *Forest, Lake and Prairie: Twenty Years of Frontier Life in Western Canada, 1842–62.* Toronto: William Briggs, 1895.

——. *On Western Trails in the Early Seventies.* Toronto: William Briggs, 1911.

——. *Pathfinding on Plain and Prairie.* Toronto: William Briggs, 1898.

——. *Saddle, Sled and Snowshoe: Pioneering on the Saskatchewan in the Sixties.* Toronto: William Briggs, 1896.

McDougall, Robert L., ed. *The Poet and the Critic: A Literary Correspondence Between D.C. Scott and E.K. Brown.* Ottawa: Carleton University Press, 1983.

MacEwan, Grant. *Sitting Bull: The Years in Canada.* Edmonton: Hurtig, 1973.

McGill, Jean S. *Edmund Morris: Frontier Artist.* Toronto: Dundurn Press, 1984.

McGregor, Gaile. *The Wacousta Syndrome: Explorations in the Canadian Langscape.* Toronto: University of Toronto Press, 1985.

McIlwraith, J.N. *The Children's Study of Canada.* London: Fisher Unwin, 1899.

Mackay, Isabel Ecclestone. "Pauline Johnson: A Reminiscence." *The Canadian Magazine,* v. XLI, n. 3 (July 1913): 273–278.

Maclean, John. *The Indians of Canada: Their Manners and Customs.* Toronto: William Briggs, 1889.

McLuhan, T.C. *Dream Tracks: The Railroad and the American Indian, 1890–1930.* New York: Harry N. Abrams Inc., 1985

McRaye, Walter. *Town Hall Tonite.* Toronto: The Ryerson Press, 1929.

Marsh, E.L. *Where the Buffalo Roamed.* Toronto: The Macmillan Co. of Canada, 1923.

Martin, Sandra and Roger Hall. *Rupert Brooke in Canada.* Toronto: PMA Books, 1978.

Miles, Henry H. *The Child's History of Canada.* 9th ed. Montreal: William Dawson, 1910. 1st ed. 1870.

Miller, J.R. *Skyscrapers Hide the Heavens: A History of Indian-White Relations in Canada.* Toronto: University of Toronto Press, 1989.

Milton, Viscount and W.B. Cheadle. *The North-West Passage by Land.* London: Cassell, Petter and Galpin, 1865.

Monkman, Leslie. *A Native Heritage: Images of the Indian in English-Canadian Literature.* Toronto: University of Toronto Press, 1981.

Morris, E.M. *The Diaries of Edmund Montague Morris: Western journeys 1907–1910.* Transcribed by Mary Fitz-Gibbon. Toronto: Royal Ontario Museum, 1985.

Morris, Peter. *Embattled Shadows: A History of Canadian Cinema, 1895–1939.* Montreal: McGill-Queen's University Press, 1978.

Morrison, James. "The Poet and the Indians." *The Beaver* (Aug.–Sept. 1988): 4–16.

———. *Treaty Nine (1905–06): The James Bay Treaty.* Ottawa: Treaties and Historical Research Branch, Indian and Northern Affairs Canada, 1986.

Moyles, R.G. and Douglas Owram. *Imperial Dreams and Colonial Realities: British Views of Canada 1880–1914.* Toronto: University of Toronto Press, 1988.

Murray, Joan. *The Last Buffalo: The Story of Frederick Arthur Verner, Painter of the Canadian West.* Toronto: Pagurian Press, 1984.

Nash, Roderick. *Wilderness and the American Mind.* 3rd ed. New Haven, Conn.: Yale University Press, 1982; 1st ed. 1967.

Neihardt, John G. *Black Elk Speaks*. New York: William Morrow and Co., 1932.

New, W.H., ed. *Native Writers and Canadian Writing*. Vancouver: UBC Press, 1990.

O'Connor, John E. *The Hollywood Indian*. Trenton, N.J.: New Jersey State Museum, 1980.

Ontario Camping Assoc. *Blue Lake and Rocky Shore: A History of Childrens' Camping in Ontario*. Toronto: Natural Heritage/Natural History Inc., 1984.

Owram, Douglas. *Promise of Eden: The Canadian Expansionist Movement and the Idea of the West, 1856–1900*. Toronto: University of Toronto Press, 1980.

Parkman, Francis. *The Jesuits in North America*. Boston: Little, Brown and Co., 1963. 1st ed. 1867.

Patterson, E. Palmer, II. "The Poet and the Indian: Indian Themes in the Poetry of Duncan Campbell Scott and John Collier." *Ontario History*, v. LIX (1967): 69–78.

Patterson, Norman. "The Indians of Canada." *The Canadian Magazine*, v. XXIV, n. 3 (Jan. 1906): 241–247.

Peckham, Howard H. *Pontiac and the Indian Uprising*. Princeton, N.J.: Princeton University Press, 1947.

Rankin, Nancy. "The Tragedy of the Red Man." *The Canadian Magazine*, v. XLII, n. 4 (Feb. 1914): 403–407.

Regular, Keith. "On Public Display." *Alberta History*, v.34, n. i (Winter 1986): 1–10.

Reid, Dennis. *Edwin Holgate*. Ottawa: National Gallery of Canada, 1976.

Roberts, Charles G.D. *A History of Canada for High Schools and Academies*. rev. ed. Toronto: Macmillan Co. of Canada, 1915.1st ed. 1897.

Roper, Edward. *By Track and Trail: A Journey Through Canada*. London: W.H. Allen and Co. Ltd., 1891.

Russell, Don. *The Wild West or, A History of the Wild West Shows*. Fort Worth: Amon Carter Museum, 1970.

Scott, Duncan Campbell. *The Administration of Indian Affairs in Canada*. Ottawa: The Canadian Institute of International Affairs, 1931.

——. "Indian Affairs, 1867–1912." Adam Shortt and Arthur G. Doughty, eds. *Canada and Its Provinces*, v. 7. Toronto: T. & A. Constable, 1913.

——. "The Last of the Indian Treaties." In *The Circle of Affection*. Toronto: McClelland and Stewart, 1947.

Scott, Marshall O. "The Pagan Indians of Canada." *The Canadian Magazine*, v. XV, n. 3 (July 1900): 204–215.

Seton, Ernest Thompson. *The Birch-bark Roll of the Woodcraft Indians.* New York: Doubleday, Page and Co., 1906.

——. *Two Little Savages, Being the Adventures of Two Boys Who Lived as Indians and What They Learned.* New York: Grosset and Dunlap, 1903.

Seton, Julia M. *By a Thousand Fires.* New York: Doubleday, 1967.

Seton, E.T. and Julia M. Seton. *Gospel of the Redman.* Sante Fe, N.M.: Seton Village, 1963. 1st ed. 1936.

Shadbolt, Doris. *Emily Carr.* Vancouver: Douglas and McIntyre, 1990.

Shrive, Norman. *Charles Mair: Literary Nationalist.* Toronto: University of Toronto Press, 1965.

Simmins, Geoffrey and Michael Parke-Taylor. *Edmund Morris:"Kyaiyii" 1871–1913.* Regina: Norman Mackenzie Art Gallery, 1984.

Sladen, Douglas. *On the Cars and Off.* London: Ward, Lock and Bowden Ltd., 1895.

Smith, Donald. *From the Land of Shadows: The Making of Grey Owl.* Saskatoon: Western Producer Prairie Books, 1990.

——. *Long Lance: The True Story of an Imposter.* Toronto: Macmillan, 1982.

——. *"Le Sauvage": The Native People in Quebec Historical Writing on the Heroic Period (1534–1663) of New France.* Ottawa: National Museum of Man, 1974.

——. *"Now We Talk – You Listen." Rotunda,* v. 23, n. 2 (Fall 1990): 48–52.

Sontag, Susan. *On Photography.* New York: Farrar, Strauss & Giroux, 1977.

Souster, Raymond and Douglas Lochhead, eds. *Powassan's Drum: Poems of Duncan Campbell Scott.* Ottawa: Tecumseh Press, 1985.

Southesk, Earl of. *Saskatchewan and the Rocky Mountains.* 1875. Reprint. Edmonton: M.G. Hurtig, 1969.

Stanley, George F.G. *The Birth of Western Canada.* Toronto: University of Toronto Press, 1961. First published 1936.

Statistics Canada. *Perspective Canada.* Ottawa: Queen's Printer, 1974.

Steele, Col. S.B. *Forty Years in Canada.* New York: Dodd, Mead and Co., 1915.

Stewart, Hilary. *Totem Poles.* Vancouver: Douglas and McIntyre, 1990.

Swayze, Nansi. *Canadian Portraits: Jenness, Barbeau, Wintemberg, the Man Hunters.* Toronto: Clarke, Irwin and Co., 960.

Taylor, M. Brook. *Promoters, Patriots and Partisans: Historiography in Nineteenth-Century English Canada.* Toronto: University of Toronto Press, 1989.

Taylor, John L. *Canadian Indian Policy During the Inter-War Years, 1918–1939.* Ottawa: Indian Affairs and Northern Development, 1984.

Therien, Gilles. *"L'Indien Imaginaire: Une Hypothese." Recherches Amerindiennes au Quebec,* v. XVII, n. 3 (1987): 3–21.

Thon, William W. *The Fine Arts in Vancouver, 1886–1930*. Master's thesis, University of British Columbia, 1969.

Tippett, Maria. *Emily Carr: A Biography*. Toronto: Oxford University Press, 1979.

Titley, E. Brian. "W.M. Graham: Indian Agent Extraordinaire." *Prairie Forum*, v. 8, n. i (1983): 25–41.

———. *A Narrow Vision: Duncan Campbell Scott and the Administration of Indian Affairs in Canada*. Vancouver: UBC Press, 1986.

Tobias, John L. "Canada's Subjugation of the Plains Cree, 1879–1885." *Canadian Historical Review*, v. LXIV, n. 4 (Dec. 1983): 519–548.

Trigger, Bruce. *Natives and Newcomers: Canada's 'Heroic Age' Reconsidered*. Montreal: McGill-Queen's University Press, 1985.

———. "The Historians' Indian: Native Americans in Canadian Historical Writing From Charlevoix to the Present." *Canadian Historical Review*, v. LXVII, n. 3 (Sept. 1986): 315–342.

Turner, C. Frank. *Across the Medicine Line*. Toronto: McClelland and Stewart, 1973.

Wade, Mason. *Francis Parkman: Heroic Historian*. New York: Viking Press, 1972. 1st ed. 1942.

Wadland, John H. *Ernest Thompson Seton: Man in Nature and the Progressive Era, 1880–1915*. New York: Arno Press, 1978.

Walden, Keith. *Visions of Order*. Toronto: Butterworths, 1982.

———. "Blue Pete and Canadian Nationalism: Vision and Experience in the Western Novels of William Lacey Amy." *Journal of Canadian Studies*, v. 24, n. 2 (Summer 1989): 39-57.

Walker, James W. St. G. "The Indian in Canadian Historical Writing." *Canadian Historical Association, Historical Papers* (1971): 21–47.

Weaver, Sally M. *Making Canadian Indian Policy: The Hidden Agenda, 1968–70*. Toronto: University of Toronto Press, 1981.

Webling, Peggy. *Peggy: The Story of One Score Years and Ten*. London: Hutchinson & Co., 1924.

Windsor, Kenneth. "Historical Writing in Canada (to 1920)." In *Literary History of Canada*, Carl F. Klinck, ed. Toronto: University of Toronto Press, 1965.

Withrow, William H. *A History of Canada for the Use of Schools*. Toronto: Copp, Clark and Co., 1876.

Young, Egerton Ryerson. *By Canoe and Dog Train Among the Cree and Saulteaux Indians*. New York: Eaton and Mains, 1890.

———. *Indian Life in the Great North-West*. Toronto: The Musson Book Co., nd.

——.*On the Indian Trail*. New York: Fleming H. Revell Co., 1897.

——. *Stories from Indian Wigwams and Northern Campfires*. London: Charles H. Kelly, 1894.

AFTERWORD TO THE SECOND EDITION

Canada. *Report of the Royal Commission on Aboriginal Peoples*. 5 volumes. Ottawa: The Commission, 1996.

Daina Augaitis, curator. *Brian Jungen*. Catalogue for an exhibition at the Vancouver Art Gallery, Jan. 28–April 30, 2006. Vancouver: Douglas & McIntyre, 2005.

Edwards, Peter. *One Dead Indian: The Premier, the Police, and the Ipperwash Crisis*. Toronto: Stoddart Publishing, 2001.

Flanagan, Tom. *First Nations? Second Thoughts*. Montreal: Mcgill-Queen's University Press, second edition 2008 (orig. pub. 2000).

——, Christopher Alcantara and André Le Dressay. *Beyond the Indian Act: Restoring Aboriginal Property Rights*. Montreal: McGill-Queen's University Press, 2010.

King, Thomas. *The Truth About Stories: A Native Narrative*. Toronto: House of Anansi, 2003.

Richards, John. *Creating Choices: Rethinking Aboriginal Policy*. Toronto: C.D. Howe Institute, 2006.

Saul, John Ralston. *A Fair Country: Telling Truths About Canada*. Toronto: Viking, 2008.

Townsend-Gault, Charlotte, Scott Watson and Lawrence Paul Yuxweluptun, eds. *Lawrence Paul Yuxweluptun: Born to Live and Die on Your Colonialist Reservations*. Catalogue for an exhibition at the Morris and Helen Belkin Art Gallery, University of British Columbia, June 20–Sept. 16, 1995, Vancouver BC.

Widdowson, Frances and Albert Howard. *Disrobing the Aboriginal Industry*. Montreal: McGill-Queen's University Press, 2008.

INDEX

DANIEL FRANCIS is a historian and the author/editor of more than twenty books, including four for Arsenal Pulp Press: *Seeing Reds: The Red Scare of 1918-1919, Canada's First War on Terror; National Dreams: Myth, Memory and Canadian History; LD: Mayor Louis Taylor and the Rise of Vancouver* (winner of the City of Vancouver Book Award); and *Imagining Ourselves: Classics of Canadian Non-Fiction*. His other books include *A Road for Canada, Red Light Neon: A History of Vancouver's Sex Trade, Copying People: Photographing British Columbia First Nations 1860–1940, The Great Chase: A History of World Whaling, New Beginnings: A Social History of Canada*, and the popular *Encyclopedia of British Columbia*. He is also a regular columnist in *Geist* magazine. Francis lives in North Vancouver, BC.